The Moral Economy

The Moral Economy

John P. Powelson

Ann Arbor

THE UNIVERSITY OF MICHIGAN PRESS

Published in the United States of America by
The University of Michigan Press
Manufactured in the United States of America
⊗ Printed on acid-free paper

2001   2000   1999   1998   4   3   2   1

*A CIP catalog record for this book is available
from the British Library.*

Library of Congress Cataloging-in-Publication Data
Powelson, John P., 1920–
    The moral economy   /   John P. Powelson.
        p.   cm.
    Includes bibliographical references and index.
    ISBN 0-472-10925-1 (alk. paper)
    1. Economics—Moral and ethical aspects.   2. Social problems.
3. Social justice.   I. Title.
HB72.P65   1998
330'.01—DC21   98-8146
                                                        CIP

To Mancur Olson, 1932–1998
insightful innovator in the quest
to understand economic institutions

Contents

Preface

In a *moral economy*, with today's technology, no one should be poor. So how did it come about, historically, that only a small part of the world is rich and a much larger part poor? Just as scientists who wish to cure cancer must study what caused it, those who wish to end poverty must find out why we have it.

Twenty-three years ago I began to think that the reasons for world hunger and deprivation lay as much in history as in economics. Without forgetting my economics, I set it aside temporarily to read voraciously in histories all over the world. Each time I came across an incident, thought, or action that seemed related to this question, I jotted it down. Thirteen years and several thousand entries later, I bought a computer and organized my notes. Only then did I feel that I could see a pattern, which was set forth in 1994 in *Centuries of Economic Endeavor*. This book explained historically why northwestern Europe and Japan had become the leaders in economic development.

No sooner had that been finished than I began to wonder how the world would fare in the future, if some of the trends identified in centuries past were extended into the next millennium. The result is the present book, which touches upon the twenty-first century and beyond. It describes the society that I consider desirable and attainable, if these world trends continue. It is not necessary to have read *Centuries* in order to understand *The Moral Economy,* however.

Since this book is addressed to both economists and noneconomists, in order to make sure I did not lapse into economic jargon, I invited a number of friends in my home town, Boulder, Colorado, mostly noneconomists who had not read *Centuries,* to read draft chapters and to meet with me monthly until the entire book had been covered. They offered many valuable suggestions. This group consisted of Earl Allen, Rich Andrews, Louise and Bob Dudley, Dorothea el Mallakh, Nina Johnson, Carl Judson, Christopher Kiefer, Howard Lambert, Mary and Fred Trembour, Jerry Van Sickle, Bob Simmons and Sarah Hartzell, Roger and Ellen Williams, and Richard Wilshusen.

In addition, a small group of outside professionals from different disciplines read the manuscript as I sent them chapters, and they too made valuable comments. These are Harold Berman, Clarence Boonstra, Ed Chesky, Bruce Hawkins, Ken Malpass, William Shropshire, Jack Urner, J. D. von Pischke, Thomas Todd, Gilbert White, Faith Williams, and Stephen Williams.

My daughter, Judy Powelson, contributed significantly by disagreeing and arguing. She persuaded me in a number of cases, causing me to change my thinking and make revisions. My son, Larry Powelson, also contributed generously of his time and his ideas.

I am also indebted to three anonymous reviewers, one of whom later admitted to being Charles Kindleberger, and to Colin Day, director of the University of Michigan Press, whose encouragement and recommendations have now improved (I think) the quality of two of my books, and to Melissa Holcombe and Mary Meade, copyediting coordinator and production manager, respectively.

It is said that every maker of a Turkish carpet purposely weaves into it one imperfection, because only God is perfect. I have not done the same for this book, believing that to do so would be superfluous.

PART ONE
The Problems of Economic Morality

Introduction

Few of us like to wash dishes, but we do it because we value a clean table. No law requires it, no inspector examines whether we have done it, no reports are filed, we are not fined or imprisoned if we do not wash dishes, and no one sues us. This book proposes an *economic* culture in which we behave morally for the same reasons that we wash dishes: doing so brings advantages to us and others, while the consequences of not doing so would be personal and painful quite apart from the law.

Moral behavior includes paying fair wages; preserving the environment; hiring without racial, gender, or other prejudices; and seeing that everyone has health care and retirement pensions. Like obeying traffic rules, as this behavior becomes routine it becomes culturally acceptable: we would do it because it would not be right not to. This book explains how a moral world economy may evolve out of the world economy we have now.

Kings and emperors, metropolitans and popes, and shoguns—powerful rulers across centuries and across the world—have tried to decree a moral society. Thomas More wrote about one. Chinese emperors touted the ethics of Confucius, Europeans and Muslims "the word of God." Today, political groups seek "peace with justice" which they would achieve by *vicarious power*. Vicarious power is exercised by voters who demand that legislators require the citizenry to behave in ways they would not voluntarily. Violations would be punished by law, not by natural consequences.

Economic morality carries two requisites. It must constitute ethical behavior according to some high standards defined by the citizenry, and it must command consensus of all people affected. By this definition, we have achieved much in the past ten centuries but we have far to go. The kings and emperors failed because their visions did not carry ethical standards on which all affected could reach consensus. Those kind citizens today who seek "peace with justice" through vicarious power usually uphold high ethical standards but run short on worldwide consensus.

Adam Smith's classic liberalism might be the foundation of a moral economy but only if economic and political powers are well distributed. If power is concentrated in a few hands, those possessing it may seize control of the world's resources through economic or political acts that defy Smith's lib-

1

eral market. These acts—dubbed "immoral" in this book— include environmental deterioration, inflaming ethnic bias, giving or accepting bribes, worsening poverty, and compromising welfare assistance, social security, and health care.

In today's democracies, the standard response to immoral behavior is to elect someone else: Labour instead of Tories, Republicans instead of Democrats, Communists instead of Liberals, or vice versa. Instead of advocating transfer of power from one group to another, *The Moral Economy* proposes that solutions to social problems are best sought in a greater *balance of power* among social groupings. If rights and obligations are redefined to reflect such a balance, Smith's classic liberal economy may provide fair resolutions. *The Moral Economy* explains how to design institutional structures that will permit conflicts to be resolved peacefully and fairly. It also shows how a moral economy and economic prosperity are mutually reinforcing.

In a previous work, *Centuries of Economic Endeavor,* I supplied a new historical explanation of why a small portion of the world is rich and a much larger portion is poor. The argument covered roughly one thousand years, during which sovereigns in northwestern Europe and Japan were increasingly forced to share their power with merchants, artisans, guilds, peasants, and other "commoners." This *power-diffusion process* enabled these groups to hold each other somewhat accountable for resources, so that they were not wasted altogether extravagantly and inefficiently. This is one reason why these areas are now world leaders in economic development and why advocates of social justice and environmental preservation are primarily found there.

Economists often—even usually—advise rulers on how to achieve full employment, widespread prosperity, and little or no inflation as if these were what the rulers want. Most rulers, however, will favor sound economic policy only if it will preserve or enhance their power. In most of the world, it will not. Therefore, most rulers, especially in less developed areas, do not accept the advice of economists without being bribed to do so by the International Monetary Fund, World Bank, or Western governments.

Classic liberalism, in which negative behavior is punished more by the market than by the state, reached its apogee in the nineteenth century in northwestern Europe and its descendants in the New World and to a lesser extent in Japan. After that the world went into a century of government intervention, also known as statism, which brought back power to the rulers. The failures of statism began to be evident by the end of the twentieth century, with Third-World economies stagnating, communism and socialism ending, the welfare state bogged down in debt, and economic inefficiencies increasingly evident. To counter these, classic liberalism is beginning to return, with new adjustments to define the areas in which government regulation is appropriate and those in which freedom of enterprise is preferred.

Three possible paths await us in the twenty-first century. One is *interventionism,* by which government taxes, subsidizes, and regulates in order to guide the people into a desirable and efficient economic organism with adequate safety nets. At the other extreme is *libertarianism,*[1] which argues that government should cease altogether to intervene in the economy, leaving charitable and regulatory functions to private agencies. One reviewer sarcastically dubbed this view as "Leave it to the Elks."[2]

The third is the moral economy. It lies in between, with a balance of power among social groupings to create the desirable medium. Environmental and other regulations are undertaken by nongovernmental organizations (NGOs) as much removed from politics as possible, while social assistance is provided through cash or voucher grants or a negative income tax. Free of governmental supervision, the recipients themselves decide upon their patterns of education, social security, health care, and other consumables.

Interventionists argue for governmental oversight because many persons would not (for example) save enough or buy enough social insurance even if they receive government financial assistance to do so. To some extent these interventionists are correct, but the governmental oversight they propose tends to exacerbate the problems. The moral economy proposes innovative ways in which needy persons may be assisted in improving their socioeconomic skills and helped toward personal responsibility, with some government finance but mainly through their own initiative. The poor themselves buy what they need with government financial help, instead of receiving a set kind and quantity of services direct from government. Corruption is diminished not by passing ever more stringent laws against it but by reducing the government power whose favors can be bought.

The institutions suggested here are possibilities, not a prediction. A few of the proposed solutions are feasible in the near term, and in fact are already recognizable in their early stages. Others may follow when the first have been achieved. The book proposes a desirable world that is historically possible if certain trends of the past millennium are continued into the next and if world power becomes more diffuse. It opens a horizon on what a distant future might bring.

At the time that I was writing this book, others appeared that more or less confirm the propositions of *The Moral Economy.* Of these, I single out three. First is Matt Ridley's *The Origins of Virtue,* which approaches the same topics that I do but from a different perspective. Ridley is a zoologist who also knows cultural anthropology and economics. In *The Origins of Virtue,* he supplies startling parallels between human and animal cultures that are similar to lessons I have learned from history.

Next is Robert Barro's *Determinants of Economic Growth,* which summarizes the post–World War II progress in growth theory and then examines, statistically, growth differences among about one hundred countries since 1965. He identifies "high levels of schooling, good health (measured by life expectancy), low fertility, low government welfare expenditures, the rule of law, and favorable terms of trade" as the main forces contributing to growth. He also shows a weak relationship between democracy and economic growth, depending on its stage. His finding of a low negative correlation between government expenditures and economic growth conforms to the findings of both *Centuries of Economic Endeavor* and the present book, and his hypothesis on democracy conforms to mine on power. But Barro chooses not to go back much in history. He does not consider the forces causing the forces of economic growth—why some areas have high levels of schooling, good health, low government expenditures, and the remaining determinants, while others do not.

Finally, David Landes's *The Wealth and Poverty of Nations* is a consummate historical work describing the evolution of what I would call moral precepts, but it fails to give proper credit to institutions, or cultural modes of behavior. For that, the nod goes to two earlier authors, Mancur Olson, who died while this book was in press (and to whom it is dedicated), and to Douglass North. Their works are cited in the bibliography.

Whoever thinks the moral economy is impossible in (say) 250 years, is asked to consider: If you were a citizen of (say) London in 1750 and someone described to you the world economy as we know it today, would you have believed it?

Chapter 1
Beyond the Twenty-First Century

When all the momentous changes in technology and social structure that we now experience have run their course, we will have created a new world society. Will this society—the total complex of who we are and how we behave—resolve our major economic and social problems? This book addresses both questions: how the morality will evolve and whether it will solve the problems. We call this new world the moral economy, because—I will argue—though it is decades or even centuries away, it embodies the climax of an evolution in economic morality that has been taking place over centuries past.

Here are some of the momentous changes. The economic world is globalizing. Even monopolies are facing competition: by using the Internet, people can buy from other countries' monopolies instead of their own. Greater access to technology and factors of production is already available, as different governments offer different conditions. If you don't like Delaware, incorporate in Luxembourg. If there are too many restrictions in the United States, try operating out of Liberia. Producers and consumers may bypass their governments and trade where they like. On the debit side, useful protections—such as for environment, safety, and health—will have to be implemented through other agencies than national governments. Many of the "restrictions," such as minimum wages and affirmative action, will be brought about in the moral economy because they are what people demand, not what government requires.

Sometimes the inadequacy of government services causes private counterparts to arise. Postal service and police are among these. Private delivery services are rapidly replacing less effective national post offices. In most western countries private police outnumber public ones.[1] The United States has three times as many private as public police officers. Central governments in the Western world are devolving activities upon state, provincial, and local governments. (Scotland and Wales have their own legislatures). The *Washington Post* recently referred to its home city as "Dullsville, USA," saying "the capital of the free world is becoming just another irrelevant, boring town," because the real activity lies elsewhere.[2]

Trade barriers are falling. The succession from reciprocal trade agreements to the General Agreement on Tariffs and Trade (GATT) through the World Trade Organization at the end of the twentieth century means that this trajectory is already in place. It is a good one, I will argue, and the moral economy will see it to its ultimate mode, after many more such steps are taken. The European Union, South American Market (Mercosur), and the North American Free Trade Area (NAFTA) are all ways of extending borders; all three have

5

plans to recruit new members. Until we discover inhabited outer space, the world is the limit.

Classic liberalism is winning in the world markets, as regulations and government intervention are dropped throughout the world. Over four decades of price supports and crop restrictions were wiped out in the United States by the Federal Agricultural Improvement and Reform Act of 1996.[3] The next century may see some hauling and backhauling on deregulation, seen as badly needed now but which may go too far. New agencies may be needed to regulate if governments fail to do so.

Governments are losing financial credibility with high, unsustainable deficits. Good, compassionate people are demanding that government supply more social services—welfare, schools, hospitals—than they are willing to pay for in taxes. They demand these services not just for the poor but mainly for middle-class persons who could otherwise afford them. Ultimately, many public services will become so shoddy that those who can afford to do so will buy them privately, and the poor will be the outcasts. In the moral economy, government will finance social services for the poor only, who will buy them on the private market with Treasury-supplied cash or vouchers. The amount will measure the degree of compassion that the better off truly feel for the less fortunate.

Corruption in government is becoming intolerable. The campaign against it is centuries old. It reached a crescendo in Britain in the nineteenth century and has reached another in the United States today. Campaign contributions are seen as both corruption and hypocrisy. Some day it will occur to someone that the answer is not to screw the lid on the kettle more tightly—more laws to control contributions—but to pour out the contents into other kettles—decentralize government and transfer power to nongovernmental organizations (NGOs). Only when presidents and legislatures no longer have the power to pass out special favors—as they will not in the moral economy—will bribery to obtain those favors fade away.

Privatization of productive facilities is now occurring in virtually all the world. In some places, this movement decentralizes power and leads to healthy competition. In others, such as Russia, it doles out the assets of socialist states among private monopolies that are just as oppressive and inefficient as the former state enterprises. Another round of failures, and a new set of reforms, must occur before this aspect of the moral economy is realized.

Land reform has led to the division among tenant farmers of vast, inefficient estates in less developed countries. In a few places, this decentralization has led to greater efficiency and higher incomes for poor people. In most others, unfortunately, governments have monopolized the fruits of land reform, snatching profits away from the poor and into the pockets of corrupt politicians. I have written about this elsewhere.[4] Corrections will come about through protests of those afflicted, but only as they attain enough power to make themselves heard.

In the United States, the Welfare Act of 1996 decentralizes welfare. But it goes too far and lacks compassion. Politicians and governments have failed to distinguish between those persons who remain on welfare for lack of motivation and those who remain because they are physically, psychologically, or otherwise unable to get off. Needed is a program run by agencies—nongovernmental ones in the moral economy—financed by government and judged by their capacity both to move the first group into productive labor and to take care of the second in dignified ways. Such a program could be passed today by a determined legislature, with sufficient prodding from the electorate. Already private corporations are offering to manage welfare on contract, but it is not clear that their operations will improve the prospects of the poor.

As dissatisfaction with public schools mounts, increasingly parents employ magnet schools, charter schools, and home education. A logical next step would be to privatize all schools—some for profit and some for nonprofit—so that parents and children have choice, opting away from systems that fail and sticking with those that work. Their choices will lead to more beneficial standards than any uniform national standards now proposed—not everyone is alike—and their choices will resolve the questions of how to learn to read, write, or solve mathematical problems and what history and literature to study. "Politically correct" will give way to student and parent choice from a wide platter. Educational loans are already in vogue. If private loan funds were offered, from which all education could be financed for all students—rich, poor, or indigent—payback might be made in lifetime mortgages. Those borrowing would finance the next generation's education by their repayment. In the moral economy, education is removed from the financial thrall of government.

All these changes are reflected in the teaching of economics. In 1997, Mankiw's *Principles of Economics* emerged, emphasizing classic liberalism, as a direct challenge to Samuelson's famous text, which emphasizes Keynesian economics and which has held primary position for fifty years. Yergin and Stanislaw show how the era of big government succeeded for a long time in both the more and less developed world, but how it finally overreached itself, and markets are replacing it.[5]

Even as these momentous changes take place, momentous problems remain. How would the moral economy handle the major problems of the day, such as poverty, environment, population growth, ethnic bias, welfare, social security, and health care? In part 1, these problems are taken up, one by one, and solutions for the moral economy are proposed—not necessarily *the* solutions, since often there are alternatives. Examples will be given to show the kinds of solutions to be found in the kind of world the moral economy will reflect.

What, When, and How

The moral economy is some future world, decades or centuries away, projected from trends that are centuries long. It is a defined culture, including ways of determining prices, wages, money supply, property, and law, and methods of preserving the environment and caring for the poor. It will have ancillary effects on education, religion, and interpersonal trust—all to be described in this book. At first blush it might seem like a whim of an author who has invented a personal utopia. Instead, the moral economy is constructed out of history, past and present. It takes account of where we have been and shows where we might be going.

Despite its emphasis on freedom, the moral economy is one of social control. However, controls are not imposed by governments that determine how society ought to be run and then pass laws to make it run that way. Rather, they are negotiated by citizen groups who determine the law, the monetary system, the manner of contracts, and labor practices, and who implement environmental practices that assure clean air and water, preserve the forests and soil, and prevent global warming and destruction of the ozone layer. The moral economy goes beyond democracy to a society of negotiation and compassion, characteristics grounded in popular will and understanding more than in governments requiring citizens to behave in ways not normal to their psyche.

Current disquisitions on the twenty-first century tend to be divided between freestyle libertarians, who believe the market alone can preserve the environment, while families and private agencies should care for the poor, and statists, who believe these goals require regulations from above. The moral economy stands between the libertarians and the statists. For readers who like to see the results at the beginning, here are some possible culminations of many intertwining projectories, for which more detail will be provided in chapter 12.

In the moral economy, any two or more individuals, anywhere in the world, may engage in any economic transaction that does not damage a third party or abuse resources belonging to others. Definitions of damage and abuse and what belongs to others must be widely agreed upon; this book provides ideas on how agreement may be reached.

The right to private property will be preserved. While some property will belong to the state, much of what is now government land will be vested in NGOs such as the Audubon Society and the Nature Conservancy that are charged, by their charters, with preserving it. Thus land will be removed from being the political football of interest groups, while outside groups will monitor compliance of the NGOs with their charters.

Common resources, such as air and water, that are currently treated as if owned by government or by no one or anyone will also be entrusted to NGOs, whose charters will charge them with determining their conditions of use and selling the rights to use them under those conditions. Their integrity also will be monitored by outside agencies.

All economic enterprise will be undertaken by citizen initiative, including schools, health care, social insurance, and similar goods, with citizen choice over which ones each person will buy and in what quantity. *Citizen initiative* and *citizen choice* may be more acceptable terms for those who associate the expressions *privatization* and *free market* with selfishness and greed, but in fact citizen initiative means privatization and citizen choice means free market.

All persons, rich or poor, will be required by law to choose and buy their own education, health care, retirement insurance, and other welfare, but with government subsidies for those who cannot otherwise afford these benefits. Consulting agencies would be available for those experiencing difficulty in choosing. This requirement is similar to the required automobile insurance in many U.S. states. Any person lacking the finances to purchase the minimum amounts will be subsidized by the state.

From time to time income will be redistributed but neither drastically nor utterly. Rather, a negative income tax is proposed in which persons in lower brackets receive subsidies from the state while those in upper brackets pay progressive taxes. Whether or not foreigners participate in subsidies for social services or in the redistributions of income remains open. The moral economy aims at a world state in which rich areas are no longer a magnet for the poor. To the extent that it succeeds in this, foreigner participation in these subsidies becomes a non-question.

The moral economy will evolve in steps. As a final step—after all the above—all persons will have the right to travel and settle in any part of the world, buying property as needed. Sovereignty over land will give way to individual ownership. One of the chief objections to unlimited immigration into Europe and the United States is that immigrants take advantage of public services that citizens have paid for. This objection is overcome in the moral economy, where users of services—citizens and immigrants alike—will pay for them in proportion to their use (although insuring themselves against sudden, catastrophic need). Another objection is that labor is usually cheaper in countries of emigration than in those of immigration. If immigration is permitted in gradually increasing quantities, this objection will gradually be overcome by the mobility of labor, which will tend to equalize wages in both places, damping the increases in areas of greater productivity but not stopping them completely.

The moral economy will train citizens to achieve social discipline in several ways. It will develop the autonomy of the individual. It will invoke positive incentive more than regulation and punishment. It will tend toward negotiation and compromise rather than confrontation and litigiousness. Citizens will take responsibility for their actions, including abuse of their bodies such as with drugs and smoking and body "improvements" such as with breast implants, as well as the risk of innocently building with materials such as asbestos, that were not known to be harmful at the time. The government may do research and supply information impartially on the basis of which citizens make their judgments, much as governments do now. But private agencies will also do this research, and the government will not force its judgments on citizens. Health insurance rates for abusers will be high to cover the high cost of treatment. The government may control activities where some might endanger others (use of guns, carrying bombs on to airplanes), and certain pharmaceuticals, such as thalidomide, that might damage unborn babies. Safety in the workplace and sexual harassment will normally be left to rules negotiated by workers and management but may require laws to control "free riders," the few businesses that would profit from the lower cost of not going along with what has been accepted by most.

Citizens trained in these principles will bring up their children in the same way, thus increasing the probability of a responsible society in the next generation. Only if the next generation agrees voluntarily to protect the environment, care for the poor, and work toward similar social goals, instead of being forced to do so by regulations and threats, will such a society be sustained.

All these are general principles, to be fleshed out in later chapters. Some will consider them "utopia" or "against human nature," but the moral economy is no utopia. Indeed, a citizen of the more developed world today, magically transported to the moral economy, would accommodate easily after some minor instruction on how to use money, go to school, ask for hospital care, and adjust to persons of different cultures.

Classic Liberalism

In the moral economy, controls will be exerted sidewise, by citizen group upon citizen group, instead of downward, by government upon citizen. Strangely, however, changes in this direction are occurring in the midst of an opposite ethos. At present, the world thinks one way—in favor of more central control—but acts in the other.

This is not unusual. In economic theory, thinking follows action, not (as we would like) the other way around. Adam Smith wrote *The Wealth of Nations* in a theoretically authoritarian environment but after England had moved toward classic liberalism for centuries. By the end of the nineteenth century, Western thinking had caught up with action, in that economic theories had become classic liberal. But in the twentieth century, the West tended again toward authoritarianism—is there a problem? let government solve it. Today, we support authoritarianism verbally but classic liberalism comes back surreptitiously.

On the one hand, an explosion of economic freedom and property rights, along with deregulation the world over, has brought unprecedented growth in world product. The ability to eliminate poverty is visible on a distant horizon. On the other hand, we fear unleashing freedom. Many believe that a shift in power to smart technocrats will marginalize the vast majority of the world's people who have never made a telephone call or do not have access to a minimally sanitary toilet,[6] and we demand government intervention to preserve the environment and to resolve social injustices. This book is intended to help us let go, to believe in what we are doing.

Depressed by economic stagnation, corruption, and extravagance and urged on by governments of industrial countries, some less developed countries seek escape by devolving industry and agriculture to the private sector. But others have been unwilling or unable to spring themselves loose from central authority. While more developed countries deregulate industry and agriculture and shift central responsibilities to state and local governments, their citizens do not easily give up the idea of the welfare state.

In the moral economy those who capitalize on the burst in technology, and who therefore have much, will share with those who have little, while the environment will be protected by agencies devoted solely to preserving it and not by a government dependent on political contributions from those who would destroy it. Social justice in employment (however one defines it) will be achieved through the free choice of consumers, not by outside rulemakers and courts. This book will show a disbelieving public how this will be possible.

The authoritarian spirit of our present society is reflected by Peter Kramer, who wrote that "the mentally ill deserve job protection."[7] He cited a competent middle manager who was deeply depressed but who was fired because a new boss wanted an "upbeat style of management-by-consensus" in which her dour personality no longer fit. She contemplated suicide. Kramer favored a directive by the Equal Employment Opportunity Commission that "employers must make accommodation for workers with mental illnesses." Inhabitants of the moral economy will also believe there are many who must be helped, but in place of mandates ordering specific individuals or companies to help them, thereby initiating acrimony and litigation, a reward system is proposed. A company hiring a mentally ill person (after adequate diagnosis) will receive a bonus from the public treasury—carrot instead of stick.

Balance of Power

How to move from the present to the moral economy is taken up throughout this book as elements of that society are presented, such as social security, health care, poverty, education, and the like. This will come up again in chapter 12, where the moral economy is described in detail. But a few general principles can be set forth now.

Theoretically, the moral economy could be established immediately in democratic countries, simply by acts of legislature, and could later spread to the rest of the world. However, acts of legislature are not usually the means to momentous changes, although they may reflect momentous changes that arise from below. Because of imbalance of power, the moral economy is not to be expected imminently. Instead, we must look toward ways of obtaining a better balance of power, some of which are described in the following paragraphs.

Government intervention will be diminished when the budgetary deficit becomes too onerous for the electorate. Some argue that budget deficits are no problem, because they provide social benefits that an expanding economy can afford. However, with the discovery over time that these benefits grow indefinitely, are corruptly awarded and inefficiently applied, and are the cause of unemployment, diminished investment, and other economic malaise, the services will gradually be privatized. This need has been discovered already in the socialist countries but not yet in France.

Private organizations will continue to be formed, gradually taking over government functions, as has been happening in schools, postal services, health care, and the like. Weaker groups will become more powerful through organization. For example, women athletes are said to be discriminated against on college campuses in the United States despite a decade of affirmative action. I have not investigated whether this is so, but if it is, I suggest that equal treatment will depend on a strong sentiment among the general populace; on groups of women in and out of colleges (including alumnae) bargaining for it; and on women athletes choosing colleges on the basis of it. Laws requiring equal treatment will not be successful unless the other conditions are in place *first*.

Corruption will be diminished—as explained in chapter 8—only when legislators find they suffer more from the corruption of others than they gain from their own. Citizens must assail politicians as part of a general system of corruption, so that to preserve his or her own power—however diminished—each legislator must vote to diminish the power of the body to which he or she belongs. For the most part, legislators have not yet thought of this strategy, but they might, within a century or so.

In the less developed world, where the cost of paperwork, licenses, and taxes to do legitimate business is especially high, many persons transact business in an "informal sector," illegal but tolerated because the economy cannot survive without it. In some countries, as much as 50 percent of the gross domestic product is estimated to be produced and traded in informal sectors. Russians could not live on their output today if it were only what the official statistics register. Expansion of the informal economy will gradually erode the regulated, formal one over all the world but especially in the less developed areas.

Economic development has historically made the poor progressively richer relative to the rich. (The common belief that this is not so results from dubious interpretations of historical and current data, as will be explained in chapter 3.) Further economic development will lead toward a more equitable distribution of income and wealth, the world over. As this happens, the poor will gain more political power and will be better able to defend themselves. The idea of "poor" will diminish, their interests will change, and they will join other groups (political parties, labor unions, lobbies, parent-teacher associations) to defend their new interests. In this way, improved balance of power will be promoted. In fact, this is already happening but may not be noticed because new "poor" always materialize.

International power struggles may happen upon moral solutions. For example, the Caspian Sea contains rich resources of gas and oil, whose ownership is in dispute among bordering countries. The present pipeline for exports runs through Russia. Because of manifold restrictions, actual or feared, some governments wish to bypass Russia with a pipeline through Iran, but U.S. politicians are divided on whether such a line would strengthen their "enemy" in Teheran. The way out would be to make gas and oil the sole province of companies whose decisions would be based on least cost rather than on politics. Such a compromise might be possible if the companies were truly international, operating in world space unlinked to any political power, a prospect we vaguely see already.

The national mood in the more developed world may gradually shift from one of reliance on government to one of individual choice. Each shift to choice—on social security, health care, education, and so on—promotes the general idea of choice, so that the next shift becomes easier. Harder cases, such as abortion and the right to assisted suicide, will become easier as the overall mood shifts its balance.

In the less developed world the growth of economic power at the base may undermine authoritarian governments that depend on mass political support. This is explained in chapter 2.

All the preceding are ways that might lead toward the moral economy, but the shift will not be easy. The current (central-control) mood calls on government to control (for example) drug usage while morality calls on parents, schools, churches, and other nongovernmental organizations to bring up children not to take drugs, with parents, teachers, and others serving as models. Researchers study the effectiveness of laws to control smoking and drugs when they should be studying families with smoke-free and drug-free children to find out how they did it.

Since the central-control mood is currently in ascendance in personal behavior, government regulation increases hand in hand with the abdication of responsibility by parents, schools, and churches. At the same time, deregulation gathers force in the economy. Some watershed may be reached where decentralizing the economy promotes the idea of decentralization as a value, so that it begins to cover personal behavior as well. This will occur, if it does, when the problems expand so much that the public becomes aware that current institutions are not solving them: paying South American governments to eradicate coca crops does not stop the drug traffic. When/if the mood shifts, the pattern will/may become cumulative, spreading from one space (drugs) to others (health care, retirement, and other elements of personal responsibility). Nongovernmental agencies would compose the rules for economic activities.

A moral society does need rules. I favor forbidding advertisements for cigarettes or psychoactive drugs, just as I would forbid advertisements saying, "Commit suicide; it's the cool thing to do." But others equally moral may differ on what the rules should be. I argue only that a moral economy requires that regulatory activities not be monopolized and politicized by government.

These paths to the moral economy may be summarized into four forces: an enhanced awareness of social problems; gradual recognition that current institutions are not working; an improved balance of power so that families and private groups replace government in areas where government fails; and the abundance of potential positive-sum moves to be made when no one has the power to stop them. Added to these forces would be the cumulative process, known in American slang as "the ball rolling."

Classic Liberalism and Interventionism

Classic liberalism—derived from the Latin, *libertas*—is the foundation of the moral economy. It calls for freedom of choice in economic transactions, personal behavior, expression, and other forms. It contrasts with *interventionism,* which would apply state controls and regulations to all of these in order to limit injustice and abuse. Although interventionism is popularly known in the United States as "liberal," it is the opposite of liberal in the generic or classical sense. (Hereafter, I use "interventionism" rather than "statism," because "statism" implies heavy-handedness. Throughout the book, I have tried to use neutral vocabulary.)

The classic liberal philosophy is founded on the idea that the most desirable world is achieved by millions upon millions of people acting independently and without great constraint from higher authority. They make billions upon billions of agreements among themselves, including economic transactions of buy, sell, invest, employ, and the like, and they establish and enforce their own modes of behavior, such as commercial rules and monetary systems.

Classic liberals argue, for example, that only with a reliable private insurance company, and no government interference, can a dependable thirty-year contract for health care be made. With Medicare, on the other hand, the government waffles, changing the terms from year to year in response to this political pressure or that, or in response to budget pressures that have nothing to do with health.

Rothschild's analogy to the rain forest is pertinent.[8] No one planned such an intricate mosaic of trees, plants, and foliage; each one found its niche after competing or cooperating with others, making maximum use of sunlight, soil, and rainfall. By the same token, in a classic liberal society individuals seek their niches, competing and cooperating with each other for resources and space, and produce an economy that makes maximum use of both of these. Central direction is neither needed nor desirable in either the rain forest or the classic liberal economy for it inhibits the individual from exercising the required initiative.

The interventionist philosophy, on the other hand, is founded on the idea that unless constraints are enforced by government, too many persons are ready to break the rules to their own advantage, destroy the environment, or prey on the less fortunate. Only government regulation will curb these behaviors, according to this philosophy. In classic liberalism, by contrast, the millions upon millions of people will hold each other accountable for the good behavior that interventionists would enforce through the government, *provided their power is relatively well balanced.* Then they can make contracts with each other that would not be changed at the whim of a new legislature. How power may become better balanced is the subject of chapter 2.

Thus *balance of power* among citizens is the key to the moral economy, such that no person or group, including the government, is able to dominate others. Instead, decisions on socially important issues are made with respect for the views of all sides, as opposed to consensus. Consensus means "of the same mind," but all citizens can hardly be of the same mind about anything. In the moral economy, one might disagree on free trade or protectionism or any other issue, but by accepting the decisions of adversaries, *given the way they feel,* one preserves a higher value, the integrity of society. Democracy is a step toward the moral economy, because unlike in earlier polities, virtually all who disagree await the next election rather than explode a bomb. The fringe element that would throw bombs is soundly condemned or considered mentally unbalanced. The ability to act in this manner requires not only a balance of power but also respect for others and a social discipline nurtured by democracy that takes centuries to become ingrained and that has not fully matured anywhere.

The moral economy is based on the philosophy that those who contravene the rules will be disciplined by the market, *but only after power has been*

so redistributed that citizen choices cannot easily be abused. The interventionist philosophy, on the other hand, relies on threat of lawsuit, fine, or imprisonment for discipline. In the classic liberal philosophy, individuals are believed
to cooperate voluntarily for the social good. Evidently Adam Smith thought
the invisible hand was the hand of God. For example: "But by acting according
to the dictates of our moral faculties, we necessarily pursue the most effectual
means of promoting the happiness of mankind, and therefore may be said, in
some sense, to cooperate with the Deity, and to advance as far as in our power
the plan of Providence."[9] I do not believe in Smith's God, but I do believe in a
social order with high mutuality of interests. In the interventionist philosophy,
on the other hand, society is believed to be strongly influenced by environmental polluters and individuals greedy for profits who will deprive laborers, minority groups, or women of their fair share and rights. In fact, both messages
are correct: there are polluters and cheats, but in the moral economy they are
held in abeyance not by regulation so much as by social institutions created
through a balance of power. These institutions will be described in detail in the
following chapters.

The Meaning of "Liberal"

"Liberal" has become confused in popular language. Strangely, in the United
States—but not much elsewhere—interventionists have come to be called "liberals," when that is the opposite of what they are. Instead, I use "liberal" in its
generic or worldwide sense, but mostly I say "classic liberal" to refer to those
who seek freedom from excessive government intervention. In Australia, the
Liberal Party is less interventionist than the Labor Party. The *New York Times*
has referred to Russia's liberals as "those who demand a less intrusive and
more accountable state."[10] I do not use the word *conservative,* which means a
person who admires time-honored virtues and vices over the speculative virtues and vices of a changed society. Modern interventionists, however, have
loaded the word *conservative* with ideological content not originally intended.

   The Economist finds that Western societies tend to be liberal in a way that
would include many political perspectives, including both Republicans and
Democrats in the United States: "a society that provides constitutional government (rule by laws, not by men) and freedom of religion, thought, expression
and economic interaction; a society in which infringements of liberty must be
justified."[11] By this definition, the West as a whole is contrasted with eastern
Europe, most of Africa, and many parts of Asia and Latin America. In the same
article, however, it concludes that "in America 'liberal' has become detached
from its proper meaning and attached to the opposite, whereas in Europe it is
merely falling out of political parlance."

Characteristically, the moral economy takes a middle path. Extreme interventionism would suppose state ownership of all property and control over all enterprise. Instead, in this book interventionism applies only to those state actions widely accepted as appropriate to a welfare state (defined in chapter 2) and not to the communism of the former Soviet Union. Interventionists define health care, social security, unemployment insurance, and similar activities as *public goods,* to be provided to everyone by the state. In addition, interventionists argue that the state must regulate private behavior to ensure preservation of the environment, an appropriate distribution of income and wealth, and equal treatment of persons of different gender, ethnic origin, religion, and sexual preference or to provide advantageous treatment for these persons to compensate for past injustices.

To avoid extreme liberalism, I do not use the term *free market* or *laissez-faire.* Interventionists often perceive the "free market" as a license to do whatever one wishes: to destroy the environment; to monopolize resources; to avoid safety regulations in factories; to abuse child labor; and to engage in other unwholesome activities for one's own profit. Classic liberals deny this definition. To us the free market merely implies freedom to undertake economic activities without "excessive" government regulation and to make choices on goods to be produced, methods of production, and prices. To avoid the intellectual baggage carried by "free market," instead I invent the term *liberal market,* or a free market modified by five qualifications, to wit:

First, if some groups, such as private corporations or a government, are "too" powerful, they will distort the market in their favor. Ways of seeking balance of power are scattered throughout this book; indeed, they are its principal focus. Second, from time to time some redistributions of income may be necessary. Otherwise, the liberal market may not cause distributions that are socially satisfactory, and therefore it may lead to discontent that is unpleasant for many and disturbing to most. Some liberals, such as Richard Epstein, disagree on this point. Third, some government regulations are necessary to protect beings unable to defend themselves (such as children, animals, and the mentally deficient) and to restrain monopoly. Most classic liberals, however, including myself, believe that regulators currently extend their jurisdiction far beyond what is desirable. Fourth, to protect itself against free riders, a liberal society should require all persons to purchase basic services such as health care, unemployment insurance, and social security—what shall or shall not be included, and how much, is open to discussion. For those who cannot afford these, but only for these persons, the central treasury should pay through cash or vouchers like food stamps, with which these services might be purchased on the private market. We should not be so inhumane as to allow someone to die or even suffer for want of health care or to starve in his or her old age. Finally, I agree with Soros that an "open society" (his term) occupies "a middle ground, where the rights of the individual are safeguarded but where there are some shared values that hold society together."[12] However, I would add that the shared values, which underlie the rules of the market, should be designed mainly by societal groups at lower levels and less so by government regulation.

The preceding definitions should be taken as reference points only, from which we all digress in practice. Nothing should stereotype an individual as either classic liberal or interventionist *in toto*. Most of us combine the two philosophies to different degrees, so that personal ideologies are found on a continuum, not at poles.

Economic Morality and Institutions

Social control in any society is enforced by cultural elements called institutions, which collectively comprise morality. Economic morality includes the rules for doing business—laws, the monetary system, modes of labor negotiation, how corporations function, and so on. It is not uncommon to say "institution" where I would say "organization," as, for example, "the International Monetary Fund (IMF) as an institution." In this book, however, institution implies behavior and organization implies a legal or social entity. The international monetary system is an institution, but the IMF is an organization. The Western educational system is an institution, but universities are organizations. The enforceability of these institutions depends ultimately on the power of the state, but before that power is called on, they function in many ways through agreements among citizens and organizations. For example, rules are made by professional associations, labor unions, schools and colleges, and clubs.

In earlier centuries, Western economic institutions (hence morality) were fashioned largely by negotiations among working groups. In the past two centuries, they have been increasingly fashioned by governments, which have therefore increasingly established our morality.

Individuals differ in concepts of economic morality—minimum wages, affirmative action, and so on. That is not the question here. Instead, whatever our differing concepts may be, this book questions whether laws intended to impose new morality will change the hearts and minds of people. Will an employer, forced by law to hire an unwanted employee, become converted to the concept of affirmative action and so bring up children to believe in it? Does this matter? I know of no research done on this question, and I do not detect any widespread concern for it. That is one reason I write this book.

In the classic liberal tradition, economic morality is (or should be) fashioned from below, by the very people whom it affects, in what I have called a *free market in institutions* (the only sense in which I use the term *free market* in this book). In the interventionist philosophy it is fashioned by a government, which may be a military dictator, a hereditary monarch, or an elected body.

The moral economy differs from most societies today not necessarily in the kind of morality envisaged, nor in the degree of social control, but in how morality evolves and is enforced.

While classic liberalism and interventionism refer to all modes of life, this book concentrates on economic philosophy, or the extent to which institutions cover our economic system and how we compose them. We enter other areas such as law, religion, and education only where they impinge on the economic.

Plan for This Book

More than show how the market can be adjusted to resolve many situations now handled from authority, this book puts worldwide technological change and classic liberalism into historical perspective. It finds that the Western world and Japan were on a course toward classical liberalism for one thousand years, a course that reached its apogee in the nineteenth century and then was reversed. It also examines a century of socialist/welfare intervention and finds that concentrated power, corruption, inefficiency, and fiscal improvidence brought it to an end, destroying the dreams of a "fairer" world administered by benevolent central power. Unfortunately, the end is divisive. Those in the seat of government, responsible for the treasury, see the impossibility of continuing all the benefits of a welfare state in the face of the public's refusal to pay higher taxes, while the public protests or riots when forced to give up these benefits. They put their taxes into a common pot and try to pull out more than they put in.

Finally, this book describes the moral economy, which captures the benefits of technological invention through classic liberalism while using sidewise checks and balances to prevent environmental damage, ethnic and gender bias, and distorted distributions of wealth. Problems that seem intractable without government intervention are resolved through the choices of millions, constrained by social institutions. A democratic government cannot solve these problems if its people do not want to do so, and if they do want to solve these problems, government need not force them. In the moral economy, governments facilitate but rarely mandate.

The desirability of classic liberalism is widely understood—in that individual freedom is a cherished value—but it is often supposed that certain major problems can be resolved only with strong government intervention. In chapters 3 to 5 we select seven such problems, to wit: (1) poverty, or disparities in income and wealth both within countries and between the more and less developed worlds; (2) growing population that may consume the world's resources; (3) environment, such as pollution of air and water, global warming, and the ozone hole; (4) ethnic bias; (5) welfare; (6) social security; and (7) health care. These chapters describe these problems and show how, if new institutions are formed, they can be resolved with discipline from the market and with minimal government intervention. Only after the solutions have been set forth, one by one, will it become clear that they have essential elements in common, and out of these mutualities the moral economy is born.

These classic liberal solutions require changes in the character, or culture, of world society, which are described in part 2. Chapters 6–9 include discussion of how accountable we are—and to whom—for the management and use of resources; how much we trust each other; how we organize property; what monetary system controls inflation and facilitates trade; how law is made and applied; how corruption is contained; what kind of tax system is needed; how citizens are to be educated; the role of religion; and finally, the extent to which government regulation is desirable. In chapter 10, the kind of people we are is summarized in terms of morality and values. Throughout the book I have mingled my findings from history with my personal experiences as economic consultant in many countries. For example, chapter 11 tells of my experiences in a decollectivizing economy, Ukraine. Finally, chapter 12 constructs the moral economy out of the solutions to the problems in part 1 and the institutions proposed in part 2.

"Take Back the Word"

Among many definitions of "liberal" in Webster's *Third International Dictionary,* the ones most pertinent to this book read as follows: (1) "not bound by authoritarianism, or orthodoxy, or traditional or established forms in action, attitude, or opinion;" and (2) "of or constituting a political party . . . associated . . . with ideals of individual, especially economic, freedom." Likewise, the *American Heritage Dictionary* describes "liberalism" as a "political theory founded on the natural goodness of human beings and the autonomy of the individual and favoring civil and political liberties, government by law with the consent of the governed, and protection from arbitrary authority."

Some have questioned whether my use of the word *liberal* or the term *classic liberal,* conveys the proper message, since it is different from the popular meaning of "liberal" in the United States. My use of this vocabulary is intended to convey two messages. The first is a plea for correct usage. The second is that Americans who call themselves "liberal," in the main, are not.

> "When I use a word," Humpty Dumpty said, in rather scornful tone, "it means just what I choose it to mean—neither more nor less."
>
> "The question is," said Alice, "whether you *can* make words mean so many different things."
>
> "The question is," said Humpty Dumpty, "which is to be master—that's all."[13]

Chapter 2
Power and the Market

To understand balance of power, we must first understand power. Power is the ability to control or influence the actions, thoughts, or speech of others. Whenever the government regulates an economic activity, it pits the power of the politicians against the power of the market. Yergin and Stanislaw refer to this struggle as "the battle between government and the market place that is remaking the modern world."[1]

The *market* consists in the collective decisions and transactions of people all over the world, weighted by how rich they are. In democracies, politicians use their power to void decisions of the market because they believe that if they do not, rich or powerful people will damage the interests of all. Let us call this "benign use of political power." Sometimes, however, they make decisions to enrich themselves and/or to preserve their power through granting favors to special interests. Let us call this "malevolent use of political power." In the moral economy, instead of trying to thwart the market through the use of any power, benign or malevolent, society tries to realign power so that citizens cannot abuse it excessively in the first place. (We cannot catch *all* abuse.) Politicians will not have the power to grant special favors, and businesses will not have the power to abuse the environment. Private welfare agencies, monitored by other private agencies, will care for the poor. They will be paid by the government, based on their success rate, not solely on the numbers of their clients. Impossible? See the next three chapters.

The market works because it is powerful, not because it is desirable. It represents not only the aggregate wishes of millions of people but also technology and available resources, none of which can be rolled back any more than the tide. Its power is grounded in these *underlying forces,* for technology, resources, and demand are hard or impossible to defeat except in the short run, but they do change over longer periods. Identifying them gradually became the foundation of liberal economics from Adam Smith (1776) to Alfred Marshall (1890). These determine the *market price* of any product, public or private, which equilibrates its supply and demand. In addition to the usual goods of the marketplace, in this book these products include all that people can supply and demand, such as protection of the environment, hiring labor or admitting students to universities without ethnic, gender, or other discrimination, adequate health care, unemployment and retirement insurance, and other items currently subject to legislation or lawsuit. All these are governed by supply (because without compensation they will not be provided) and demand (because people are willing to pay for them). The market price is what clears the market, equilibrating supply and demand.

21

In the moral economy, behavior is promoted by citizens not having the power, for the most part, to behave immorally. For this to come about, some of the underlying forces must be changed, over time, to bring a new distribution of power. Citizens will then supply the new social order freely rather than being required to do so by political or legal action, though some laws may be necessary to curb those who would take undue advantage of their freedom. Far better to harness the market than to thwart it.

On the supply side, underlying forces include technology of production and availability of factors of production (land, capital, materials, and labor) and the distribution of rights to these. On the demand side, they are the strength of consumer desire for a good or service, compared to other goods that consumers might buy, and the magnitude of the consumers' wealth. (Rich people can demand more than poor people.) The market price of bananas depends, on the supply side, on the extent of plantations; the availability of workers; the technology of picking, storing, transporting, and retailing; and the ability of those in charge to manage and sell. On the demand side it depends on how strongly consumers want bananas; how much money they can spend on them; and their alternative ways to spend that money, such as in buying oranges.[2] Invention (which means new technology), saving for more capital goods, new alternative opportunities for pickers, changes in consumer taste, and redistributions of wealth will change the underlying forces and therefore the market price.

However, if one has the power to set money prices high by international commodity agreement, to forbid producers to hire whom they wish or to pay wages below a minimum, or to tax banana exports, one can substitute a contrived price for the market price. The battle between political power and market power is begun. Consumers and producers both try to thwart the contrived prices. Consumers may buy fewer bananas—they might switch to oranges. Producers may increase their production but be unable to sell at the higher prices, so bananas rot. Though the market price continues to exist, it is invisible, and buyers and sellers seek evasive ways to restore it or else to produce or consume their second choices. These ways are wasteful, as any battle is wasteful—they use resources that would have been saved had prices not been contrived.

When the market brings "injustice," whatever one's definition, changing the results by contrived prices will not correct the situation, except for short periods. Only by changing the underlying forces can "justice" be obtained. For example, those with political power who believe the market does not supply the proper quantities of social security, food and housing for the poor, income for farmers, and so forth, often legislate contrived prices, such as minimum wages or ceilings on health care premiums. Government direct provision of these services, financed by taxes—which are not market determined—also amounts to contrived prices. However, producers remain constrained by technology and scarcity of inputs, and consumers do not change their preferences in the short run. A Muslim *hadith,* attributed to the Prophet, says it all about underlying forces: "Only God can fix prices."[3]

In the battle between government and producers/consumers, contrived prices cause social tensions: some suppliers are required to provide more than they freely would, or to hire some workers when they would prefer others or not to hire at all, or to be deprived of their resources by taxes, inflation, or fines. Contrived prices also cause inefficiency, in that evasive tactics use resources in the evasion alone, thus causing less output than would have been possible with given inputs at market prices. Economists call these *distortions* of the market, which lead to *deadweight losses.* The "obvious" answer, to achieve "justice" by paying cash to the poor or oppressed—make them richer—and to leave *them* free to buy needed services in the market, is not selected because citizens want to maintain their vicarious power over the poor, as we will see in the next section.

Vicarious Power

Respect for government in the Western[4] world reached a low ebb at the end of the twentieth century. Polls indicate lack of faith and the belief that politicians are self serving and corrupt, that government is wasteful and inefficient, and that government caters to undeserving special interests. At the same time, paradoxically, Westerners are entrusting more to government than ever before—schools, unemployment insurance, social security, welfare, environmental protection, and health care. Does it not seem odd that the voters should grant increasing power to those they believe have abused it so flagrantly?

The explanation lies in *vicarious power.* Citizens not themselves in government wish to hold power over other citizens through their elected representatives. They wish to make decisions for others that in classic liberalism would be made by the individuals directly concerned. Strong citizen sentiment holds that certain services should be available to all—everyone should be granted the same system of education, the same health care, the same social security pensions, and the same opportunity for welfare in case of need. Any who spurn these services in favor of private substitutes must still pay taxes to finance the public ones. Every conscientious voter tends to feel that he or she has the right answer about what educational system, what health care, how much social security, and so on, and it is only necessary to elect politicians of the same sentiment. The idea that each person should decide for himself or herself how much and which of these services to buy and should foot the bill for them, although with government help for the poor, finds little support. Yet citizens become impatient when the bureaucrats debate endlessly, cannot agree, and enrich themselves and their cronies through the power that the same citizens have bestowed upon them.

Vicarious power can be just as destructive as other power. Kindhearted, unselfish people who direct the behavior of others by government regulation tend to step well beyond constructive boundaries. They deprive other citizens of their rights to negotiate their own rules, such as over welfare, housing, health care, affirmative action, social security, education, and similar "good things." Vicarious power holders are like parents who direct their children's choices, even as they grow up. The societies of the Western world, as they become increasingly dependent on government, risk becoming—over the next two centuries—like children who have never learned to bargain and decide for themselves.

Vicarious power significantly influences analyses of political decisions on the major problems discussed in the next three chapters. It will also play a role in creating the institutions of the moral economy, as will be seen in part 2.

The Consumer and the Market

Who gains by the power of the market? The consumer, for whom real prices are reduced when the market rules. The real price of a product is its nominal (money) price compared to those of other products. Its real price declines if its nominal price goes up by less than general inflation. If real prices do not go down when they should, the consumer in the liberal market goes to competitors or buys different products. This ability will be increased further as the Internet becomes more widely used and as tariffs are reduced worldwide: in the moral economy the consumer will choose from markets everywhere. Often consumers are thought of as the least powerful of actors, since they are not organized in guilds or unions. In fact, their feet—walking away from overpriced or inferior goods—give consumers great power, unless the politicians, through government monopolies, quotas, or tariffs, prevent the exercise of that power. The consumer will also gain through a liberal market in air and water since these benefits may be obtained more cheaply and more thoroughly than they are now in the interventionist society.

All these principles—on the relative powers of the market versus interventionism—apply to central governments and private enterprise alike. Throughout eastern Europe and the Third World, governments are divesting themselves of economic activities that have failed. Why did they fail? First, lumping them together under the same management made no more sense than inefficient combinations in a private firm. What qualities found in the commander in chief of the armed forces make him or her the best CEO of health care? Second, other inefficiencies of interventionist management—corruption and extravagance—

have been so wasteful that taxes and borrowing to cover them are no longer tolerated by the electorate. Third, governments in the thrall of powerful groups that would destroy the environment for their own benefit do not create an ecologically safe world. (Witness the degree of pollution we now have.) Fourth, by selling public enterprises the governments gain a one-time increase in resources with which they can pay part of their overwhelming debts.

Clean air and water, preservation of forests, and other ecological objectives also have market prices, although they are more difficult to discern beneath the layers of distortion imposed upon them. The market price for protecting the air and water from pollution also depends on underlying forces, such as who has the right to use them; the incentives of right holders to protect them; the technology of protecting them; and the desires and wealth of persons who would "buy" or usurp the right to damage them. Just as ownership of a banana plantation is a property right, so also will air and water be protected only when those who have incentive to protect them—such as the Audubon Society or Nature Conservancy—own established property rights, guaranteed by law, and are not dependent on the goodwill of their supporters. At present, the "property rights" over air and water belong to governments by default, and these governments are swayed by their own selfish interests or the interests of those with power to elect them or bribe them.

In primarily market societies, the market performs functions that pass unnoticed until they are suddenly absent. When collective farms were initiated in the Soviet Union in the early 1930s, central decisions "had" to be made on such mundane things as the size of peasant farms, since peasants were not allowed to base these on market principles such as unit cost of planting large versus small areas, choice of crop, and the like. Instead, committees in Moscow divided the peasants (without seeing them) into three types—rich (but not the "too rich," since kulaks had been deported to Siberia or elsewhere), middle, and poor, deciding on different size plots according to the peasant, not according to the production. Billions of bureaucratic hours were spent on millions of picayune decisions—Stalin, who knew nothing about peasants, offered his ideas—which in market economies would have been made by peasants negotiating with each other.[5] Now consider the hours of bureaucratic time spent today in the more developed world on deciding the type and quantity of health care, social security pensions, education, and so on, that each person should receive, according to age or social classification. All these could be decided in far less time, and more agreeably, if the government simply gave money to those who could not otherwise afford these services and left the negotiations to them. Here is the power of the market.

In summary, virtually all that we now see as major problems can be resolved in a classic liberal society with the market as adjudicator; the power of the market is so great that any other method—such as contrived prices, prohibitions, and punishment—induces distortions that damage the economy and society and in the end turn out to be ineffective; and the consumer loses from contrived prices. However, changes in underlying forces, including income distribution, will be needed to assure fairness.

Many classic liberals have already declared victory for the power of the market, such as Fukuyama in his exaggerated "end of history."[6] Others have argued that the rush of technology, especially the Internet, which enables people the world over to defy government regulations and make their own arrangements with each other, implies victory by the end of the twenty-first century. Some have even said the nation-state is dying because multinational corporations, workers, and consumers transcend its boundaries. However, considering the ways in which powerful people have controlled the mechanisms of economics, and how they now try to control the Internet, I am not so sanguine. I believe the nation-state has enough stamina to keep it alive for the medium term, say two to three centuries. In the longer run, say a millennium, the power of the market will surely defeat political and even monopoly power, for underlying forces cannot be resisted forever. By the year 3000, however, a whole new configuration of technology and social and political forms may be ascending, which we cannot now foresee, and the same or a new power struggle—between the market and those who would control it—may be in place.

Intervention by the Private Sector

It is often presumed, incorrectly, that classic liberalism is associated with private firms and interventionism with government. However, a classic liberal society cannot exist without rules and property rights enforceable by governments, while on the other hand interventionism—or directed deviation from market prices—is often practiced in private business. Many American firms, being monopolies or semimonopolies, or protected by government regulations, earn *rents,* a technical economics term meaning excess profits stemming from monopoly or other situational or political advantage. Sometimes executives have shared these rents with workers by paying them higher than market wages while contenting themselves with lower salaries than they could earn elsewhere. International Business Machines (IBM) was famous for this practice. Whether they did so out of fairness or to assure worker loyalty is debated. With shifting technology, deregulation of many industries, freer world trade, and the rise of competitive firms in Asia and elsewhere, however, these rents were diminished; many rent-seeking firms could no longer defy the market and stay in business. In 1994, IBM was forced by world competition to raise executive salaries if they wanted to keep top-of-the-line managers, and they could no longer afford to pay secretaries more than the going wage elsewhere.

In Japan, loyalty to the firm, with lifetime employment expected, has been promoted by this same practice. The gap between the lowest- and highest-paid employees in Japanese firms has been much less than in the United States. However, the increasing competition of firms in other countries, especially in Asia, has led the Japanese to deviate from both lifetime employment and sharing rents within the firm.

In the United States, the gap between the highest-paid CEO and the lowest-paid menial worker is probably widening. With deregulation and more competition from abroad, both the CEO and the laborer are increasingly paid according to their separate (marginal) productivities. Most CEOs are paid more because they are believed to increase the efficiency and profits of the firm. David Balkin, a professor of management, says more is required of American CEOs than of CEOs in Japan or Europe. "They need to have leadership, a vision, and bring diverse people together on a large scale." They must "also possess political skills and interact well with the Wall Street investment community. Public speaking and the ability to lobby government regulatory boards are also important."[7] The scarcity of such persons causes their high salaries.

Controversy simmers over this, however, with publicized cases of CEOs who have been paid well despite poor performance. If profits increase because the general economy is improving, CEOs may be rewarded for what they did not achieve, just as presidents may be. More on this in chapter 6.

Many believe the gap is an injustice—their concept is of "fair" wages rather than wages according to productivity or market. Rather than injustice, I sense an unfortunate situation that can be corrected only by addressing the underlying forces: by creating more CEOs through education and experience—an increase in their supply will bring down their wage—or upgrading workers, again through education and culture. The forces leading to the "unfair" condition illustrate how the power of the market, fair or unfair, ultimately overrides political power. Recognizing this, we should move our concern away from "protecting" workers through contrived prices and direct it toward upgrading their skills.

The size of the firm is another arena in which changes in technology and globalization of markets have compelled producers to pay more attention to the market. How many different activities should be carried out under the roof of a single management? Should AT&T produce computers as well as telephones? Should a firm produce its own supplies and parts, or should it buy them? Should it run its own cafeteria or call in an outside restaurant chain? Market, or underlying, forces would require that where combinations of activities bring economies in management, they should be brought into the same firm; where they do not, separate firms are called for. Management guru Peter Drucker has argued that "large companies were hard to manage—if not unmanageable—unless they decentralized into small and autonomous units."[8]

The 1970s and 1980s saw many takeovers. If a firm were mismanaged, such as by charging prices different from the market, its profits would decline; its stock would lose value; and an outside group, believing it could better the situation, would buy up the low-priced stock, take over, and re-form the firm to the profit of stockholders (themselves), employees, and customers. Such opportunities, however, are often erroneously predicted or taken for power reasons rather than market or are otherwise done to excess. If takeovers do not conform to market principles, a reversal becomes likely. In the 1990s, many American firms were "downsizing" and "outsourcing," which together are the opposite of takeovers. For example, new communications make it possible to acquire inventory "just in time" from outside sources instead of manufacturing and storing it oneself, so the supply of inventories becomes outsourced. If management selects the wrong size firm, with the wrong number of activities under one roof, the penalties in a liberal market are losses and possible bankruptcy. Takeovers and downsizing are the results. Herein once more lies the power of the market.

Downsizing and outsourcing do not in themselves decrease employment, as some wrongly think. The same (or new) activities occur, just by different actors. Often a department split from its parent becomes an independent company, taking with it the same employees. In some cases, employees are without work until they find placements in the new firms. Overall unemployment in the United States has not increased with downsizing.

The Power-Diffusion Process

To approach balance of power, we continue a process of power diffusion long existing in the West and Japan. In the millennium ending in the nineteenth century, people of lower socioeconomic levels in northwestern Europe and Japan wrested power from kings, emperors, church, nobility, and shoguns to create societies of interest groups that balanced each other tolerably, curbed extravagances moderately, and held each other accountable—to a degree—for the use of world resources. In *Centuries of Economic Endeavor,*[9] I called this the *power-diffusion process.*

Beginning as far back as the ninth century CE, and increasingly as the Middle Ages progressed, both Japan and northwestern Europe were becoming pluralist societies, possessing many economic interest groups. These included not only emperors, kings, religious orders, nobility of different ranks and properties, government servants, knights and other military, but lower-level groups such as guilds, monasteries, village associations, and peasant warrior bands. The formation of these groups was not unique, since interest groups exist all over the world. Unique to Japan and northwestern Europe was the extent to which these groups bargained corporately, as organized bodies, across social lines, or "vertically."

For example, two upper-level groups (say, king and nobility) would contest land, power, or anything else. A lower-level group (say, peasants) would ally itself with either king or nobility, exacting power or privilege as its compensation if its side won. I call this process *leverage,* because the weaker group levers its power on the coattails of the stronger. If its side lost, it would bide its time until the next occasion. Through many thousands of vertical alliances with leverage, over centuries power became extended to more and more groups in northwestern Europe and Japan. By holding each others' extravagances within limits, the groups allowed entrepreneurship to flower and complex organizations to be formed, while war was increasingly held in check. Galbraith wrote of this process as "countervailing power," which he applies to corporations in *American Capitalism.* I have extended it to cover the entire economy.

Diffusion of power also helps limit warfare. Powerful rulers like Henry V or Henry VIII, Hitler, Mussolini, and Saddam Hussein are far more likely to wage aggressive war than are democratically-elected governments with separation of powers. From this I hypothesize that placing power in the hands of government, even for benign purposes such as social security and health care, or for economic development, gradually builds up to the probability that such governments—to exert or strengthen their power, or to flex the muscles of rulers—will some day initiate a war.

In Japan and northwestern Europe—unlike in the rest of the world—the institutions of cooperation were forged primarily by the parties concerned, who bargained corporately one-on-one. Contract and commercial law was written primarily by merchants and guilds; the monetary system was fashioned by lenders, borrowers, and traders, and so on. Not only were labor conditions negotiated by employers and workers, but so also were the procedures for bargaining. In the rest of the world, by contrast, these institutions were mostly handed down by sovereigns. In their bargaining, the Japanese and northwestern Europeans built accountability, or checks and balances, into their systems to prevent abuse by powerful parties. Roughly speaking, the same accountability did not mature in the rest of the world, for the sovereign resisted limiting his power. The result was that Japan and northwestern Europe led the world in economic development. Many examples of this process, a more detailed explanation of why it happened only in northwestern Europe and Japan, and an argument for its relationship to economic development are all found in *Centuries.*

With modern democracy, however, the same two or more interest groups that used to negotiate directly began instead to rely on government to make and enforce their rules of conduct. Governments moved to control private monopolies. Governments found ways to advance the welfare of their citizens at the expense of foreigners. In the United States, a great depression called for centralized action, or so it seemed. Because of all these occurrences, the world passed into decades of government intervention whose full implications are only now being appreciated.

It turned out that the government and the law are not—as some political theorists supposed—merely the arbitrators for citizens and enforcers of rules. Bureaucrats assumed powers of their own, becoming themselves interest groups intent upon keeping and expanding their territories. While some of them acted honorably and effectively, for the most part their inefficiencies, corruption, extravagance, and unfairness became intolerable to much of the general public, which responded with the move back toward classic liberalism. Whereas before the nineteenth century the main struggle was to limit the prerogatives of sovereigns, for the next millennium it will be to contain the expanding prerogatives of elected government officials, while again forging a balance of power among free-acting interest groups so that none will dominate the rest.

Robert Samuelson finds an additional negative in the political shift toward central authority. In the 1960s, he states, "conflicts then bubbled up from the depths of society, and the political superstructure—the president, Congress, other elected and appointed officials—tried to grapple with them. By contrast, today's conflicts often are consciously nurtured (if not created) by political leaders and elites."[10] "Nurtured conflicts" arise out of the growing need of politicians to maintain their power; one way to do so is to promote an increasingly adversarial society that calls on them to defend polarized positions.

Whereas corporate bargaining by interest groups, one-on-one, appears to be the characteristic of the power-diffusion process historically, the twentieth century has shown that the same process may occur by the spreading of mass protests among unorganized groups and individuals in an incipient democracy. For example, power in Peru in the 1990s was concentrated in a president (Fujimori) and the heads of the military and intelligence service. Fujimori achieved great popularity by standing up against guerrilla warriors such as the Shining Path (Sendero Luminoso) and by storming the Japanese embassy that had been taken over, in 1996-97, by other guerrillas, called Tupac Amaru. However, his power eroded when he could not stand up to the other two members of the trio. In deference to them, in 1997, he clamped down on a prominent journalist who had revealed a plot by "the national intelligence agency to secretly record the telephone conversations of dozens of politicians, business executives, and journalists."[11] This was but the last straw in a number of similar abuses that mobs took to the streets to protest.

They could not have done this a few decades ago. Only when economic power becomes widespread at a basic, nongoverning level may massive protests against arbitrary authorities serve the same purpose earlier undertaken by interest groups negotiating vertically. The Peruvian example might easily be a harbinger of power diffusion in China and other emerging areas in the twenty-first century.

The holder of inordinate power is like a cancer in the human body. When it first appears, "there are tens of thousands of other genes which will thrive if they accidentally stumble on mechanisms that will cause the suppression of the selfish mutant."[12] Thus most cancers die. But if the cancer cell grows to the point of dominating others, it can destroy the body of which it and other cells are parts. This book maintains that holders of inordinate power of any sort, both private and government, are like cancer cells of any sort. They tend to overcome the resistance of other members, finally destroying their own society. Witness the Soviet Union.

In summary: uniquely in northwestern Europe and Japan, interest groups with "relatively well balanced power" negotiated the rules, such as commercial law and the monetary system, in such a way that no group, including government, could dominate the others. Since the resulting institutions could not be distorted to serve individual interests "excessively," no group could spend resources "extravagantly." (Quotation marks indicate that meanings are subjective.) The efficiency of such a system contributed to economic development through the following steps: power diffusion leads to classic liberalism; which leads to economic development; which leads to more egalitarian distributions of income and wealth, more concern over environmental protection, population restraint, gender and ethnic equality, and income, health, employment security. This is a rough order of things, to which there are many exceptions and qualifications. In the twenty-first century, the same process may occur through massive pressure by dissatisfied citizens who have achieved a spread of economic power wide enough to offset that of the state.

The power-diffusion process should not be taken as a complete theory of economic development, however. Instead, it complements other theories, such as Schumpeter's classical roles for business cycles and entrepreneurs, the cultural theories of North and Olson, and geographic theories of Kamarck and Diamond, all of which I admire and in some parts agree with. Economic development is enormously complex, and no simple theory can explain it.

What can be said is that the greatest economic development has occurred, and continues to occur, in societies that tend toward classic liberalism and that liberal economic development brings with it distributions of income closer to equality (though never reaching it), plus increasing concern for social and environmental problems. These propositions will be defended in the next three chapters.

The History of Liberalism

Arising in the seventeenth and eighteenth centuries in Europe, liberals were those who wished to *liberate* the people from the control of monarchs and the nobility. These were the pursuits of writers like Hume, Smith, and Locke, while they were opposed by conservatives who saw value in the elitist order, such as Hobbes, who favored "liberalism" under an absolute monarch, and Burke, who favored "orderly" change. The nineteenth century was the "age of liberalism" in the West, as new industries were formed after the industrial revolution, and as price-controlling guilds declined. In that century the same liberals who favored freedom of enterprise also attempted to correct its defects. Liberals first fought for free popular education, factory acts limiting child labor, antitrust laws, and price regulations for "necessary" monopolies such as public utilities. These reforms were all intended to strengthen the liberal society, and because of them liberals became known as reformers or "progressives."

By supporting Roosevelt's New Deal and a host of other social reforms in the twentieth century, however, American liberals took a new turn. All these reforms implied government intervention that went beyond strengthening freedom of enterprise. Although democratically arrived at, the reforms were not necessarily achieved by consensus or even with respect for the feelings of dissidents, and it is still disputed whether they served more to divide or to unite the society. American "liberals" kept their name, however, as they became more interventionist.

However valuable these reforms, they revert to an earlier ethic—*sovereign dispensation*—which contrasts with the liberal market. In medieval times, kings and nobility obtained their consumption goods through taxation, monopoly privilege, and regulations in their favor, not by buying them in the liberal market with incomes derived from their employments. Interventionists, who would today ask the state to supply unemployment insurance, health care, social security, and other goods, have reverted to sovereign dispensation, except that the people as a whole have replaced the king and nobility as sovereigns.

In short, the difference between the classic liberal and the interventionist ethic does not lie in whether advocates are humane—will or will not help the poor or protect the environment, do or do not advocate social security, health care, and the like—nor in the amount of resources to be devoted to such activities. Rather, it lies in whether the government will finance them with cash or vouchers such as food stamps and leave the individuals to choose their amounts and their suppliers, bargaining for lower cost (the classic liberal ethic) or whether the government itself shall supply these services (the interventionist ethic), as does the government of the United States in social security and Medicare.

Whether one is classic liberal or interventionist depends not only on what the rules are but on how they are made. A classic liberal, under the definition of this book, will not wish a rule to be adopted, or law made, or civil judgment issued, without widespread agreement. In the interventionist philosophy, on the other hand, this respect for others is subordinated to obtaining the "right" mode of behavior, whether it is widely agreed upon or not. For example, the classic liberal would seek a compromise on smoking in public places, preserving the rights of smokers to smoke and of nonsmokers not to be bothered by them. The interventionist might have smoking banned for health reasons, regardless of the feelings of smokers.

Those who make critical national decisions enjoy a feeling of importance that I have called "power as a consumer good," as opposed to "power as a capital good," which yields a money income. President Kennedy is reported to have said his was the best job he had ever had. Some take power in stride, as if it is their natural attribute, but many a middling government official, who yesterday spoke with someone who spoke with someone who spoke with the president, senses exhilaration at being close to the center of power, akin to the "high" of a stimulating drug. This is my subjective judgment, made not from research but from having lived among middling officials and even having been one myself.

Two Rules on Power

The message on power diffusion can be summarized in two rules:

1. *Power expands until other power stops it.* Hosking expresses this rule with respect to Russia: "Expansion comes to an end only when Russia fetches up against another power capable of offering effective resistance and of affording a predictable frontier, so that future relations can be conducted on a diplomatic rather than a military footing."[13] I have merely extended this rule to apply to power in all contexts, not just territorial.

2. *Holders of excessive power accumulate resources excessively and prevent the economy from functioning optimally. They are the principal causes of underdevelopment, spoliation of the environment, and poverty.* This rule applies no matter who are the power holders: feudal lords, dictators, business corporations, or democratically elected governments.

The expansion of government power is an example of rule number 1. In the democratic world of the twentieth century, in which economies became too complex for all groups to sit down in a single room, decisions previously negotiated among groups were entrusted to the legislature as their representative. However, branches of government began to take on powers of their own, quite apart from those of the interest groups. They no longer served as pure referee but acted in such a way as to preserve their own power. The resulting economic decisions often became different from those that might have been negotiated had only the interested parties, or their representatives, met face to face.

Here is an example: in 1996, my home city of Boulder, Colorado, having passed an antismoking ordinance applicable to all restaurants, argued that actors on the stage of a dinner theater should not be allowed to smoke, even though smoking was called for in their script. Letters to the newspapers questioned whether—with wars going on in Bosnia, the Middle East, and Chechnya, and hunger in many parts of Africa—taxpayer resources devoted to arguing this case in court were well spent. ("Don't you have something better to do?") In a liberal market, either the patrons of the dinner theater would not care about actors smoking, or if they did they would attend a different theater. Instead, one must suppose that strict enforcement of the ordinance served the latent function of making the enforcers feel important. (Because of pressure from constituents, in this case the council eventually made an exception for actors.)

Another example: in 1995, Barbara Williams, a small restaurant operator in Gettysburg, Pennsylvania, who was careful about the environment—always recycling, never putting toxic waste in the trash—was charged, under the Superfund Law, with having dumped her garbage in a landfill in which toxic waste was found. "The law carries 'strict liability,' which means that once the government proves Ms. Williams used the local dump, she will be deemed guilty."[14] On its face, the law would appear to be unconstitutional, since it would deprive Ms. Williams of her property when no guilt on her part could be proved. But the cost to defend herself would be so great that she might find it cheaper to pay her "share" of the fine. The greater question, however, is why the Environmental Protection Agency—presumably an impartial arbiter seeking justice—is so lacking in compassion as to charge her in the first place. The only explanation that comes to me is that they have the power to do so; their power has expanded (by rule no. 1) into an area where no other power has yet stopped them; and exercising that power gives them a kind of "high."

Still another example is the announcement of the International Monetary Fund, early in 1997, that in its negotiations with Argentina, it will give its seal of approval based not on the economic criteria that had previously been its only basis but also on evidence of "good governance, as emphasizing spending on health and education, overhauling the tax system, improving court practices, strengthening private property rights and opening Government ledgers."[15] Later in the year, both the IMF and the World Bank announced that hereafter the ability to control corruption would be a criterion for their lending.[16] After the East Asian crisis of 1997-98, the Fund began making demands for revised corporate structures and corporate regulation.[17] All these may be worthy goals, but proponents of the moral economy—who prefer these "goodies" to be created through citizen power—will resent "Big Brother" strengthening the power of government to regulate them. How will the IMF and World Bank make judgments that normally require an immersion in the affairs of member countries far beyond the tolerable? These are examples of organizations expanding their power until other power stops them.

The same kinds of questions arise with programs such as social security. If all contributors and beneficiaries in social security were to negotiate with those ready to offer pensions—both the government and private insurance companies—would they all decide on precisely the same system as the one supplied by the government, or would there be variations? In a liberal market, decisions on social security, prices, wages, production, safety regulations, and rules to protect the environment are negotiated among the groups concerned and not by a "benevolent" government enjoying its power.

The Welfare State

The twentieth century saw the rise and fall of socialism and the rise and twilight of the welfare state. A *welfare state* is one that provides its citizens with certain services—such as health care, unemployment insurance, and old-age pensions—by sovereign dispensation. A country may be more or less of a welfare state depending on the extent and quantity of these services. When I refer to Japan and the West as classic liberal societies, for example, I refer to their classic liberal attributes; when I refer to them as welfare states, I refer to their welfare attributes. Thus a country can be partly one and partly the other.

The welfare state anywhere has four major problems. First, it caters to everyone, not just the poor—everyone receives health care, social security, and so on—which means that poorer people are being taxed to support these services for wealthy corporate executives, entertainment stars, and highly paid athletes. But second, and more serious, governments always promise more than the people are willing to pay for. Therefore, they always renege, ultimately. Every government in Europe, and Canada as well, is denying health services it once promised; queues and postponements are increasing; and the future will probably see more of that. In New Zealand, an eighty-year-old welfare state, which had provided its services in part by borrowing abroad, was reversed in the late 1980s when its credit ran out in world markets. In the elections of 1996 in Australia, both parties recognized the need to cut down on the welfare state to balance the budget. In the United States, safety in work offices—which used to be decided by bargaining between unions and employers—is now the province of the Occupational Safety and Health Administration (OSHA). OSHA's activities are cut back for want of funds; the muscle that unions have not exercised recently has become flaccid; and workers are at risk. Social security is an empty fund, containing only government IOUs: one pocket owes the other. Because of baby boomers, by 2020 social security will no longer be able to pay the retired with the contributions of the still-working. The third consequence is that funds intended for the welfare state can be diverted into other budget categories such as war. Clearly this has happened to the social security fund in the United States. Fourth—the most significant consequence to my mind—is that the welfare state robs citizens of their autonomy and creativity in those areas where it supplies services.

This final consequence is highlighted in a book on death and dying, in which Dr. Timothy Quill writes about one of his terminal patients: "Her professors [in her PhD program in Psychology], who shared her disdain for traditional educational methods, were engaged in the scientific study of the relative educational efficacy of *enhancing versus controlling a learner's autonomy*"[18] (emphasis added). This patient died of cancer in 1992 at age 37, but she had taken control of the dying process, made the best of what she desperately did not want, and turned it into a beautiful experience.

That patient (my own daughter) applied to her death her observation about authoritarian professors, who would limit a student's autonomy, in contrast to those who would enhance autonomy to encourage creativity. The doctor might either abandon the terminal patient to die on her own or help her convert death into a cooperative experience of doctor, patient, religious persons, family, and friends. The enhancement or control of people's autonomy applies to many fields of social action, not the least of which is economic development.

The welfare state is in twilight, for the same reasons as socialism earlier: inefficiency, corruption, and its inability to fulfill its promises. More importantly, the welfare state assumes responsibilities that have in the West traditionally belonged to the people, either by voluntary collective action or individualism. It controls rather than enhances the autonomy of its citizens. As this has occurred, the people forget how to defend themselves and lapse into a condition that psychologists call "learned helplessness." When the state fails them, they have lost. For examples, see chapter 11 on Ukraine.

Profit

To many, the principal argument against the classic liberal society is that its economics is driven by profit, and profit is immoral. It is associated with greed, manifest in executives who fail in "corporate responsibility." They see only their own narrow interests and not those of the community as a whole, caring little for the environment, for example. They raise their own salaries sky-high while downsizing their companies by firing workers. Greed also refers to technicians who take undue risks, monopolies that destroy their competitors, ostentatious display such as the Trump Tower, and physical abuse of workers such as illegal immigrants.

But greed does not correlate with a system, such as communist, socialist, free enterprise, or other. Instead, I prefer to treat greed in chapter 10, on morality. There we ask the hard questions of this paragraph: whether business morality, that would maximize profits, is different from personal morality toward our fellow human beings. Is compassion lacking in business but present in government? In the current section we limit ourselves to the economic functions of profit and their limitations.

Every society requires a means to determine which goods and services will be produced and who will get them. In interventionist societies, particularly socialist, sovereign dispensation is the method chosen—the government chooses. In free-enterprise societies, on the other hand, profit is the driving force. Many years ago, Paul Samuelson wrote in his *Economics* that every day the right quantity of groceries arrives on the shelves of every grocery store in New York; they are regularly sold, little is wasted, and few stores run out completely: "all this is undertaken without coercion or centralized direction by any conscious body!"[19] This marvelous but daily routine is achieved by the profit motive: grocers, dairies, farms, and all others involved produce the quantity needed at the lowest possible cost in order to maximize their profit.

If someone is earning too high a profit by market standards, someone else will start a rival business, provided that firms may be initiated freely or shut down by their owners or creditors, a classic liberal principle. The new competitor will offer the same goods at a lower price, or better goods at the same price, or some combination, forcing the original producer to reduce price and profit. Profit after these adjustments is the market return on capital invested, in the same manner that wages are the market return for labor.[20] The quest for profit causes productive resources to flow into those fields where demand exceeds supply and away from those where supply exceeds demand. Thus profit is the regulator that causes the right goods and services to be produced, in the right quantities and at the right prices, to meet demand at reasonable cost.

The profit motive does not always lead to prices and wages that we consider "fair." A great gap remains between the wages of the highest-paid CEO and the lowest-paid worker. Monopolies distort the market, yielding profits not in accordance with the principles of the preceding paragraph. I recognize these imperfections but put off their discussion until chapter 10, where we will consider private versus business morality.

The profit motive conserves resources. Firms consuming more resources than necessary are driven out of business by competitors conscious of cost. Socialism failed mainly on this point: it operated with goals other than profit maximization, and the resulting waste drove governments and state-owned enterprises into near-bankruptcy, at great cost to the natural environment. As this book goes to press, the advanced countries are about to bail out a number of east Asian countries where the profit motive was subordinated to lax credit policies: not being disciplined by profit as a measure of value, businesses in these countries wasted these billions of dollars. When a grocery shopper compares prices among stores, he or she is responding to the profit motive: to seek the greatest surplus for the family with a given amount of resources. In an interventionist society, spending units are accountable to overseers and regulators, whose duty is to make sure that waste is minimized, but who are themselves corruptible and often lack incentives for efficiency. In a classic liberal society, they are accountable to the market, which performs the same function—with some corruption and inefficiency, but not nearly so much, because the person who cheats is likely to be the one who pays. More on accountability in chapter 6. More on East Asia in chapter 12.

By responding to profit a competitive society creates more resources than it consumes. If a firm produces goods worth $5,000 in the liberal market, at a labor and capital cost of $4,000, it has created $1,000 more of resources than it has consumed; its profit is the financial counterpart of this real surplus.

Finally, I believe profit as a motive is overstated by those who oppose it in principle. Many entrepreneurs are motivated by professional satisfaction as much as by profit, although profit is necessary for their survival. Some economists have questioned whether profit is a motive at all, noting that a large enterprise does not possess a monolithic brain that forecasts the results of every choice by its profit projection. Instead, numerous decisions are made by individuals who try to maximize their own positions rather than the profit of the firm.

In summary, interventionists often associate profit with greed, inconsiderateness, environmental destruction, and other bad things. Drawing on economic theory, classic liberals think profit is merely the regulator of which goods are produced, who can buy them, what prices are paid, and who receives the income associated with the production. Any of these activities may be associated with greed and inconsiderateness, but they may also be associated with acts of generosity and kindness. Which rules in any case depends on personal characteristics and not on "the system." Socialism—for many years lauded as the "ideal" society by those who opposed profit making—turned out to be characterized by extreme greed, intolerance, and brutality.

Chapter 3
Poverty

In an efficient, compassionate, and just society, with present resources and technology, no one need be poor. The world possesses the resources to feed, clothe, and house all its people adequately. That we do not do so—this chapter argues—is mainly the result of illiberal societies. An illiberal society arises out of skewness of power—both explicit and vicarious—or monopoly, lack of trust among people, warfare, and other cultural inhibitions, which slow economic interaction. To understand this, we must examine poverty separately in the less developed and the more developed areas.

Economic theory tells us that a classic liberal society leads to a maximum economy: the greatest value of goods and services that can be produced with given resources and technology. Economic history shows that a classic liberal society also leads toward a more nearly equal distribution of income and wealth. In either case, unfettered individuals—including the poor—have the intelligence, perspicacity, and sense of cooperation to join voluntarily in positive-sum moves that eliminate poverty, provided no one prevents them from doing so. Possible obstacles are conglomerations of power, either private or public, or a culture that forbids its members from making economically advantageous moves.

Some attribute poverty to the low intelligence of the poor. However, many of the poor are no less intelligent than the rest of us and are capable of taking initiative. The burst of entrepreneurship among Chinese peasants and the increase in agricultural output after the Deng reforms of 1976 are prime examples. Gray cites the entrepreneurial experiences of many African tribes in adapting to European invasions.[1] Harms tells a similar story for central Africa.[2] De Soto and Dietz and Moore have studied the successes of the informal sector in Peru.[3] Herrenstein and Murray argue on the other side, that poverty is associated with low intelligence. However, the statistical methods of these authors have been shown to be faulty, so their results are not persuasive.[4]

The Gap between the More and the Less Developed World

We do not know when the gap between nations began. It is likely that ancient Greek and Roman societies had greater incomes and wealth than did African and Asian societies, but we have no solid information. Probably the gap widened in the Middle Ages—with technological improvements in agriculture and manufacturing in Europe—but the big differences appeared after the industrial revolution of the eighteenth and nineteenth centuries. Japan joined the more developed countries in the twentieth century, but the foundations for its membership were laid from the seventeenth through the nineteenth, as the institutions of economic development were forged. Marxists argue that the gap resulted from Europeans stealing slaves from less developed areas, colonizing them, and buying their raw materials at very low prices to make their own industrialization possible. However, those countries that did most of this—Spain and Portugal in the Americas and Russia in eastern Europe—were the slowest to develop, while those, like England and the Netherlands, where innovations in technology, industry, and finance were concentrated, became the leaders. Enlightenment thinking and liberal trade played their part.

Comparisons of gross national income per capita in 1995 are shown in table 3-1, where the gap reflects the difference between richest and poorest. The gap is not a blank, however, for other countries are scattered through it.

The Internal Gap

Not only do we find a gap between groups of nations but within nations. The distribution of income and wealth has always been more highly skewed within

TABLE 3-1.

Gross National Product Per Capita for Selected Countries

(in U.S. Dollars, 1995)

South Asia	350
Sub-Saharan Africa	490
China	620
Algeria	1,600
Russian Federation	2,240
Latin America and the Caribbean	3,320
The Gap	
United Kingdom	18,700
Hong Kong	22,900
United States	26,980
Germany	27,510
Japan	39,640

Source: **World Bank,** *World Tables* **1997:214-15.**

the less developed areas, which include northwestern Europe and Japan in the Middle Ages. As economic development advanced in these areas, so the internal gap (the gap within countries) narrowed. Where economic development was slow or nonexistent, as in the rest of the world, the internal gap remained wide.

Historical records are not systematic—scattered studies of particular places at particular times use different kinds of information, generally incomplete. Yet subject to these uncertainties, we must come to some opinion on the relationship of underdevelopment to income distribution.

From time to time we read nostalgic essays that assume harmony, equality, and willingness to share wealth in ancient hunting-gathering tribes. Nothing in archaeological studies or historical records confirms this. For example, studies of the ancient Maya show that common people were smaller than the ruling classes and did not live as long.[5] From the beginning of written history until the nineteenth century, reports of maldistribution are many, but I quote only a few: "The disposable wealth of the Greek world came to be concentrated . . . in able and ambitious hands."[6] In Rome of the first century CE, an unskilled worker might earn four sesterces a day, but Cicero considered fifty thousand sesterces too meager for a gentleman.[7] In 1427, 10 percent of the people in Florence, Italy, owned 68 percent of the total wealth, while 60 percent owned only 5 percent.[8] In Turkey in the sixteenth century, "members of the military-administrative group controlled by far the greatest wealth and economic resources."[9] In seventeenth-century Italy, "the building of magnificent cathedrals at a time when hospital beds were so scarce that the sick had to be piled up two or more to a bed reflects the unequal distribution of wealth."[10]

Three writers—Gregory King in 1688, Joseph Massie in 1760, and Patrick Colquhoun in 1803—attempted to quantify the distribution of wealth in England, and although their figures are largely guesses, they correspond with much anecdotal information. All three agreed that the richest of the population (nobility, gentry, and rentiers) had annual incomes of about fourteen hundred times those of the poorest (soldiers and laborers).[11] These are the extremes. Comparing the ordinary nobility with ordinary workers, "King estimated that the average noble family had an income over fifty times greater than that of an army officer, and a hundred and fifty times greater than an ordinary seaman."[12]

Less Developed Areas: The Internal Gap Remains

With modern measurements, it is now clear that the distribution of both wealth and income is still more skewed in less developed than in more developed countries. In the early 1970s, a number of countries were studied by different researchers. These studies, which were compiled and summarized by Shail Jain of the World Bank, show high indexes of disparity within the less developed countries at that time.[13] The few studies done since then show little change. For example, a Brazilian economics institute showed in 1998 that "the richest 20 percent of the Brazilian population still hold more than 60% of the nation's wealth, while the poorest 20% account for about 2%."[14] Casual observers and newspaper reports about the urban slums, the deprivation experienced by farmers in Africa, and the munificent homes of the rich reinforce the statistical studies.

After examining many historical reports, as well as current data, I have come to believe that income and property distribution in ancient times was highly skewed everywhere—a few powerful people virtually held an enormous proportion and did not share with lesser folk, such as serfs and slaves; that distribution has become more egalitarian along with economic development; and that today it is still highly skewed in the less developed areas but has become more egalitarian in the industrial world.

Why has the internal gap stubbornly remained in the less developed countries?

Less developed countries share certain characteristics in common, whether they are present-day less developed, as in Asia, Africa, and Latin America, or less developed of an earlier time, as in Europe and Japan of the Middle Ages. All these characteristics may also be found in the more developed world but not nearly to the same extent as in the less developed world. In this book, I will argue not simply that these characteristics correlate with low per capita income, which they do mainly but occasionally do not, but that *they constitute the basis for a new definition of lesser development.* The characteristics that define lesser development are the following, albeit in different proportions in different areas and different eras:

> *Concentration of power.* A small elite possesses the power to direct many aspects of citizens' lives, including their right to do business, to employ others, and to own land or other assets. Severe restrictions, all the way to outright prohibition, may be placed on some or all of these. The governor of the central bank and the minister of finance jointly have far greater power over monetary policy than do their counterparts in more developed countries and furthermore are apt to act in collusion rather than as counterpoises to each other, which is the case in more developed countries. In some countries, bosses—in Mexico, *caciques*—command local populations. Constituents are expected to vote as they are told and to obey in other ways. Those who do not do so may suffer physically or be eradicated.

> *Government monopolies.* Up until only a few years ago, government monopolies covered a wide range of products deemed to be of "national importance," such as oil, railroads, airlines, cement, fertilizer, agricultural credit, and numerous others that in the more developed world are sold in the private market. These were justified as

belonging to "the people," but in practice they were operated by the few for the benefit of the few. Prices were set, often capriciously, in the capital city, far from the areas where operations occurred. Therefore, they were not necessarily related to cost. In the 1990s, many of these monopolies have been privatized—ownership presumably spread among the many—but the fact that privatization is dictated from above and forced by financial necessity, rather than arising from below, makes them historically suspect. For example, many are sold into private concentrations of power that may be as corrupt as the government concentrations.

Poor accounting and accountability. These government monopolies, and private businesses as well, often do not adhere to standards of auditing and accountability to creditors and stockholders that are found in more developed countries. Government and business assets may be siphoned into the pockets of the small elite. The distinction between private, business, and government assets is often not clear.

Governments in disarray. Where the economy depends heavily on the actions of the state, as in most less developed countries, any disarray in the government itself, such as through confrontational disputes among the ruling elite, or armed repression, may slow the economy. "Nearly three years after American troops and aid began pouring into this country . . . the Haitian Government is all but paralyzed by internal squabbling that has left the economy moribund and the populace irate."[15]

Human rights. A greater degree of personal cruelty is found in less developed than in more developed areas, such as torture of political prisoners or guerrilla and terrorist actions that disrupt the lives of others. Torture was common in medieval Europe: during the Inquisition, prisoners were burned, flayed, and had their bodies pulled apart. "In village games [in fourteenth-century France], players with hands tied behind them competed to kill a cat nailed to a post by battering it to death with their heads, at the risk of cheeks ripped open or eyes scratched out by the frantic animal's claws."[16] Torture is found in more developed countries today, but when it is disclosed, it is usually met with wide publicity and public disgust, in contrast to the less developed world where—barring an especially egregious event such as the Argentine "dirty war" (see chapter 10)—it is often routine.

Confrontation and violence. Again relative to more developed countries, extreme positions are more likely than moderate ones, and violence may be a first rather than last resort for conflict resolution. In some countries, warfare is endemic: while there may be periods of peace, the threat of low-level war and violent acts is always present.

Authority by position rather than experience. An official may be considered an authority merely because he or she holds a position. For example, a minister of education appointed as a political favor thinks he knows more about how to teach seventh grade than the teacher in the field. The same for the minister of economy with respect to business, the minister of agriculture with respect to farming, and so on. These officials will impose curricula and regulations that do not make sense to the person in the field. Meetings between government officials and their subordinates tend to be one-way conversations, with the official (almost always male) stating his views and not seeking subordinates' opinions. (I have experienced this myself many times as a "subordinate" economic advisor in less developed countries.)

Capriciousness. Government regulations are often passed or enforced in one year and repealed or ignored in the next. Forecasting a business budget becomes difficult. Taxes and subsidies change from year to year. This quality is also found in more developed countries but surely to lesser extent.

Unclear law and arbitrary enforcement. Law is not always clear. Frequently a law, on the books but widely ignored, is suddenly enforced against a political opponent. Imprisonment or execution are frequent ways to get rid of political opposition.

Business restrictions. Price controls are common, and firms are sometimes not allowed to close down when they are unprofitable. Compensation for several years ahead may be required for workers being fired, with or without cause, a practice that discourages firms from hiring them in the first place. In many countries, agricultural products must be sold to government monopolies at prices lower than market, while inputs (fertilizer, seed, credit) are obtained from other government monopolies at high prices. The resulting squeeze on farmers has caused many to give up agriculture and move to city slums. Richard Stock and I documented this situation for over twenty countries in *The Peasant Betrayed.*

Restrictions on freedom of speech. The governments in less developed countries place restrictions on speech and press far more than is the case in more developed countries.

Public versus private, and corruption. In many countries public offices are treated as private property. In medieval England and France, offices were regularly sold by the monarch, and crises would arise when he wished to dismiss a person who had bought an office. Murder is an occasional means of dismissal in less developed countries today. Holders of offices routinely sell their services—sales that would be described in the more developed world as bribery or corruption—

and the right to disobey a law, as in drug traffic. Payrolls of both government and government enterprises are often bloated with sinecures and fictitious appointments.

Absence of invention and scientific discovery. Although entrepreneurship abounds in areas of lesser development, few scientific discoveries arise.

Little caring about environment. Environmental problems are the concern of the rich, according to much thinking in less developed countries. The rich caused these problems by their earlier industrialization, and their proposals for world controls are taken as a way to suppress the poor. The poor countries should be allowed their share of pollution to catch up, and only when they become rich—which is not yet—should they restrain themselves. They do not see the environment as a mutual problem of rich and poor living in the same world.

High population growth. Although it is now declining, the rate of population growth has long been greater in less developed than in more developed countries. Since all less developed countries had low rates before the seventeenth century, one reason for the current surge may be the spread of medical and health innovations from more to less developed areas. Demographers predict that populations in less developed areas will increase for another half century before the rate of increase approaches zero.

Widespread urban slums. Masses of people congregate in slums, living in anything from cardboard boxes to shacks made of leftover materials. In some countries the government bulldozes the slums occasionally, to "improve" the cities for tourism or to force the occupants to move back to the country. Rarely do they move en masse, however, and the slums crop up again elsewhere.

High unemployment. Casual observers see many people walking or loitering in both urban and rural areas, apparently without gainful employment. One wonders where they receive their sustenance.

Social service programs that do not work well. Many governments in less developed areas have passed laws providing retirement security, health care, and unemployment insurance. Closer inspection, however, reveals that retirement allotments are inadequate, health care poor and available only after long waits, and unemployment insurance nonexistent in practice.

Shorter life expectancy. Because of poor health and sanitary conditions, malnutrition, and other living conditions, life expectancy is shorter in less developed than in more developed countries.

Communication. Less communication occurs among social groups in less developed than in more developed countries. Accounting disclosure is not well developed among businesses, nor is disclosure in general of activities and data that in more developed areas are considered to be of public concern. The elite frequently have little idea of life in the villages; governments and guerrillas rarely talk to each other, and peasants are sometimes classified wholesale as guerrillas when in fact they have not been engaged in any political activity. Guatemala is an extreme case of this, although recent events—the election of Arzu as president— offer a possible improvement.

Poverty. Economists think of countries of low per capita income as less developed. Because economics has recently restricted itself mainly to quantities measurable with numbers—some economists have even said that if something cannot be measured it does not exist— they have focused on low income and largely ignored the other attributes of lesser development.

Informal economy. Because of all the previously mentioned restrictions, "informal economies" have sprung up in many less developed countries: goods that are made and traded freely but illegally. Sometimes these are countenanced because the nation could not live without them. Because they are always subject to arbitrary enforcement of the law, however, they encounter costs of avoidance.

As the "less developed countries" were brought to the attention of the Western world after World War II, it was presumed that their plight was due to lack of capital. President Mobutu of Zaire (now Congo) referred to his country as "undercapitalized," not "underdeveloped." This lack was to have been redressed by loans from the World Bank and foreign aid programs of the United States, Canada, Japan, and European countries. Fifty years later the problem is still severe. Today's shibboleth is privatization. Indeed, recent reforms have shown startling results in Chile, Argentina, India, China, and elsewhere. There is no doubt that a classic liberal market is effective. All today's reforms had been tried in Asia and Africa in earlier times, however, at the insistence of European powers, but they had failed in the long run because the cultural attributes, as listed previously, continued. The characteristics of lesser development surfaced again in east Asia, especially South Korea and Indonesia, with financial crises in 1997 and 1998—see chapter 12. Will today's reforms succeed nevertheless, as the exceptions in history? We do not know yet.

I submit the above set of cultural traits not just as characteristics of less developed areas but as a new definition of *less developed.* Not all low-income countries have all these qualities—countries vary greatly—but we must not accept low income as the single indicator of underdevelopment anyway. Rather, let us classify as less developed a country that has many of the traits just mentioned, of which low income is one. Because some of these characteristics are found also in more developed areas—human rights violations, racial cruelty, violence in urban ghettos, police torture, capricious tax changes, and more— let us refer to the *characteristics of lesser development* rather than to less developed countries.

Often these characteristics—especially the concentration of power—are deceptively couched in terms of protection to workers and the underclass, but in fact they weigh so heavily upon producers that companies may be driven out of business unless subsidized by tax money. Then the workers and underclass lose as well. The economy operates at a low level of efficiency, unable to produce enough for the needs of its people. India is an extreme case:

> The rules oblige companies to offer benefits such as pension funds, health insurance, crèches, subsidised canteens and clinics. . . . permission to sack workers in firms employing more than 100 people must be obtained direct from state governments. Only very rarely is permission granted. . . . Firms with more than 25 workers have to inform official labour exchanges of any vacancies, and fill them from that source. This gives armies of civil servants a vested interest in the system, and offers valuable opportunities for graft. . . . firms of a certain size . . . must notify the authorities of changes to job content or employee status. Some states forbid any such changes unless every worker consents to them. . . . In many firms . . . workers are granted not just lifetime employment but employment in perpetuity: when a worker retires, his job goes to a son, relative or other nominee. . . . Denied permission to retrench, [firms] face the possibility of closure. But the government has thought of that as well. Closing a firm is forbidden by law.
>
> India has so many thousand "sick companies" . . . [but the] system keeps them struggling on for years with subsidies (including cheap power), tax breaks, debt forgiveness and other life support instruments. . . . firms have enormous incentives to avoid growing and, if possible, to remain invisible to the authorities.[17] [They also have incentive not to start up in the first place, and this fact aggravates unemployment.]

The distinction between more and less developed areas is relative, depending on the degree and quantity of these characteristics. Economic models frequently specify development as caused by investment and by personal skills acquired by education and of underdevelopment as caused by their lack. But these models show ingredients, not underlying forces; they are like saying the causes of steel are coal and iron. The real question is: What leads to the need for steel and technology or to behavior conducive to economic development?

Mancur Olson has convincingly set aside the familiar explanations of underdevelopment—lack of resources, skills, or knowledge—by showing that these do not correlate with development or underdevelopment anywhere. Many of the least developed countries are rich in mineral resources, and "the world's stock of knowledge is available at little or no cost to all the countries of the world."[18] He has shown that emigration from less developed countries, which might encourage a higher marginal productivity of labor by making labor scarce relative to capital, does not in fact do so, empirically. He also has shown that "endowments of human capital between the poor and rich countries . . . account for only a small part of the international differences in the marginal product of labor." By process of elimination, he arrives at differences in policies and institutions as the only logical explanation of the gap. Thus he reaches the same conclusion that I do, that institutions make the difference. Even so, he posits two principles at variance with my findings.

First, "if enough voters acquire more knowledge about what the real consequences of different public policies will be, public policies will improve and thereby increase real incomes in the society."[19]

Second, "the best thing a society can do to increase its prosperity is to wise up. This means, in turn, that it is very important that economists, inside government and out, get things right."[20]

However, I would argue that the events implied by these two principles will not occur unless the characteristics of lesser development are already alleviated.

Let us consider Olson's second principle first. Many times the World Bank and International Monetary Fund suggest sound policies, which are refused by the host government unless it is "bribed" to accept them with a Bank loan or Fund advance. Why do they hesitate? Because Bank/Fund policies may bring market strength, hence more power to the producing classes and less to the rulers. The heady feelings that power brings them—control over others, media exposure, admiration, and going down in history—in the mind of the rulers often outweigh the financial benefits of a classic liberal society. While Bank/Fund policies would have brought what the country needed, they would have caused the opposite of what the leaders wanted. The leaders had indeed "wised up" by getting things right according to their own interests rather than those of the country as a whole.

I call this the Philip II syndrome. Why did Philip II, king of Spain 1556-98, not wise up to the high probability that he might have achieved even greater tax revenue, in addition to his "take" from the New World, to finance the projects most dear to his heart—retention of the Netherlands and defeat of France and the Ottoman Empire—if he had encouraged entrepreneurship and markets? After all, he had close enough contact with England and the Netherlands to understand the successes of those policies. Olson argues that medieval rulers ("stationary bandits") maximize their revenue if they give their subjects just enough goodies to keep a stable society peaceful;[21] by inference, Philip II should not have taxed producers too heavily, and if he did so anyway, he had not wised up. I suggest, instead, that Philip cared little about the economic development of Spain or the prosperity of manufacturers or workers. His principal concern was his own power, which would have eroded in favor of the manufacturers had he allowed them more liberty.[22] In a modern case of the Philip II syndrome, just as this book is being published President Suharto of Indonesia is refusing to undertake economic policies prescribed by the International Monetary Fund, that would be favorable to his people, because (among other results) they will diminish his own power.

Now turn to Olson's first principle, that if the mass of voters knew the consequences of policy they would insist on improvements. We might suppose that education is the answer. However, if a Third-World peasant learns to read and write and then studies economics and political science and is then given the choice to vote for the correct policies that he now understands or for don Fulano, who will pave the sidewalk in front of his house, guess whom he will vote for?

Overturning the political culture of less developed areas is far more complex than advising their governments and educating their citizens on proper economic policies. The euphoria currently experienced in the West about policies and privatization of industries in the less developed countries and in eastern Europe is apt to last for less than a century unless the power balance shifts in those areas. For the most part, these countries still carry the dominant characteristics of lesser development.

More Developed Areas:
The Internal Gap Narrows over Long Periods

Before the industrial revolution, the Western world manifested the great gap between rich and poor that is characteristic of lesser development. After about 1850, however, disparities began to narrow, and the narrowing continued for over a century. By 1976, the internal gap between rich and poor was smaller than it had ever been historically, while for less developed countries it was still wide. While we do not have hard data on distributions, the tendency toward greater equality is presumed from the rise in real wages relative to the real return on capital, which has remained about the same. The sequence is roughly as follows. Technological innovations, which introduce new products and reduce costs, increase the profitability of enterprises. The marginal productivity of labor rises, so workers demand a share of the profits. So long as they do not reproduce themselves as fast as capital accumulates, laborers become scarce relative to the capital that would employ them, and they can demand higher wages. This was the pattern in the United States until about 1976.

From 1947 on, we have data on the percentage of national income earned by each quintile (20 percent) of U.S. families, from poorest to richest. In figure 3-1, the shares of the quintiles are arrayed from poorest to richest, left to right. From 1950 to 1975, the share of the richest declines, then rises sharply. During the same period, the share of the poorest increases, then declines. The gain by the richest after 1975 occurred largely at the expense of the middle brackets, since the increases of the rich more than offset the declines of the poor. Similar changes have been noted in Britain.[23]

Figure 3-1.
Percentage Distribution of Household Income
by Quintiles, United States, various years, 1947-94

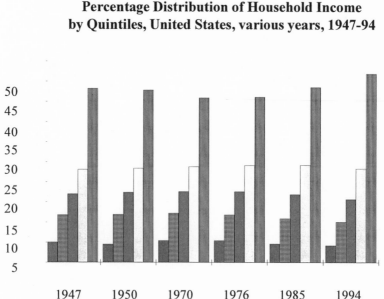

1947   1950   1970   1976   1985   1994
SOURCE: U.S. Census Bureau: http://www.census.gov/hhes/income/ histinc/f02.html, last revised 29 September 1997.

From about 1850 until 1976, the classic liberal society was doing what it was supposed to do: bringing income distribution closer to equality. Why, then, does the share of the richest rise suddenly after 1976? Even though labor productivity in the United States has increased over the past two decades, albeit slowly, many argue that productivity has not been translated into higher wages, unlike earlier in the century, but instead into higher profits.

Alan Greenspan, chairman of the Federal Reserve, stated that "the growing inequality of income in the United States could become a 'major threat to our society,'" while Nobel laureate Robert Solow "warned of a society 'which might turn mean and crabbed, limited in what it can do, worried about the future.'" Kevin M. Murphy, winner of the prestigious John Bates Clark Medal in 1997, has written eighteen papers with sophisticated statistical analysis to show that the main cause of the widening gap in wages is the growth in demand for skilled labor compared to the rise in supply and decline in demand for unskilled.[24] Hacker roundly enforces this position with a challenging book revealing the declining rate of productivity growth in the United States, which affects the unskilled more than the skilled, and may be a source of the increasing inequality shown in figure 3-1.[25] Do these events portend a fundamental change in the socio-economic structure that will reverberate into the twenty-first century, or is this a temporary aberration, from which the earlier trend will be restored? History does not usually make sudden changes—*Natura non facit saltum* is the theme of Marshall's famous book on *Principles of Economics*[26]—so why now?

To approach that question, we must first examine the statistics. Figure 3-1 represents income distribution by families, not by individuals. We do not have data for individuals. Suppose a man and woman, married, are earning $25,000 each, for a family income of $50,000. They divorce, becoming two separate families. Statistically, average family income has decreased from $50,000 to $25,000, although in fact no change has occurred in the income of either. In another example, assume four persons, of whom two earn $75,000 each and the other two $25,000 each. The difference between the average income of the upper and lower pairs is $50,000. If the two higher-income people marry, and so also the two lower-income people, the new families are earning $150,000 and $50,000 respectively, so the difference in average family incomes has increased to $100,000, while the individual income of each one has not changed.[27] Since the divorce rate in the United States has increased greatly in two decades, and since men and women—rich or poor—tend to marry in the same income class, and because more women are working now than two decades ago, the phenomena of these two examples may explain the entire seeming increase in income inequality. Finally, the decline in the share of the poorest quintiles, and the rise in the share of the richest, has not been steady from 1976 to 1995. In some years, the reverse occurred. Shifts, one way or another, in any short period may be explained by random events, not necessarily by a new trend.

But several other factors are at work. Some persons in all brackets are moving up, and some are moving down, for several reasons. First, the increasing role of high-technology products, especially computers and software, has created a demand for trained workers greater than the supply, so their wages are bid up. Second, businesses have been downsizing. Tasks that earlier required two or three workers now require one or two. Third, the use of computers causes formerly skilled jobs to become unskilled—it takes less aptitude to follow a computer program than formerly was required for middle-level management tasks. Fourth, with the globalization of the economy, lower-skilled jobs are moving abroad, sometimes entire industries. One gap has not been increasing, however: wage rates based on ethnic origin and gender. For the same skills and training, women and minorities in the United States are now earning wages almost the equal of white males for similar work. Given a few more years of this trend, equality will be achieved.

Many have argued that real wages have declined since 1976. Hacker[28] and Madrick both attribute this decline to a slowdown in productivity growth, which may however be no more than a reflection of the United States shifting from an industrial to a service society. Productivity in services cannot be expected to increase as much as in industry and is also difficult to measure. Both of them—and others as well—cite declining real wages as a reason why families resort to having two earners. An alternative explanation might be that women want to work for reasons of equality and pride, thus causing an increase in the supply of labor that has dampened wage increases. Madrick adds that "unequal wages are, to a large degree, based on a class system that favors those privileged enough to attend college, where they acquire not rare skills so much as good work habits, the right credentials, and a sense of how a college graduate should behave."[29] The argument weakens, however, by assuming that the "class system" has become more rigid in years in which it has probably become more flexible.

To me, the most probable explanation lies in the supply of labor—increasing rapidly—compared to the supply of capital and technology—increasing but not so rapidly as the labor force. By 1998, however, the ebullient American economy was ready to absorb more labor: unemployment fell, wages rose, and some economists were predicting a return to the old pattern of economic development favoring all income groups. It is very difficult to beat the demand/supply explanations.

Whether real wages have actually declined in recent decades depends on the statistical series used. Most wage series do not take account of fringe benefits, such as health and life insurance and amounts paid into pension plans. Disparities in family incomes, as in figure 3-1, do not take account of government entitlements, including social security and welfare. In an earlier situation when social security and health insurance were not available through employers or government, wages had to be higher so employees might pay for these benefits. Now that these are supplied outside of wages, employers may pay less cash to workers—that is how the market works—while the real value of worker compensation remains the same or rises. Accounting for the total cost paid by employers for labor, including all social benefits and social security taxes, the Employment Cost Index in the United States increased by 70 percent from 1982 to 1995, while the consumer price index (CPI) increased by 58 percent.[30]

Thus real wages deflated by the CPI, including all benefits and payroll taxes, on average increased by about 12 percent, or roughly 1 percent per year. However, according to a panel of economists headed by Michael Boskin for the Senate Finance Committee in December 1996, they increased even more. This panel charges that in recent years the CPI overstated the annual inflation rate by 1.1 percent, mainly because the Bureau of Labor Statistics used a "fixed market basket" based on the years 1982-84, whereas changed patterns had enabled consumers to obtain far greater real value in 1996 than was measured by that standard basket. In Boskin's own words: "Instead of falling by 13 percent, real hourly earnings have risen by 13 percent from 1973 to 1995 . . . median real income over the same period grew 36 percent, not the puny 4 percent in the official statistics that deflate by the CPI."[31]

The Boskin panel's conclusion has not gone unchallenged. Moulton,[32] whose work is reviewed approvingly by Madrick,[33] argues that the Bureau of Labor Statistics (BLS) already made adjustments in the CPI of the type that Boskin argued that they should, to cover changes in quality, consumer preferences, and substitutions of products. However, Gordon and Griliches, members of the Boskin panel, reply that the adjustments made by the BLS were deficient statistically.[34] Even expert statisticians and economists will not understand all the intricacies of this debate without studying in great detail the work of the Boskin Commission, and of Moulton, Madrick, and others, which is not within the scope of this book to do. Rather, for most of us the answer must lie in complementary data, such as the Employment Cost Index and the Federal Reserve studies in wealth, which show increases in real income and wealth for most Americans. In addition, it would be most unusual for a strong period of growth such as that experienced by the United States in the 1990s not to be accompanied by rising wages. We may reasonably surmise, therefore, that real wages have not fallen in the past two decades, and—given other related data and our general knowledge of what happens during prosperity—have probably risen considerably. Gordon and Griliches point out that "98 percent of American households own an average of 2.2 color TV sets, and 78 percent own at least one VCR." A recent report by the Employment Policy Foundation found that in ten out of thirteen categories of particular household goods, the *poorest* 20 percent of households in 1993 was better off than the *average* American household in 1970. Such relationships could not occur if the CPI were not undervalued.[35]

Figure 3-1 shows *relative* shares in national income, not *total* shares. All identifiable groups in the United States except one—single women with children—increased their wealth between 1983 and 1989, according to the Federal Reserve, which conducts studies of wealth sporadically.[36] This includes identifiable racial and ethnic groups, in which men and women are listed separately. In fact, wealth for minorities grew faster than for whites, although the base differences remain large. The percentage of families owning their own homes also increased for every income bracket—even those below $10,000—between 1983 and 1989, except for incomes from $50,000 to $99,999.[37] Also, *in real terms, personal income per capita in the United States in 1995 was two and one-half times the corresponding income of 1929.* This means that, for every automobile the average family could buy in 1929, it could buy two and one-half automobiles in 1995; for every trip abroad in 1929, two and one-half in 1995, and so on. Changes in relative prices of goods might decrease some to (say) two instead of two and one half, while increasing others to (say) three. Furthermore, all income groups gained. Therefore, why do we hear that poor people, especially in urban ghettos, have a very hard time subsisting today?

There are several reasons. First, building codes prevent people from constructing substandard houses, so they are driven into homeless shelters instead. Second, automobiles are not the same now as in 1929. Upgrades are required, culturally and often legally, so more has to be spent for what is a better product but is still considered minimal in today's society. Third, the incidence of single parenthood is much greater than in 1929, with child-care responsibilities and other cultural factors that discourage unwed mothers from finding jobs. While the poorest quintile is improving its real income on average, some within that quintile have sunk to the bottom. Fourth, the drug culture of the inner city, and higher crime rates, cause difficulties in economic mobility. Fifth, at least until 1996, the welfare program sidelined many persons who would lose benefits if they were to take jobs. Sixth, upwardly mobile persons from the inner city have moved to the suburbs, leaving a core that has lost its constructive role models.

This sixth reason is the most serious. Although one may doubt that the mass society is moving toward greater disparities or that real wages are really falling—and I do doubt both of these—nevertheless urban ghettos in the United States are deteriorating. William Julius Wilson writes of the disappearance of jobs from the ghettos. Where thriving communities stood fifty years ago, with bustling businesses, people gathering socially, and schools and churches bursting with energy, now stores are boarded up, schools closed down, and streets almost deserted, and the remaining population is living in fear of violence, crime, and drugs. He attributes the change to the out-migration of jobs and people. "The economy has churned out tens of millions of new jobs in the last two decades. In the same period, joblessness among inner-city blacks has reached catastrophic proportions."[38] Remaining residents do not have the means to transport themselves to the suburbs, where the jobs are. Wilson's article is poignant and true, but his proposed solutions are more of the same: restoration of the federal contributions to cities and a reinstatement of the large public works program instituted by Roosevelt in 1935. These might be useful, but they are more of "we" (the affluent) doing things *for* "them" (the poor). In chapters 5 (on welfare) and 9 (on education) I will propose opportunities for education, training, and counseling that the poor may themselves select, but that would be financed by government funds.

Conclusion

Poverty and wealth for the coming centuries will take on different faces at different levels. For less developed countries, the main hurdle will lie in overcoming the characteristics of lesser development, especially the concentration of power. Powerful people prevent poorer people from undertaking new businesses or deprive them of their earnings. Rulers are reluctant to loosen the reins, for they might lose the control they enjoy in running their horses. The principal force for change—a slow one—will be the poor themselves, as they become more valued players in liberal economic systems. Within the more developed areas, some are worried about the evaporation of the middle class, since a society segmented between rich and poor would not be stable. But this eventuality assumes that the experience of two decades will become permanent. My own projection would be that once this particular restructuring is complete, to take account of the new information, and once the low-skilled jobs have moved abroad—not all of them can go—there will be a return to the historic trend of a decreasing gap as overall incomes rise. This will not happen automatically and especially not for those stuck in urban ghettos. The more developed areas will require a much better educated citizenry, greater openness for entrepreneurship and innovation, and greater scope for the price mechanism. All of these have occurred historically, at least up until the last century, and we need only restore and reinforce the trend. For the gap between more and less developed countries, the problem will be one of unrest, violence, and resentment against power. Governments of more developed countries and international agencies will be called upon to arbitrate and resolve these differences, against their wills and better judgment. Only through overcoming the characteristics of lesser development, however, will poorer countries take advantage of potential positive-sum moves, to be found in increased trade and investment, worldwide.

Chapter 4
Environment, Population,
and Gender and Ethnic Bias

Is a classic liberal society capable of solving questions of environment and resources, population growth, and ethnic or gender discrimination? Or is governmental intervention needed? This chapter describes these problems and suggests how a classic liberal society might approach them.

The argument is both ideological and institutional. On the ideological side, it notes that the major durable reforms of history have commanded almost universal consensus. If not, the problems continued until/unless virtually all sides agreed or history overtook the problems. Therefore, it posits that almost universal consensus is also required for enduring solutions to today's problems. Such consensus is achieved only by individuals and groups negotiating with each other and not by majority rule of governments, with festering wounds for a minority. In a classic liberal society consensus is a prime mover.

On the institutional side, agreed-upon ways of behavior are the results of these negotiations. They include the rules for determining who may live where, for the conduct of business, and for other social encounters. These rules define the legal system, the monetary system, modes of labor negotiations, and how corporations function, as well as education standards, methods of population control, government, and many more. While most institutional changes are set forth in part 2, those appropriate to the problems of the present chapter appear here.

Environment and Resources

Pollution

Environment problems include attaining clean air and clean water, proper use of land and forests, and whether and how to intervene in global warming and the ozone layer. There are more, but we need only a sample. All over the world, land and forests are being abused, especially in the less developed areas. Here is but a small number of the many reports continuously appearing in the newspapers. The governments of Suriname and Guyana have contracted with investors in Asia to lumber their ancient forests, depriving thousands of indigenous people and tropical species of their habitats.[1] Peasants have destroyed forests in India.[2] The rain forest in Bolivia is falling before commercial exploiters.[3] Tropical forests everywhere are being destroyed faster than ever before.[4] The Government of Brazil is squandering "its" forest, selling it to those who pay for privileges.[5] Mahogany forests in Brazil are sold off by the native Kayopo people, whose chiefs spend the proceeds on ranches, luxury cars, and airplanes.[6]

Large sections of rain forest in Peru have been sacrificed to drug crops.[7] "From Dickensian factories [in Egypt] . . . what wafts southward is a toxic cocktail that by most estimates shaves four points from the I.Q. of the average Cairo child."[8] Vast forest fires in Indonesia in 1997, caused by reckless logging practices, dealt carcinogenic smog to wide areas of southeast Asia.[9] The tiny nation of Nauru has destroyed its island by strip-mining guano, so that residents may have to abandon their country and move to a different island.[10] Dictator Ceausescu of Romania drained the wetlands feeding the Danube to plant 140,000 acres with wheat and rice and ordered the shooting of pelicans and cormorants who were eating the fish. The project failed, but not before serious damage to plants and wildlife that scientists from many countries are now trying to reverse, at immense cost. The much-touted economic growth of China is built on ecologically disastrous practices and will soon encounter its limit.[11] Bulldozers, tractors, and chain saws are destroying teakwood in Myanmar (Burma), after the British system of thirty-year cycles was set aside.[12] Centuries-old encroachment has destroyed the forests of Costa Rica.[13] Tutsi cattle herders, returning in 1995 after long exile in Uganda, invaded the national parks of Rwanda, driving out wild game. Eventually these cattle will die of starvation.[14] The World Bank has reported that industrialization, population growth, and subsidization of water has caused a severe water crisis in Africa.[15]

The erstwhile socialist countries destroyed resources prodigiously. Chernobyl is the most notorious case, but others abound. Vast pollution has spewed forth from heavy state-owned industries. "It is no accident that the world's most polluted countries are socialist," a World Bank executive stated.[16] Environmental laws are frequently not enforced. In an ill-conceived scheme to plant monoculture cotton in the desert, the Soviet government diverted the Syr and Amu Rivers into the central steppes. Dozens of dams and thousands of miles of canals were built in politically favored districts. Pesticides and defoliants contaminated the water so that mothers who breast-fed their babies risked poisoning them.[17] Even this foul water evaporated from the reservoirs and leaked out of the unlined canals. The Aral Sea, fourth largest lake in the world, now in Kazakhstan and Uzbekistan, became an "ecological calamity." The fishing industry is destroyed, shores are barren, and wildlife killed off. Pollution has also caused the collapse of fisheries in the Black Sea: Bulgaria, Romania, Russia, and Turkey are all affected. A dramatic decline in life expectancy in Russia was reported in 1995, caused not only by Chernobyl but also in part by the many nuclear tests and waste dumps. The general stress of sudden political and economic change is also cited as a reason. Here is a further report from 1990:

Take Eastern Europe, the dirtiest, most degraded region on Earth. Eighty percent of East Germany's rivers are contaminated, and some of its citizens breathe air polluted 50 times above safe limits; two-thirds of Poland's trees are damaged, two-thirds of its rivers too dirty even for industry; 80 percent of Bulgaria's farmland is threatened by erosion, 25 percent of its animal and plant species are threatened. Throughout the Eastern bloc life expectancy has been dropping, with millions suffering from environmentally induced disease. Some Eastern Europeans expect to live a decade less than Western Europeans.[18]

In the village of Badui, China, just below a site where a state-run fertilizer factory spills its waste:

One third of the peasants in this hamlet in Gansu province in western China are mentally retarded or seriously ill. Most people die in middle age, the women report unending miscarriages and stillbirths, many of the children are trapped in toddler-sized bodies that they never grow out of, and even the goats totter and stagger into trees as they go blind and insane.

. . . a boy named Wei Hanyun, only 29 inches tall—the height that an average American baby boy reaches at 12 months, but Hanyun is 8 years old . . . mentally retarded as well . . .[19]

Nor are the more developed areas exempt. The United States government directly or indirectly subsidizes submarginal mines that leave their debris untended, the overgrazing of cattle lands, the excess cutting of timber, and chemical pollution on sugar lands such as the Everglades in Florida.[20] In northwestern United States and in Canada, ancient forests such as ponderosa are being replaced by strains less resistant to insects.[21] Salmon-spawning grounds are being depleted.[22] A diversified forest sustains much wildlife, whose life cycles are interrupted by clear-cutting. Space photos show the forests of the northwest to be "so torn up by clear cuts that their ability to support a variety of species is threatened."[23] Although the area may be replanted and look lush to the casual observer, its character is forever changed: it has become a tree farm instead of a forest. Acid rain, arising from emissions of sulfur dioxide and nitrogen oxide by industries in the eastern and central United States, has caused some deaths and a large number of respiratory illnesses and has destroyed entire populations of fish in eastern lakes. Similar effects have been discovered in Europe. Flood damage from major rivers, such as the Mississippi, is exacerbated by heavy development close to the shores. Wetlands that used to sop up much of the cyclical increase in flows have been drained. Government insurance and other rescue programs encourage development by reducing cost for the developer. There is social cost but not private cost.

The Solution: Pay the Cost

Each of the preceding problems arises from farms, industries, or other groups drawing on common resources for which they do not pay full price. In some cases, they have been granted privileges by government. In others they have appropriated resources because no one would stop them. Full price would have been the amount necessary to restore the resources to their previous condition, or—if they could not be restored—to compensate others for their losses of common property, if others were willing to accept, or to refrain from the appropriation if they were not. If full price were charged, many industries would find pollution and destruction too expensive.

This condition is what Garrett Hardin has called "the tragedy of the commons." No one wants the disastrous results. However, each person who draws on common property pays only a tiny share of the costs—that person's appreciation of the devastation—while extorting a significant personal benefit. One who cuts down trees in a common forest cannot save the trees others are cutting down, so he might as well take his share. One who takes antibiotics excessively may know that she contributes to developing viruses resistant to them, but her damage is tiny compared to her perceived benefit, and she cannot stop others from using them. A resource held by a government or industry with little appreciation of the future—economists would say "high time discount"—is sold cheaply or consumed extravagantly, as with teenagers who take up smoking with little heed to its life threat fifty years later. The forest's time horizon is centuries, the government's until the next election. The problem will be resolved if and only when every person pays a private cost equal to the burden he or she has inflicted upon the entire community and when some "owner" of the resource is required by its charter to calculate a realistic time discount.

Government regulations embody the first of recent attempts to control these problems. In the United States, the Clean Air Act of 1967, with subsequent amendments, has set air-quality standards for hazardous substances, giving the Environmental Protection Agency (EPA) responsibility for enforcing them. This act recognizes that a certain maximum air pollution is permissible—we can live with it, or Nature will purify it. But who has the right to pollute up to the permissible limit? The Clean Air Act of 1990 allows the EPA to award salable permits to pollute. Suppose the permissible amount of some hazardous material is 10,000 units, but ten companies emit a total of 15,000, say 1,500 each. Suppose under the act each company is granted rights to emit only 1,000 units, so the aggregate will be brought down to the permissible amount. But Company A, for whom reduction would be very costly, can buy 500 pollution rights from Company B, which might reduce its emissions more cheaply. B is left with only 500 units, while A may continue to pollute up to 1,500. A gains because the price it pays to B is less than its would-have-been cost to reduce its pollution. B gains because the price it receives from A is greater than its cost to reduce its pollution by another 500. The hazardous materials are kept within the permissible limit. In this way, the market encourages those companies that can reduce their emissions more cheaply to do so. In 1997, the EPA announced that salable pollution rights had contributed to a 30 percent drop in sulfur dioxide emissions from major polluters.[24]

Several obstacles arise. First, acid rain created on the east coast of the United States falls largely in the Atlantic Ocean, where it does less damage than the same amount from Ohio, which falls into the Adirondack forests. The trade-off for permits to emit sulfur dioxide in the two regions might be calculated, but the great diversity of pollutants—from coal, oil, gasoline, automobiles, and fossil-fired electrical power plants—will lead to controversy over permissible amounts of each. If the damage from coal and oil is substitutable but one damages more than the other, whose calculation of the trade-off will be accepted? Second, once rights are defined, administration will be a Herculean task. Third is a question of fairness: why should an excessive polluter be given the "grandfather" right to pollute any amount at all, just because he or she has been polluting all along? Wood fires were not grandfathered in Pittsburgh; they were forbidden outright. An ancient right was taken from homeowners and handed over to automobile drivers, whose activity was not curbed. This was politically easy because homeowners and automobile drivers for the most part were the same people. It will not be so easy when the people are different. Fourth, the political pressures of polluters may jeopardize any government control program, which may be repealed or scaled back after a new election. In 1997, New York State offered pollution permits, which had been awarded to state agencies or bought from private firms, free to outside firms if they would settle in New York.[25] This kind of subsidy distorts the liberal market. Instead of giving out-of-state firms cash to settle in New York—which might be politically unacceptable—it does so deceptively by giving them pollution permits instead.

None of these problems is insurmountable—they may be solved by negotiation, but the details need not be worked out here. Taking our cue from the Clean Air Act, we must find the answer in requiring polluters, grazers, miners, and woodcutters to pay the full cost of their actions. The full cost is the difference between the value of a clean environment and a degraded one; the value of clean air and water rather than dirty; of protected forests and grazing land over those that are damaged, and so on. In each case, a little bit of damage does no harm—cost is virtually zero—such as smoke from a bonfire if the air is not otherwise sullied, or some grazing or tree cutting, whose effects will be replaced naturally. Who is to decide what is reasonable and what is excessive?

In all countries, the central government has proved itself a poor decider. It is all things to all persons. In the United States, the federal government represents cattle interests, lumber interests, automobile drivers, and environmentalists not alike but according to political influence. Other than preserving its own power, government has no inherent interests; rather, it reflects those of constituents. Occasionally a true statesman or stateswoman will take a stand on conscience, but mostly government reacts in proportion to vote-producing capacity or contributions to election campaigns. If industries contribute enough, the recipient politician will not force them to pay the full cost of their pollution. If this were not so, we would find presidents and Congresspeople willing to sacrifice their offices to do the right thing.

The two major parties bundle their policies. While each—Republican and Democrat—has certain traditional constituents and a certain ideology that inclines its bundle in one direction or another, nevertheless each fine-tunes the bundle to bring the most votes, dropping one policy if its opposite will be more lucrative in votes and paying little heed to "marginal" policies, or those not strong enough to swing blocs of votes. Thus most politicians will stand on major issues such as abortion, women's rights, minimum wage, the economy, and trade, marginalizing the environment where it is not a vote swinger. In many cases, only if environmentalists are strong enough to defeat a representative will that politician yield to their interests. Democracy is not like going to a grocery store, where one may decide separately how many bananas, how much sugar, and how much of everything else one wishes to buy. If one wishes to "buy" a policy on women's rights, one may be forced to accept the candidate's policy on cutting trees, whatever that may be. And, of course, the candidate knows very well how the voter is limited.

Regulating agencies often go to excesses. While their purposes—such as preserving wetlands—are laudable, they have the power to make life costly to other people at no expense to themselves. James Bovard cites one case in Nevada, in which housing "developments in the midst of cactus and parched earth [were] classified as 'wetlands' because standing water [could] occur for 7 days in a hole dug for a foundation."[26] He also describes other cases of tiny portions of land being declared wetland, to the great cost and inconvenience of their owners, in contrast to "lavish agricultural subsidies [that] have encouraged farmers to plow under millions of additional acres of wetlands."[27]

The solution, in the moral economy, would be to unbundle the policies and let limited rights be bought on the market. Public land might be deeded to a number of nongovernmental agencies, such as the Sierra Club, the Audubon Society, or the nature conservancies that exist in many states. Each of these would be required by its charter to maintain its land in certain ways and dedicate it to certain uses, such as camping and hiking. It might allow cutting, grazing, or mining to the extent that these activities are rehabilitated by a generous Nature or by the restorative actions of the grazers/cutters/miners. Mining lands would have to be reforested or replanted. By auctioning off these rights to the highest bidder, it would assure payment of full cost, while its own lust for power would be curbed by its charter limitations. The agency would finance its activities with the income from hikers' fees or grazing, mining, or woodcutting permits. Since the land would no longer belong to the government, its use would not be compromised by the political interests of the party in power. Three deterrents would prevent the agency from abusing its trust. First, if it sold off its pollution rights at too low a cost, it might itself go out of business, with its land taken over by another agency. Second, if it violated its charter by selling too many rights, it might be brought to court by any interested outsider. Third, its profit might be capped by its charter.

A step in this direction was made in 1951, when Nebraska courts ruled that legislatures could not discriminate against nonagricultural applicants for leases of land that had been deeded to states upon their admission to the union, for the purpose of financing local schools with their proceeds. In 1982 the Oklahoma supreme court ruled that "a state may not use school trust land to subsidise farming or ranching." In 1996, "two environmental groups, Forest Guardians and the Southwest Environmental Centre, both based in Santa Fe, paid $770 to lease a 550-acre tract of land in north-western New Mexico. It was . . . the first time that an environmental group has won a preferential right to lease state grazing land."[28] Since payment of annual rent to the state for the use of land is similar to paying taxes on land owned, the principles of the moral economy become an easy next step. In 1997, Mark Munro suggested in the *New York Times* that environmental groups should be allowed to buy federal timber and preserve it, instead of the Forest Service limiting sales of timber to logging companies and subsidizing them by "selling timber at below-market prices and by building roads to enable these companies to cut the trees."[29]

Air and water might also be assigned to nongovernmental agencies, that would charge for pollution. The Clean Air Act is a good model, but it would be still more effective if the air were not the "property" of the government—to be auctioned off by politicians dependent on the campaign contributions of polluting industries—but rather the "property" of a nongovernmental agency whose sole interest is to keep it pure to a degree specified in its charter and whose directors have no interest other than in doing their job well. Their performance would be judged by results—how pure the air or water is—and not by the methods they prescribe, such as reducing automobile emissions by so much. They too would be subject to court challenge by any outsider who felt they were not performing adequately.

Global Warming and the Ozone Layer

Some environmental problems are confounded by uncertainty. If we had all the facts, we would know our course. However, decisions must be made under a veil. The possibility of global warming and the role of the ozone layer are two of these.

Global Warming

While carbon dioxide and other "greenhouse gases" help maintain the earth's warm temperature by keeping the sun's infrared radiation from escaping into space, a gradual buildup in these gases, presumably because of human activity, may be causing them to do their job all too well, with the result that the earth is warming. If the warming continues, rainfall patterns will change, affecting agriculture, and polar ice caps will melt so that seaside cities may be inundated.

Reports presented at a meeting of 120 governments in Berlin in 1995 found that average global temperature has risen about one degree Fahrenheit in the past century, for which, the scientists argued, carbon dioxide and other greenhouse gas emissions are the principal cause. At current rates the average global temperature would rise three to eight degrees Fahrenheit in the next century.[30] Dr. Benjamin Santer, the chief author of this finding, prepared models to predict the warming and cooling in different parts of the earth. Measured differences, he says, correspond with what the models predicted, and the same models can be extended to predict changes in temperatures in the future resulting from human activity. If they "are right . . . the human imprint on the climate should emerge more clearly in the next few years. . . . he expects 'very rapid' progress in the search for the greenhouse fingerprint."[31]

Dissenters favor the natural-cycle theory. The chairman of the Harvard-Smithsonian Center for Astrophysics asserts that the increase in greenhouse gases has been spread over the last century and most of the small earth temperature rises since 1880 had occurred before gases from human activity were being emitted. "The ecosystem itself dwarfs human activity in generating or absorbing carbon dioxide."[32] The eleven-year sunspot cycle has been blamed by some scientists. Sallie Balliunas, an astrophysicist at the Harvard-Smithsonian Center, "and her co-workers studied records of the past 120 years and found the Sun responsible for up to 71 percent of the Earth's temperature shifts. When other factors were added to their research model, that figure rose to 94 percent."[33] Charles Harper, planetary scientist at Harvard, criticized the inter-governmental report for being based more on deficient computer models than on ground-based temperature records during the period in which greenhouse gases were mainly emitted. These records, he says, "imply relatively low to moderate sensitivity of climate to fossil fuel burning." Thus, he argues, we have the time for more needed research before seriously cutting back on fossil fuels.[34] Richard Lindzen of MIT concurs, arguing that carbon dioxide by itself does little to increase temperature, a fundamental point of physics; only with some amplifying substance would the degree of warming predicted by the panel occur. The most likely candidate for this substance would be water vapor—also a heat-trapping gas—which the models assume would be held in greater amounts by a warming atmosphere.[35] But, argues Lindzen, this assumption is unwarranted, and therefore the models are flawed. Patrick Michaels, professor of environmental science at the University of Virginia, argued that the Santer model had taken into account only half of the known factors influencing the greenhouse effect and that when all were taken into account "the correspondence between the model and reality vanishes." Furthermore, he pointed out, "satellite-measured temperatures . . . find a statistically significant cooling trend in the lower atmosphere since they started taking measurements in 1979. . . . The satellite data also match up perfectly, on a year-to-year basis, with temperatures measured in the lower atmosphere by weather balloons." [36]

History supplies the evidence for the natural-cycle theory. Records of the quantity of ice on Alpine glaciers are available for more than a century, and historians have examined transportation and agricultural records much farther back. From 800 to 1200 the earth's climate was warmer than it is today. The Vikings traveled in open sailboats with no cabins. Passes that were open to people and animals in the Middle Ages are ice-clogged today, and in the seventeenth and eighteenth centuries, after a period (1450-1850) known as the "Little Ice Age," Swiss farmers complained of glaciers damaging their crops. At one point, the people of Chamonix feared that the glacier Mer de Glace would destroy their church, and a painting of 1740 shows it encroaching upon the village. However, in the past century it has retreated by almost a mile. Danish scientists Friis-Chistensen and Lassen explain these changes by long-term variations of sun spots, whose reduction causes cold on earth, while greater sun activity causes warmth. Morris of the Environmental Unit in the Institute of Economic Affairs, London, argues that the sun's long-term activity better explains climate changes than do greenhouse gases.[37]

To comply with the Rio treaty of 1992, in which nations agreed on a goal for reducing greenhouse emissions, the presidency in the United States initiated a voluntary program by which corporations would undertake energy-saving improvements, trees would be planted, and automobile emissions curbed. By late 1995 it was clear that the goals of the Rio treaty would not be met, and more stringent regulations were agreed[38] at another international conference, in Kyoto in 1997. At time of publication, it is not clear that these will succeed.

But the challengers still point out that the levels of greenhouse gases have fluctuated over centuries, and the current buildup may be only part of these natural cycles. Robinson and Robinson of the Oregon Institute of Science and Medicine support the sunspot theory, pointing out that the solar magnetic cycle length correlates very closely with the earth-temperature deviation from the 1951-70 mean.[39] Furthermore, they argue that increased carbon dioxide in the atmosphere not only does not contribute to global warming but has major environmental benefits, accelerating the growth rate of plants and allowing them to grow in drier regions. To reduce it—as proposed in the Kyoto agreement—will do economic harm with no ecological benefit.

Ozone Layer

The ozone layer, which protects earth and its people from skin cancer and other damage by the sun's ultraviolet rays, is diminishing; a big "ozone hole" has been found over Antarctica and other areas as well. Chemicals called chlorofluorocarbons (CFCs), which have long been used as refrigerants and in aerosol spray cans, and others such as nitrous oxides from fertilizers have destroyed ozone molecules, increasing the hole. The United States has banned the use of CFCs, and in 1987 thirty-six nations signed a treaty to protect the layer through gradual reduction of destructive chemicals. Some are optimistic that ozone loss may be reversed at the beginning of the next century.

Others challenge this analysis, arguing that natural forces such as volcanic eruptions—Mount Pinatubo in the Philippines in 1991 and 1992 is cited[40]— spew forth a far greater quantity of ozone-destroying chemicals than does human industry. The ozone layer increases and decreases in long-wave cycles, this argument goes, and we have been measuring it only since 1970.[41] We happen to have hit the downswing of a cycle, and if we do nothing the cycle will turn again.[42] In the meantime, we might sacrifice much human satisfaction, from refrigerants and other industry, and induce unemployment, for no valid reason. The challengers argue that "no observational evidence [is available] that man-made chemicals like CFCs are dangerously thinning the ozone layer over most of the world."[43]

On the other hand, the Union of Concerned Scientists argues as follows:

The vast majority of the scientific community agrees that a hole in the ozone layer has opened over the Antarctic every austral spring since the late 1970s, permitting harmful ultraviolet radiation to reach the Earth; that this ultraviolet radiation will lead to various human health problems and damage to plants and animals; that the hole is caused by human-made ozone-destroying chemicals; and that ozone depletion is occurring at all latitudes (except the topics) during all seasons.[44]

What to Do?

Global warming and the ozone hole present similar conundrums. In each case, there are an economic and a social advantage to paying no attention to them: jobs, conveniences such as refrigerators, and all other activities that contribute to the build up of carbon dioxide or the destruction of the ozone layer. These activities have gone on for so long and have built up such human dependency that cutting them off suddenly might bring extreme hardship to many. On the other hand, there is a risk—not yet proved—that ozone depletion might be life threatening, or earth threatening. One answer would be to do more research until decisions can be put off no longer. Many would favor this, but others say the time is already here.

Yet research should not be discounted. One possible savior is the fuel cell— based on a principle invented in 1839 by William Grove—which can create electric power out of hydrogen and oxygen. Although the fuel cell was considered until now to be prohibitively expensive, the demand for pollution-free sources has caused scientists to work on reducing its cost. A commercial fuel-cell bus is expected in the same year this book will go to press, and—it is claimed—a commercial car competitive with gasoline-powered vehicles may be ready by—hold your breath!—2003. Such a vehicle would emit no noxious pollutants such as carbon monoxide and oxides of nitrogen and would significantly reduce greenhouse gases without eliminating them entirely.[45]

As long as the ozone hole and global warming remain as threats, they should be unbundled, or removed from politics. Because of its conflict of interest, a government subject to "bribes" (campaign contributions) by interested parties should not be the decider. Nor should regulators eager to demonstrate and extend their power. Rather, we should establish two nongovernmental agencies, one for global warming and one for the ozone hole, which would be composed of both scientist-specialists and lay citizens. Each would be charged, by its charter, with taking into account the risks and acting in a conservative way. Each risk should be weighted according to both its severity—earth threatening is very severe—and the likelihood of its happening. A conservative way means paying greater attention to severity than to likelihood.

While such nongovernmental agencies contain their own moral hazards, of becoming too powerful themselves, nevertheless they might be controlled by outside monitors more effectively than governments can be controlled. If the alternative is governments, consider the following, written after the United Nations global warming conference of 1997:

[C]ommittees of nations bickered for days but were unable to agree on concrete proposals in three critical areas: cutting emissions to head off global warming, protecting forests, and increasing aid to poor nations who are ruining their environments through uncontrolled development.[46]

In 1997, a group of two thousand economists, including six Nobel laureates, found that "there are many potential policies to reduce greenhouse-gas emissions for which the total benefits outweigh the total costs," with "policies which are either inexpensive (such as encouraging consumers to buy energy-efficient appliances) or worth implementing whether or not global warming proves to be a problem (such as reducing subsidies to fossil fuels)."[47] Such win-win measures are clearly the place to start. They also recommended internationally tradable budgets, similar to permits under the Clean Air Act in the United States, so that each country—with a specific budget in reduction of greenhouse-gas emissions, might trade its internationally respected budgetary rights with other countries—or, by extension, firms in one country with those in another. Finally, they recommended that "governments should shift more of their spending on energy research into renewable sources of energy (which are still more expensive than fossil fuels, even though the cost of wind and solar power has been falling steadily.)" Such policies would be easier to implement if authority were granted, internationally, to nongovernmental agencies rather than to governments subject to pressure by special interests.

These agencies—once removed from the political process—might auction off rights to create a limited number of global-warming or ozone-depleting substances. They would be subject to the same accountability as other pollution agencies: they would have to raise their own funds by selling rights, and they would be subject to court challenges if they misbehaved. Unfortunately, it would be difficult to judge them by results—the amount of global warming or the extent of the ozone hole—since not enough is known about natural versus human causes. They might be tempted to sell too many rights in order to increase the agency's income. These problems can be alleviated, though not permanently solved, by making the salaries of administrators independent of agency income, and by creating citizens' bodies to oversee their work, and by putting a cap on the allowable profits of the agency.

No one should underestimate the political and international hurdles faced by these ideas. Vested interests would oppose them, especially those of governments in the less developed world that declare that the environment is not their problem. Governments in both more and less developed areas that currently enjoy and profit from their own power would be reluctant to yield that power to nongovernmental agencies, especially international ones such as would be needed for global warming and the ozone hole. Nevertheless, we start with the political process we have, and the battle must be fought through that process, which—if successful—would spawn new organizations and institutions more capable of handling these problems than the ones we now possess.

Population

At the time of the Roman Empire (14 CE), world population was about one quarter billion. Not until 1600 did it double, to about one half billion. In another two hundred years it had doubled again. It took only 125 years for yet another doubling, and by 1962 it had reached three billion. It is projected to double again in thirty-eight years, to six billion in 2000.[48] About 90 percent of the recent increase is in the less developed countries. Among these, the highest percentage increases (3.1 percent per year) are in Africa, but the greatest absolute amounts are in Asia, where the population base is much larger. These figures have given rise to disaster predictions, as in Paul Ehrlich's *The Population Bomb*, and Garrett Hardin's *Living within Limits*. Alarm over such increases poses several questions. First, does population growth immiserate people? Will there be enough food? Second, will the environment deteriorate with such high rates of growth, through overgrazing, overcutting of forests, or urban pollution from masses of human beings? Third, people in more developed areas are concerned over immigration from the less developed: whether foreign workers— Turks in Germany, Algerians in France, Mexicans and Asians in Los Angeles—are changing the cultural face of home areas and whether these low-wage workers are taking jobs from citizens. Fourth is fear over imbalance: will Asia, Africa, and Latin America overwhelm Europe and North America? Fifth, though the population growth rate is positive, is the rate itself increasing, staying the same, or tending to fall? Before considering what to do about population growth—what institutions are needed—let us examine the premises for these concerns.

First, is there enough food? Lester Brown of World Watch Institute shows that beef production fell from 1950 to 1989 and that grain output has slowed and become less predictable. From this, he concludes that "food yields are shrinking as populations grow."[49] A World Bank study of 1997 confirms that "increases in yields of major cereal crops, including wheat, rice, and corn, are expected to slow in the next 25 years, following already slower growth since 1982."[50] By using aggregate data from the United Nations Food and Agricultural Organization, on the other hand, Amartya Sen finds that not only is food supply growing faster relative to world population but food is becoming cheaper relative to other goods.[51] Because he uses aggregate estimates rather than Brown's selective perception, I am persuaded by Sen. Furthermore, the greatest increases in world food production are occurring in India and China, where they are most needed. The world's people are now in a better position to buy food than ever before. "A new United Nations study [in 1996] has found that the world's population is growing more slowly than was expected."[52] An independent study by *The Economist* reaches the same results.[53] Julian Simon has found that, except for short periods explained by drought or other calamity, the world's food supply has been growing by a greater annual percentage than population for the last 200 years.[54] If people are hungry, he concludes, it is because they are poor, not because the world cannot feed its growing population. Dennis Avery of the Hudson Institute has also estimated that the world is capable of feeding two billion people more, "mainly on the good land diverted from crops by government policies in the U.S. and Argentina."[55]

Some areas do not grow enough food for their populations, but so long as income per capita is increasing—as it is in virtually all the less developed world except in some countries in Africa—food can be bought on the international market. Despite increased incomes over-all, poverty has worsened in pockets in less developed countries, a worrisome problem but not one associated with population growth. Nor does population growth explain declines in African incomes, although both occur simultaneously. Nor does it explain why poverty increases in urban slums while a country at large may be becoming richer, as is surely the case in Brazil. These explanations lie more in the conditions of lesser development, which were discussed in chapter 2.

Second, will the environment deteriorate? Yes, as populations impinge on woods and fields, and as urban industry pollutes the atmosphere, especially in less developed areas. Mexican plants along the U.S. border *(maquiladora)* are particular villains, because strict environmental laws are not rigidly enforced. Still, this pollution would probably have happened with economic growth even if population had not been increasing. (It is a problem, but we must get the blame right.)

Third, the great immigration from less developed areas into North America and Europe is indeed changing the cultural composition of some areas. But it is probably due not so much to the population growth in less developed areas as it is to increasing employment opportunity in the more developed areas. The poorest people—in India and China—do not have the means to travel to the more developed areas. Those who do travel usually pay, occasionally extortionary sums. The question is not a population one but one of how the world's land is to be used and of whether anyone in the world should have the right to settle in lands anywhere in the world. Is the fear of cultural dilution akin to the hated "ethnic cleansing" in Nazi Germany or Serbia/Bosnia? No, it is usually neither violent nor genocidal, but it does embarrass a society where multiculturalism is a value.

Fourth, is the world becoming unbalanced, with too many people in less developed relative to more developed areas? In 1650 and 1750, 78 percent of the world's population lived in Asia and Africa.[56] After the industrial revolution, European population grew much more rapidly than elsewhere, so that by 1962 the Asia/Africa proportion had diminished to 64 percent.[57] Then it began to rise again, to 71 percent in 1994, and the United Nations predicts a further increase to 78.5 percent by 2050. This is not much above the 1650-1750 figure. If the experience of Europe is repeated in Asia and Africa, rising incomes will cause growth in those areas' populations to taper off by mid–twenty-first century, and the proportions may remain the same thereafter.

Fifth, what are the data on world population increase? In the early 1950s, the world total fertility rate averaged 5 (the number of children per woman in a lifetime). By 1977-80 it was 4, by the early 1990s 3, and today 2.8 and falling.[58] The world population growth rate peaked at about 2.4 percent in the middle 1960s; since then it has declined to the neighborhood of 2.0 percent. If it continues to fall by the same rate—there is no assurance of this—it will reach zero, or a constant level, sometime in the twenty-first century. In the meantime, however, world population will grow so long as the rate is positive.

Some propose government solutions. The most extreme has been that of China, where committees examine the personal lives of villagers, inquiring about and directing their contraceptive methods. They have also mandated abortion. Those who violate the principle—one child per family—may be denied access to jobs, housing, and education for their children. By 1997, however, Chinese population had declined for three years in a row, possibly because of economic growth, and the government began to allow two-child families.[59]

Less extreme are the programs of Bangladesh, Indonesia, and Zimbabwe, where government workers persuade women to use birth control. In Zimbabwe, eight hundred bicyclists fan the countryside for this purpose.[60] Both extreme and less extreme programs are deemed successful in some countries, in that population growth has decreased since they were put into effect. Others, however, propose that with greater freedom of women to participate in education and the economy, population increase will diminish voluntarily. They cite not only the history of Japan and the West, where this is what happened, but also the decrease in birth rates in less developed areas by about one-third since the mid-1960s, from an average of six children per woman to four, or "about halfway to replacement level."[61]

Sen suggests that the success in China, where net population growth has been reduced to zero, might not be explained at all by the coercive, cruel methods. Instead, the improved access of women to education and jobs may have led them to reduce their fertility. In Jamaica, Thailand, and Sweden, new access to both of these have been associated with declines in fertility rates, to 2.7 children per woman, 2.2, and 2.1, respectively, compared to China's 2.0.[62] They have moved toward China's level without any of China's invasions of privacy and coercion.

Nordhaus approaches the question from an economic perspective. "If the earth is reaching its carrying capacity because of land or food or energy shortages, where are the warning signs? Why have economic growth rates increased rather than slowed in the last two decades virtually everywhere? Put differently, if the globe is reaching its limits on land and resources, the increased stress should be accompanied by rising prices of land, food, and energy. But these prices have been declining relative to labor for two centuries and particularly over the last 15 years."[63] From 1980 to 1993, world population[64] and world cereals output[65] both increased by approximately 25 percent. Using extrapolations of declining fertility rates separately in more, less, and least developed areas, Eberdstadt projects that world population will start to decline between 2040 and 2050 and thereafter will shrink by about 25 percent with each generation.[66]

In two articles in mid-1997, Williamson and Higgins,[67] and Mason, Lee, and Miller[68] suggest that the demographic transition may be a boon to the East Asian "tigers" (South Korea, Taiwan, Hong Kong, and Singapore). In 1990, the youth-dependency ratio (percentage of population of working age, say twenty-five to fifty-nine, relative to the dependents, both younger and older) was quite low, say in the neighborhood of 30–35 percent depending on country. As population grows along with economic growth, this ratio increases—more working people supporting fewer dependents, both younger and older, proportionately. These authors project the ratio to approach 50 percent in many countries by 2050. During this proportionate "bulge," the working group—with fewer dependents—may save more and even begin exporting capital, thus spreading economic growth throughout the world. By the end of the century, the bulge will diminish, and the proportions may be similar to those of more developed areas today.[69]

Finally, some demographers are concerned about the *decline* in population in rich areas, even as total world population rises. In thirty-three countries of Europe, plus a few elsewhere such as China, South Korea, and Canada, the fertility rate (average number of children born to a woman during her lifetime) was less than 2 (the number required to keep population from decreasing), and each year more countries join the "club."[70] If fertility rates fall in the rich countries, the economic development of poor countries may suffer from loss of markets.

The facts that world food supply is not only not short but is growing at a greater rate than population; that environmental degradation relates more to industrialization and agricultural practices than to population growth; that the distribution of world population is returning to earlier proportions; that a bulge in the youth-dependency ratio in the east Asian tigers may even promote their economic development; and that improved standards of living and, above all, education lead to a tapering of the growth rate and perhaps a decline in Europe and North America, all these remove the case for panic but not for long-term introspection. Government family planning is popular, but it succeeds only where a desire to limit the number of children is already in place. The moral economy should tilt toward a reasonable, noncoercive program of education on population control, plus considerable emphasis on those activities that will lead toward decreased demand for children, such as education, health, and improvement in the welfare of women. How all these may happen are the subjects of part 2, where they are taken up as culture change, with wider implications than those of population control.

Inequality

In *South Pacific,* Rogers and Hammerstein created a ditty about how we have to be taught at a very early age to fear people of different skin shades. Whether race-consciousness or ethnic identity is cultural, as they implied, or whether it is genetic, has been and will be a subject of spirited debate. Not debatable is the fact that scarcely a culture, if any, lacks a sense of ethnic identity.

"The feeling of distinctiveness *vis-à-vis* outsiders is both ancient and basic, and 'national' consciousness is thus formed in terms of the relationship to others."[71] The pervasiveness and stubborn durability of ethnic identity throughout history and into the present day lead to the hypothesis that in addition to one's individual identity, each person's psychological stability requires belonging to some social group, which is usually an ethnic group.

The need for a group identity explains the enticing enlistment into street gangs of inner cities, which has been known since Roman times and probably before. All the tribes of early Europe—Celts, Alemanni, Goths, and others—along with Scots, Irish, and English divided into clans and other groupings. The same has been historically so for Chinese, Mongols, Magyars, Japanese, Southeastern Asians, Indians, Middle Easterners, and Africans. If we named all the tribes that divided into groups and clans, we would probably have named all that ever existed.

Ethnic groups endow their identity with a heroic past. Many African tribes refer to an "original settler" who early on claimed their land. For Judeo-Christian tribes, this role is played by Adam and Eve; for Hindu tribes by Manu. The past may include periods of greatness: for the Turks, the Ottoman Empire; for the Serbs, the battle of Kosovo; for the Jews, the settlement in Israel; for the French, the Revolution; for the Americans, independence from Britain and (later) the conquering of the western frontier. Monuments are constructed to these periods of glory.

Ethnic identity is associated with sovereignty over land. If the Arabs or the Jews want land in the Middle East, why must they conquer it? Why do they not merely buy it? The same for residents of Northern Ireland and other irredentist regions. But when maps are drawn on ethnic lines, each ideal map is usually incompatible with those of rivals; "each treats as anathema any arrangement dependent on the good faith of the other."[72] The idea of sovereignty over land arose because ethnic groups felt themselves threatened by others whom they wished to keep out. In describing the origin of nations in eastern Europe, Wandycz writes:

> A Hungarian chronicler of the thirteenth century defined a Hungarian as a subject of the king, born in the country, and drawing his descent from the land. Two centuries later in Bohemia, Jerome of Prague stressed the religious element, declaring that common blood, language, and faith were ingredients of the nation. By this time there was a tendency to restrict the term nation to "noble" or "political nation" that excluded the toiling masses. . . . A xenophobic attitude . . . was an early phenomenon.[73]

Characteristics emphasized by ethnic groups often include a common religion, common language, clothing, speech, marital and burial customs, and above all ideology or ways of thinking, all of which make one feel "at home" with one's ethnic group. Symbols, such as flags, reinforce the comfort.

All these positive characteristics turn negative as ethnic groups clash with each other over land, military, and economic advantage. A senator in Washington, DC, will vote for a law bringing an economic advantage, in tariffs or trade restrictions, to a person in California over another person in Japan, when she has seen neither of them and has no reason to appreciate one more than the other except residence. The Californian might even be Japanese American.

For centuries in widely disparate areas, commerce, or soiling the hands, was disdained by the upper classes and left to "outside" ethnic groups. Sometimes these groups staked out trading areas because only their kinspeople were trusted. Here are a few examples out of innumerably more. In ancient Persia, Parthians left trade to Syrians, Arabs, Babylonians, and Greeks.[74] In medieval Europe, Jews and other ethnic minorities excelled in commerce and finance because these were the occupations left to them.[75] Japanese historian Yosoburo Takekoshi likens the Kamigata people, from the provinces around Kyoto, to the European Jews in a similar history.[76] External trade in seventeenth-century Turkey was conducted by Jews, Armenians, Greeks, and Lebanese.[77] In nineteenth-century Egypt, only ethnic minorities were trusted to do banking because they had no connections with local corruption.[78] In Africa, trading groups have been ethnically defined—Harms writes of these for the Upper Zaire basin, where networks defined by ethnicity facilitated both trust and trade monopolization.[79] In Kenya, Uganda, and Tanzania at the time of independence, commercial enterprises were managed mainly by Indians; in West Africa by Lebanese. In his book *Trust,* Fukuyama cites ethnicity, giving rise to "communities of shared ethical values,"[80] as a major force in trust among those engaging in commerce.

As ethnic groups have claimed both trading and land monopolies, conflicts have become harsh and have advanced into hatreds. Here are some samples of ethnic hatreds that have interfered with trade and nation building. Aristotle thought that Greeks were superior to other peoples, some of whom should serve Greeks in slavery. For eleven centuries up to 939 CE, China and Nam Viet (Vietnam) continued wars and mutual hatreds. "In Ireland [before the eleventh century] the tribalism of its communities made it impossible for kingdoms to submerge their differences and loyalties to a degree sufficient to allow provincial monarchies to evolve easily."[81] In the twelfth century the Germans applied the name "Slav" (for "serf") to their eastern neighbors as a sign of contempt.[82] In twelfth-century Sicily the Normans and the Arabs coexisted in an armed peace, with riots and marauding attacks.[83] Italians of the fifteenth century "commonly accused Germans . . . of carrying the evil odors of the Empire wherever they went."[84] In sixteenth-century Spain *moriscos*, descendants of Islamic settlers, were subject to hatred, suspicion, and finally expulsion.[85] Rwanda and Burundi developed rigid class distinctions between Tutsi overlords and Hutu serfs in the seventeenth and eighteenth centuries,[86] which continue with bloodshed today. Tribal distinctions and warfare prevented Africans from uniting against common foes during the period of European colonization.[87]

Ethnic pride carries a positive connotation, racism a negative one, yet they mean the same thing. Strangely, the emphasis has shifted in some more developed areas in the twentieth century, particularly in the United States. Ethnic pride has become more positive, and racism more negative, while continuing to have the same intrinsic meaning. In the United States, civil rights and antidiscrimination laws call for equality of voting and other rights. The federal government lets contracts in favor of ethnic minorities even when their bids are higher than those of nonminorities, thus imposing on taxpayers an extra cost in the name of equality. Employers are frequently sued under the civil rights laws if they appear to favor dominant groups over minorities. Districts have been redrawn to ensure the election of minority candidates. Educated Europeans and Americans of a century and a half ago would have been astounded to hear of these events, which for them were utterly beyond the horizon. Why should all this happen in the twentieth century and never before in history? Why in the West and not elsewhere? We will return to this question in the next subsection.

The history of discrimination against women is similar. Hesiod, Greek poet of the eighth century BCE, regarded women as a curse sent by Zeus, who were necessary only to keep inheritance within the family.[88] In ancient Egypt, women could own and inherit property and engage in trade, but they did not hold government office and probably could not read or write.[89] Among the Salic Franks, women could not inherit property, because their holdings would belong to their husbands and be lost to the clan.[90] "For the good order of the human family, [Thomas Aquinas] argued, some have to be governed by others 'wiser than themselves'; therefore, woman, who was more frail as regards 'both vigor of soul and strength of body,' was 'by nature subject to man, in whom reason predominates.'"[91] Women could not succeed to the throne in France,[92] although they could in England and Scotland. In several European societies, men addressed their wives in the familiar form, but wives used formal vocabulary for their husbands. [93] In 1558, John Knox published *First Blast of the Trumpet against the Monstrous Regiment of Women,* in which "he drew on a seemingly inexhaustible fund of near misogynist sentiment in the Bible, ancient philosophy, the pagan classics, and the church fathers to defend the widely held belief that both divine and natural law opposed the rule of women over men."[94] In sixteenth-century Russia, "the Household Code *(Domostroi)* emphasized the wife's subordination to her husband's authority and declared that a husband may whip his disobedient wife."[95]

Although organizations of and for women were formed during the French Revolution, they suffered a setback with the Napoleonic Civil Code of 1804. "Not only Bonaparte but also the vast majority of drafters, legislators, and jurists believed that woman was weak, fickle, frivolous, and in need of protection."[96] In Confucian principles of conduct, dating to the fifth century BCE in China, women and children have been subordinate to the father of the family. In legal codes throughout the centuries Chinese women have been excluded from disposing of family property. This principle was adopted into Vietnamese codes in the nineteenth century, although apparently it was not much practiced.[97] Even in the late twentieth century, Chinese women have been kidnapped, beaten, and gang raped, then sold into slavery.[98] The mania for boy babies in both China and India today has probably led to female infanticide; in both societies men are significantly more numerous than women.[99] "Women in Iran ride in the back of the bus. They are banned from studying mechanics or electrical engineering, from traveling in the country without their husbands or fathers and from serving as judges because Islamic clerics call them too emotional."[100] In Pakistan, a woman's testimony in court is given half the weight of that of a man. In Africa until colonial times, men frequently bought their wives from other tribes, treating them and their children much like slaves. A few African societies have been matrilineal; property was inherited through women but was managed by their husbands.

Just as it did for minorities, equality for women has taken a leap forward in more developed areas in the twentieth century, especially in the United States, first with the women's suffrage movement and then with civil rights laws similar to those accorded to ethnic minorities. For whatever the prejudices that remain—and there are many—nevertheless the equal treatment of women and minorities has taken a great jump in the twentieth century in the Western nations. Why then and why there?

Cultural Diversity and Affirmative Action

Noting that Western nations, along with Japan, are the most advanced economically, we come to an intriguing hypothesis: that cultural *diversity* is a "good thing" in the economy, yet cultural *distinction* is a "good thing" in promoting self-respect and identity within a group. The world may be heading toward complete economic equality of persons of diverse cultures and both genders but toward ethnic identity in areas of religion, belief in other lives, hero worship, ritual, eating habits, burial customs, clothing, songs, history, and other noneconomic traits. Imagine a world of complete equality in economic opportunity but cultural distinctions in ways that allow individuals to maintain their historic group identities. This is the moral economy. More in chapter 12.

Already in the United States, some firms are finding that cultural diversity leads to competitive advantage. "They may be more attuned to an increasingly diverse population of customers. Equally, firms which continue to favour white men will find themselves fishing in a shrinking pool of potential employees. . . . [Also] heterogeneous firms will be better placed to form global alliances and strike international deals. . . ."[101] "Much of corporate America has decided that having a diversified workforce can be a business asset. A recent study found that nearly three-quarters of the 50 biggest firms in America had 'directors of diversity' or 'diversity managers' whose job is to modify corporate culture so that it suits the needs of all employees. . . . A diversity industry, charging fees as high as $10,000 a day, runs sessions on valuing differences, . . ."[102] In a multicultural workforce, diversity training may help to reduce tension and encourage creativity, thereby increasing productivity.

These gains, however, are offset by many stories of continuing discrimination against employees or potential employees because of ethnic origin. For example, Hochschild found, in samples, that 50 percent of African American home buyers and 20 percent of African Americans applying for entry-level positions experienced discrimination, from real estate agents and prospective employers respectively.[103]

Affirmative action—or the laws that mandate preferences for minority groups in businesses and universities, or that redraw political districts to assure minority representatives—has had a mixed record. On the one hand, many members of minority groups have achieved economic, social, and political advancement only because of the new laws. Davidson and Grofman provide a compendium of these in *Quiet Revolution in the South.*[104] "[I]n interviews with the Federal Glass Ceiling Commission, a bipartisan group studying diversity in the workplace, a majority of chief executives acknowledged that federal guidelines had been crucial in maintaining their commitment to a diverse work force"[105] that they later found advantageous. "David Phillips says he owes just about every job since his college graduation in 1971 to affirmative action—from his first position as bank examiner through his climb to director of corporate finance at Stride Rite Corp." Oliver Lee, "son of an illiterate garbage man with a third-grade education, . . . ,was plucked from an all-Black junior high in Savannah, Ga., in 1965 to attend Cheshire Academy, a Connecticut prep school."[106] Lee attributes his becoming a successful lawyer to many steps taken because of affirmative action laws. The stories go on and on.

On the other hand, many businesses have been subject to heavy, unnecessary costs because of overzealous federal regulators. Bovard has a book full of such examples, covering not only affirmative action but other types of regulation. "The EEOC [Equal Employment Opportunities Commission] sued the Daniel Lamp Company in 1991 for allegedly discriminating against Blacks. The company was in a Hispanic neighborhood in Chicago and relied on Hispanic organizations to refer job-seekers. All of the company's twenty-six employees were either Black or Hispanic. The EEOC ran a computer test, compared Daniel Lamp to much larger employers within a three-mile radius, and informed the company it was guilty of breaking federal laws because it did not have 8.45 Black employees. The EEOC based its lawsuit on the complaint of one Black woman who applied but was not hired. The EEOC 'demanded that Daniel Lamp not only pay her back wages of some $340, but also that it spend $10,000 on advertisements to detect other Blacks who might have answered want ads, and to pay them another $123,000 in back pay.'"[107]

Daniel Lamp is but one example of many, in which employers were informed that they must hire someone other than the ones they had considered most qualified. The EEOC demanded that Exxon hire employees with drug addictions—they were a "disabled group"—despite a long-standing company policy of not doing so.[108] In a classic liberal society, it is assumed that employers have better knowledge than the central government of the needs of the company for employees and are better equipped to judge an applicant's capabilities. Where an employer may be prejudiced by ethnic origin or gender, such prejudice would put him at a competitive disadvantage compared to others not so prejudiced, because he would draw from the smaller pool. The market would then punish those who discriminate.

Why, then, did the market not punish those many employers who discriminated against African Americans in the South of the United States before their behavior was proscribed by federal laws? Probably because discrimination was universal, demanded by white customers and white employees alike. No competitors would interfere. With the formal end of that era, the remaining discrimination—let us not underestimate it—will now be subject to the market and human conscience, which may well be a greater force for affirmative action than punitive laws.

Did the formal end of that era depend on federal intervention? Surely it was accelerated, and those who suffered may not have been willing to wait another ten to twenty years. I favored the intervention at the time and would again under the same circumstances. Yet, why did anyone care enough to bring on that intervention? If a democratic society demanded that its government enforce antidiscrimination laws, would not that same society ultimately have reduced its discrimination without those laws? I would hypothesize that the era formally ended because economic development had reached the stage in which further growth demanded bridging the cultural gap, and the bridge—which may take two or more centuries to build completely—was begun.

Affirmative action by law brings other problems. Some minority persons, fully qualified for employment or university careers, find others believing they may have achieved their places by legal favoritism. One Stanford candidate refused to specify minority status in his application because he did not want to be accepted under that stigma.[109] The laws have given rise to other groups demanding similar minority preferences, some of them extreme, such as overweight persons who sued movie theaters for wider seats.[110] One estimate showed that two-thirds of the United States could claim preferential status.[111] Another study showed that affirmative action in industry had not helped poorer African Americans—no greater African American employment overall—since the preferences went to wealthier African Americans with political connections. Many of these had accepted government contracts at a 10 percent preferential bid, then hired white-owned firms to perform the contracts, and themselves pocketed the difference.[112] Lawsuits over employment discrimination increased 20 percent per year, 1992-96, leading one judge to complain, "The Federal courts are becoming flooded with employment cases . . . We are becoming the personnel czars of this nation's public and private institutions," [113] an exaggeration perhaps but an indication of the tendency. To help balance its budget, Brown University eliminated four varsity teams, two men's and two women's. The women sued. Under the Athletics Disclosure Act, Brown was ordered to prepare a profuse amount of data on sports participation, at university expense of course; altogether, it spent more on its defense than it saved by eliminating the four teams.[114]

Reverse discrimination has been charged: white students turned down for university places in favor of African Americans who were less qualified academically. Some of these suits have succeeded and some not, lending an air of uncertainty to the law. Beginning in 1995, the courts began to take a narrower attitude toward affirmative action, permitting it only where specific discrimination had been proved, not just general categories as previously.[115] In 1994, an appeals court disallowed an African American–only scholarship program.[116]

Finally, we ask What is the purpose of affirmative action? Is it to increase opportunities for employment, education, and political access for minorities? Or is it to change the hearts and minds of racist people, so they will share their spaces with all persons regardless of race, creed, and color and bring up their children to do the same? These are distinct questions, and it is not clear that a strategy to achieve one will also achieve the other.

In a classic liberal society, the inclination tilts toward individual choice, with persuasion and competitive pressure, not toward proscription and punishment. Granted that ugly discrimination persists, it is questionable whether it will be eliminated through fines, imprisonment, or forcing the hire of persons the employer considers unqualified. Rather, enlightenment on questions of ethnic origin, gender, and sexual preference arises out of economic advancement, which is promoted more in the classic liberal society than in any other type, and pressures by churches, schools, colleges, and citizen groups. Many universities and business houses are already choosing affirmative action policies on their own: businesses that see advantage in a diversified workforce and universities wanting to expose their students to students and faculty of different cultures. Boston Latin School, a prestigious preparatory school, had a policy—not required by any government or court—"of reserving 35 percent of its slots in the seventh grade for Black and Hispanic students." A white student complained of discrimination. The Supreme Court, correctly, ruled in favor of the school.[117] Some of these efforts have even been reversed in the courts, which—inconsistently— sometimes punish a defendant for not giving preferences to minority groups and sometimes punish one for doing so. The zealousness of regulators who extend their power into situations not envisaged by the lawmakers, and the enormous expenses of litigation, adds to the discomfort and waste. Far better that the courts and the government leave the effort to enlightened citizen groups, through pressures, strikes, or manifestations like the marches sponsored by Martin Luther King, Jr. Such actions can be more effective—without the negative side effects—than those of a punitive government and courts.

In 1995, the University of California regents decided to stop admitting students, hiring professors, and awarding contracts on the basis of race and sex. In 1996, the state government passed Proposition 209, which reads: "The state shall not discriminate against, or grant preferential treatment to, any group on the basis of race, sex, color, or ethnicity, or national origin in the operation of public employment, public education, or public contracting," wording that closely follows the Civil Rights Act of 1964.[118] Minority applications to the flagship university at Berkeley dropped off, but they picked up in the less demanding state colleges.[119] Berkeley responded in 1997 by announcing plans to expand its partnership program with fifty low-performing high schools throughout the state, to improve the probabilities of minority students qualifying for the university.[120] Late the same year, the Supreme Court refused to review Proposition 209. In fact, Proposition 209 called for a polar reversal: first, affirmative action had been mandated (by the federal government), then it was prohibited (by the state). Such mandating and such prohibiting are both contrary to the moral economy. Accepting that cultural diversity is desirable in employment, schools, and other civil society, the moral economy should have no laws commanding it or prohibiting it but should leave churches, families, civil rights groups, employers, and others to make decisions according to their consciences. Civil activists would then work on the consciences of their communities instead of on the legislature. They would create morality instead of obedience.

Conclusion

Although the three problems in this chapter are worldwide in scope, concern for them has mushroomed mainly in more developed areas. India's laws of affirmative action are an exception. Each problem is acknowledged in the less developed areas, and platitudes are expressed in meetings of international organizations, but the impetus for reform comes from more developed areas. In a study of forty-three cultures of industrialized nations, Inglehart shows that when people are safe from hunger and other threat to physical survival, they become more concerned for self-expression, individual rights, and the quality of life, including environment, population, and ethnic equality, and less so for personal security.[121] From this we ask: Is economic development a prerequisite to recognizing and resolving the problems of this chapter? Surely development is no cure-all; it does not cause the problems to go away automatically. I will argue, however, that a greater degree of economic development than is currently found in most of the world is a necessary but not sufficient condition for resolution of the problems.

Chapter 5
Welfare, Social Security, and Health Care

For all its devotion to *liberté, égalité, fraternité* and its long history of enlightened political thought, France often operates more like an elective monarchy than a democracy. Between government and governed lies little more than a void.

The Economist, December 16, 1995

Privatization and the Downsizing of Government

In the paradox of vicarious power, in the Western world, citizens are entrusting more and more economic activities to governments that they increasingly mistrust. And they object to paying the taxes to finance all the government activities they demand. As a result, budgetary deficits have pushed governments to privatize state enterprises and turn some activities back to the market. Their attempts to do so, however, bring on protests and rioting from those with vested interests in these activities.

In 1960, governments of the rich industrial countries taxed or borrowed 30 percent of gross domestic product; by 1997 the corresponding figure was 46 percent and still rising.[1] In Sweden, Belgium, Luxembourg, and the Netherlands, governments now spend approximately 50 percent of gross domestic product. The figure for most other European governments resides in the 40 percent decile, with only a few in the 30 percent decile. For the United States and Canada, it is less than 25 percent.[2] In 1995: "Unable to afford the bill, the [Swedish] government is reining in the welfare state. The high costs of maintaining generous benefits are seen as a drag on the economy."[3] A year and a half later: "What Welfare State? Swedes Ask Sourly . . . Burdened by a yawning budget deficit . . . Sweden has been struggling to slim its welfare state these last few years."[4]

In many countries, complaints are heard that government services are not adequate or are discriminatory. In 1986, French students rioted against proposed reforms that would permit individual schools a greater voice in selecting students.[5] In 1995, they were clamoring in the streets for more professors, larger classrooms, and improved libraries, with of course no increase in taxes.[6] In Germany, "desperate farmers [in the east] accuse their government of bankrupting them by cutting subsidies and by allowing West German producers to flood the market."[7] After giving a lecture in the University of Córdoba (Argentina) in 1995, I learned that students were planning a strike. Why? I asked them. For two reasons, they replied: in solidarity with provincial civil servants who had not been paid for three months, because of lack of funds, and in protest against a proposal by the government to charge student fees when public higher education had heretofore been free. They did not see the conflict.

Many government deficits have been high. In the Maastricht accord of 1991, members of the European Union agreed to limit their deficits to no more than 3 percent of gross domestic product (GDP). By dint of unpopular austerity, increased taxes, and some imaginative accounting adjustments, eleven nations announced in February, 1998, that they had met the test.[8] In the United States, the annual deficit has been decreasing for several years, but it was still greater than 3 percent of GDP until 1995, when it dipped below that mark. By 1998, a balanced budget was announced.

So long as deficits are positive, even though they may decrease, the debt piles up. "The chief executive of Scandia, one of [Sweden's] largest insurance firms, announced that his firm would shun Swedish government bonds until politicians came up with a credible program for dealing with the debt problem."[9] In the United States, the federal debt has more than doubled from $1,562 billion in 1985 to $3,460 billion in 1994.[10]

The increase in debt causes higher government interest payments. For the most part, these are transfers from poor to rich, since the former also pay taxes while the latter hold most of the government debt. In the United States, federal interest payments increased from $154 billion in 1985 to $212 billion in 1994 and are expected to continue rising for at least the next decade.

Let us now consider three prominent government services: welfare, pensions and social security, and health care.

Welfare

History of Welfare in the United States

Kaus classifies the history of twentieth-century welfare in the United States into seven phases, which I have combined into five:[11]

Mother's Aid (1911-35). All but eight states paid single mothers for parenting. But critics complained that desertion by fathers was encouraged and subsidized.

The Roosevelt Revolution (1935-60). The Federal Relief Emergency Program, established by President Franklin D. Roosevelt (FDR), supplied "direct relief," a cash dole. Being persuaded, however, that people receiving assistance should work, FDR initiated the Works Progress Administration to provide jobs creating works of national importance, such as highways, bridges, and improvements to national parks. Unemployment insurance, social security, and other social legislation were passed. For families where the breadwinner was "dead, disabled, or absent," cash grants were provided under "Aid for Dependent Children" (ADC). In 1939, this program was brought under the aegis of social security and was renamed "Aid to Families with Dependent Children" (AFDC), and in 1996 it was replaced by "Temporary Assistance for Needy Families" (TANF).

The Growth of Restrictions (1960-68). By 1960, "absent fathers" characterized 64 percent of AFDC families. Many were calling AFDC a subsidy that encouraged desertion by fathers. It was widely believed that welfare caused the situation it was designed to alleviate. Abundant restrictions were placed upon it, including "preventive" and "consultative" services for the poor. Midnight calls were made on recipient women to make sure they did not have "male callers." A public outcry attacked the ways in which welfare agencies, both state and federal, patronized and paternalized recipients.

The Cash Grants Proposals (1968-78). In response, cash grants to the poor were advocated by both classic liberal and interventionist thinkers, including Milton Friedman, James Q. Wilson, John Kenneth Galbraith, Sargent Shriver, and Daniel Patrick Moynahan. Presidents Nixon and Carter advanced guaranteed income plans in 1969 and 1977, respectively. These did not pass, for they were not supported by Congress, which would have lost its power over the poor, or by the voters, who would have lost their vicarious power.

Workfare, Time Limits, and Cutoffs (1978-present). With an explosion in welfare, and much dissatisfaction with its "eternal" nature, both major political parties have agreed that reform is needed. President Clinton promised "to end welfare as we know it," and Republican members of Congress have proposed cutting it severely. A study by the Cato Institute showed that when recipients enrolled in all programs available—AFDC, food stamps, Medicaid, housing, nutrition assistance, and energy assistance, none of which was taxed—the pretax equivalent of their earnings, based on a presumed forty-hour week, ranged from $5.50 per hour in Mississippi to $17.50 in Hawaii, and in thirty-nine states it was more than $8 per hour, a "probable reason why recipients prefer welfare to work."[12] A law of 1996 "ends a federal guarantee of aid to the poor by shifting responsibility to the states, requiring work and imposing a five-year lifetime limit on benefits."[13]

Welfare reforms have encountered a seemingly intractable problem. On the one hand, it is amply demonstrated that some recipients cannot work, because of mental illness, drug addiction, low intelligence, or utter inexperience, and aid cutoffs would precipitate starvation and homelessness. Often these are single mothers—who would take care of the kids?—whose children would suffer through no fault of their own. For example, Jason de Parle wrote the story of Mary Ann Moore, who truly tried to get off welfare but found it excruciatingly difficult to find a job and then to hold it, mainly because of factors in her personal life, such as separation from her husband, an earlier cocaine habit, and child care. Even if she worked despite these obstacles, the "bottom line" was that welfare had paid a total of $985 a month, while a job paid only $775 after taxes.[14] Advocates of such persons argue that any cuts in government aid for child care, school lunches, health care, or food stamps would be inhumane —and they are right, unless the cuts are compensated. Furthermore, aid cuts will not induce people to work when they cannot.

On the other hand, we find documented cases of welfare abuse and of unwise laws. Tom Holt writes how he—a good earner with no need for a welfare check—takes his two children to a government-licensed child sitter and finds that, whether he likes it or not, "the government is determined to give our sitter $1,390 a year, . . . courtesy of the $1.5 billion Child and Adult Care Food Program."[15] The Supplemental Security Income (SSI) Act classifies children who do not behave in an "age-appropriate manner" as eligible for disability benefits. Thus "parents have an overpowering incentive to sign their kids up for SSI, since they receive payments of $458 a month or more, with no strings attached. Stories abound of parents coaching their kids to misbehave in school or fail their tests."[16] Social Security Disability Insurance (SSDI) has classified drug addiction and alcoholism as federally subsidized disabilities, thus providing incentives to acquire these "disabilities" rather than the means to conquer them.

Finally, the president, Congress, and bureaucrats spend hours of their time and millions of taxpayer dollars debating whether this or that generic case is eligible for welfare, whether welfare ought to include medical insurance or not, what constitutes a disability, and whether or not there is discrimination in such and such a program.

Welfare in the Moral Economy

In the moral economy, on the other hand, the success of welfare is judged by its results, not by its inputs, just as in the liberal market an automobile is judged by how well it works and not usually by the method of manufacture.

The government would invite a large number of private welfare agencies to "adopt" welfare clients, at the initiative of the client. These might be existing charities or churches, or new agencies either for profit or nonprofit. Eligibility of clients would depend on assets and annual income being below a certain amount, but no client would be required to dispose of newly-acquired assets in order to remain eligible, nor would a client lose eligibility until his or her after-tax income had reached a level somewhat greater than the initial one. One does not have to immiserate oneself completely to qualify for welfare, nor does one get cut off immediately upon finding a job. An agency would lose its own eligibility if it turned down a client who met the criteria. Each agency would presumably be staffed with counselors skilled in psychology, drug addiction, child care, job hunting, and other needs of persons on welfare. The decision on which of these to employ would be up to the agency, which would be judged by performance, not by whom it employs. Agencies might test clients for aptitude and train them in appropriate skills or might sometimes help them acquire financing and start small businesses. Already a number of private agencies perform these services, which may be modeled after small-scale loans and services supplied to clients, often rural women, in less developed areas.[17] But not nearly enough exist. If the welfare client was not satisfied with the services of an agency, he or she might shift to another one.

Each agency would receive a cash grant for each welfare client it accepted, plus a monthly allotment to support the client. The agency's objective would be to get the client off welfare by reaching a certain standard of job and income and holding the job for a certain period of time. In the meantime, it would support the client in cash or vouchers or might not support the client at all during the job trial period when the client earns a wage. Vouchers, redeemable only for specific services, such as food, housing, health care, and the like, would be used if the agency did not trust the client to spend cash well. Purveyors of these services would redeem the vouchers at the agency. To avoid the perverse incentive of keeping a client on welfare so the agency would collect more money, the monthly allotment would be kept a bit below the expected cost for client housing, food, health care, and so forth. The agency would make up the difference by drawing down the initial grant, whose amount would be calculated on an average expected time period. If the client is released before a "normal" period elapses, the agency would earn a profit from the grant; if the client takes longer, the agency would lose. Thus the agency has incentive to prepare the client to enter the job market as soon as possible and to stay there. Nevertheless, the cash grants should be large enough to cover the expectation that a certain percentage of clients will be unable to support themselves in any event. These would be continued indefinitely, on the principle that our society is rich enough and compassionate enough that no person must starve. This proposal will not come cheap, but if we wish to solve the problems associated with welfare, we must pay the cost.

Within certain statutory limits, the amount paid to support the client would be determined by the agency. An agency that paid too much would go bankrupt; an agency that paid too little would lose clients. In these ways, welfare would be restored to the liberal market, with government participation limited to providing the funds according to law. Legislators and executives would lose their power over the lives and behavior of welfare clients. A prototype for the moral economy is a program, "Pathways to Independence," run by Marriott International, which provides learning and work experience for welfare clients. "Over 90% of those who start classes finish them, and almost 80% of those people still hold their jobs after a year."[18]

In the Welfare Reform Law of 1996 in the United States, responsibility for welfare programs devolves upon the states, with federal assistance and some federal requirements.[19] No state may provide welfare for any one person for more than two years at a stretch and more than five years in a lifetime, although various loopholes may allow states to assist hard cases from other funds. While popular with voters in an election year, this program has many defects. First, while releasing the states to experiment with new ways, it nevertheless constrains them with time limitations. Second, the permissible exceptions are vague and will surely lead to litigation. Third, many poor people, unable to work for physical or mental reasons, may be driven into poverty, along with their children. Fourth, states may compete with each other to provide the least amount for welfare clients, so as not to attract them to reside in the state.

On the other hand, it is possible that some state will come up with an innovative program—even one resembling the moral economy—that might overcome these remaining obstacles. For example, giant companies are entering the race to run welfare programs under contract from states; Texas is letting a five-year contract to a big company to run the entire state welfare system.[20] No one yet knows how such contracts would work. Furthermore, "no company can be expected to protect the interests of the needy at the expense of its bottom line,"[21] and the possibility that clients would be "dumped" under the false assumption that they had been "rehabilitated" is real. Nevertheless, such contracts may be the first step toward privatizing welfare, while lessons from failures may bring it closer to the moral economy.

At the time of publication of this book, the White House is objecting to Texas's initiative, arguing that "only state employees can be charged with the task of determining who is eligible for Medicaid health coverage and food stamps."[22] Clearly their concern is still with inputs—who will or will not perform the service—rather than outputs, or how well the service is performed.

Pensions and Social Security

My retirement income comes from two main sources: a teacher's pension and social security. The teacher's pension was accumulated over the years through contributions by my employers and me; it was invested in income-earning assets such as stocks and bonds of private companies plus a few government bonds. The social security was also paid over the years by contributions by my employers and me, but its proceeds were blown up over Vietnam and Iraq or have otherwise financed the government deficit.[23] My teacher's pension is a contractual obligation, contingent on profits earned by corporations. My social security income is not a contractual obligation; Congress and the president can abolish it any time they dare; it is paid not out of profits on current production but from the social security taxes on younger workers. When the baby boomers (those born right after World War II) reach retirement age, with fewer young workers per retiree, the burden of social security taxes per worker will be so great that the new crop of workers will surely be unwilling to pay. Then our politicians must decide whether to reduce social security pensions, increase the wage tax as much as they can, raise the retirement age—how high?—or pay pensions out of general government revenue, as proposed by Princeton economist Alan Blinder.[24] If they do the latter, both deficit and interest payments will increase, with more transfers from poor people to rich bondholders.

In 1997 a presidential commission, deeply divided among three options for the United States, presented all three, leaving the choice to Congress: (1) investment of some assets of the social security fund in private equity securities, (2) diversion of part of the payroll tax into mandatory personal retirement accounts, and (3) increases in both payroll tax and the age at which benefits start.[25] About choice (1), one dissenting member of the commission wrote: "Our strongest objection . . . involves the proposed government investment of social security funds in the private equity markets. Over a 15-year period starting in 2000, the government would accumulate $1 trillion (in 1996 dollars) in equities, thus becoming the single largest investor in private capital markets. . . . [I]t is not clear that social security administrators have any competence as investment managers."[26]

In Japan, the number of working contributors to social security is expected to decline from 5.1 per retiree today to 2.4 in 2025.[27] The same situation affects governments in Europe, where "greying populations are undermining their pay-as-you-go state retirement schemes. These governments [also] pay pensions to retirees out of the contributions from current workers. As the proportion of old people rises across Europe, such schemes are fast running out of money."[28] This fact has led several countries to consider privatizing their social security by "selling" their pension liabilities to private insurance companies. How does one sell a liability? By giving an asset—such as government bonds—in compensation. Insurance companies might finance the pensions with their interest income on the bonds. But they might also sell those bonds and invest the proceeds in private companies, from whose interest and dividends they would pay the pensions. In final analysis, the government would have to pay the interest and redeem the bonds at maturity, a process that would increase the national debt on paper; but the national debt is actually much greater than the figures show now, because it ought to include the present value of the implied liability on social security for the lifetimes of current recipients. Social security's actuaries estimate this, for beneficiaries for the next seventy five years, at about $21.3 trillion.[29] Alternatively, the government might sell some of its assets to pay the insurance companies. In the United States, these assets might include government land, but sales of this would raise environmental questions, which might be resolved if the land were sold to environmental agencies such as nature conservancies (see chapter 4). Citizens might make taxdeductible contributions for this. Once the new system is inaugurated, workers and employers would invest their social security funds with the private insurance companies, and pensions would be contractual obligations based on current profits of enterprise.

Suppose an insurance company should fail? Failure could be insured against by a second layer. Participating companies might sell portions of their liabilities to other companies, to spread the risk, or they could reinsure, just as fire insurance companies do. If a fire insurance company has insured too many buildings in a given city, it would fail if the whole city should burn. To guard against this, it often reinsures—sells its policies or buys guarantees to cover them—through insurance companies in cities with different patterns of risk. Risk may be spread, but it is never eliminated in an uncertain future; even leaving social security funds with the government becomes increasingly risky. I would prefer the risk of investing my pension funds in productive corporations rather than with a government that changes the payoff by majority vote and has not staked productive assets to back it up. I would spread the risk by choosing a fiduciary that invests in many corporations and reinsures. But those with more power than I have forced me into the investment that I consider more risky and with a lower return.

The government of Chile has privatized social security. Workers are required to pay 10 percent of their income, but may pay up to 20 percent, for investment in a private agency.[30] Payments are taxdeductible, and reinvested earnings are not taxed. At retirement, the worker transforms the investment into an annuity by a private insurance company of his or her choice. A worker may retire at any age and convert the pension plan into a lifetime annuity or other kinds of payback. If the savings in the plan are insufficient for a reasonable retirement, the government will supplement them out of general revenue. Government rules for diversification of investments prevent the companies from taking undue risks such as with derivatives.[31]

After sixteen years, however, this model is "beginning to show some strains."[32] High marketing costs and poorly diversified portfolios led to negative returns in 1995 and low returns in 1996. Some would therefore argue for reinstalling a government system. While I see logic to their reasoning, nevertheless governments also renege on agreements. Therefore I prefer the classic liberal approach, which is to overcome these problems by publishing the returns of pension funds, just as mutual funds do, as education in financial responsibility, and by competition.

In Britain, Tory administrations have been gradually reducing the government's role in pensions through the state earnings-related pension system (SERPS), encouraging employees to opt out of that system and into new private-sector pension funds. This change has occurred smoothly since the early 1980s, so that now the British do not face the same pensions time bomb as other countries.[33] Recently the governments of Argentina, Bolivia, Colombia, and Peru have also established private pension schemes to replace those of the state.[34]

By contrast, the Mexican government's cradle-to-grave social security is in deep financial trouble. Since its creation in 1943 this system "has evolved into a life-long security blanket that includes hospitals in which one out of every three Mexicans is born, and a chain of 16 funeral parlors."[35] It also collects and manages retirement pensions; to cover all this, Mexican workers are taxed more than 25 percent of their salaries. In 1995, faced with estimates that the system will be bankrupt by the year 2002, President Zedillo proposed privatization, and the lower house of Congress approved the establishment of individual retirement accounts, to be privately managed, beginning in January 1997.[36] The new system is now in effect, but it is too early to judge success.

Company pension plans are little better than government plans. Companies notoriously contribute their own stock to these funds rather than investing in diversified securities. This is similar to the U.S. government investing social security funds in its own bonds. If the company goes bankrupt, the worker's job and savings disappear at the same time. Furthermore, companies frequently underfinance pension schemes or "borrow" from them to supply their own needs, counting on a pay-as-you go plan to make up the difference. *The Economist* refers to this practice as managers pillaging their companies' pension funds.[37] A Brookings Institution study showed that from 1983 to 1989, company pension funds earned less than stock market averages and extorted high management fees.[38]

In the United States a government Pension Benefit Guaranty Corporation (PBGC) was established by the Employment Retirement and Income Security Act (ERISA) of 1974 to pay the pensions of retirees if employers who paid premiums to it should go bankrupt. By 1992, economists were predicting that this corporation would have to call on a taxpayer bailout to cover its obligations.[39] In 1994 Secretary of Labor Reich denied that pensions were underfunded, citing the ERISA, which "requires that pension plan money be invested solely in the interest of the workers participating in the plan, and for the exclusive purpose of providing benefits to workers, retirees and their beneficiaries."[40] However, in quoting the law rather than citing the data, he ignored a finding of the General Accounting Office of 1993 that "the cost of failed pension plans taken over by the PBGC . . . is 58 percent higher than companies had reported."[41]

Another disadvantage of company schemes is the "golden handcuff," by which companies may penalize employees who change jobs by refusing to vest a portion of their funds in them. In 1992, a worker lost his rights to a pension because the steel mill employing him closed one year too soon.[42] Finally, why the U.S. taxpayer should guarantee obligations that rightfully belong to business corporations is a question explainable only in terms of power interests in the interventionist state.

In summary, all three choices of the 1997 presidential commission, and the Blinder proposal as well, follow the philosophy that government is ultimately responsible for managing the retirement funds of citizens. The moral economy, on the other hand, adopts the philosophy that while individuals should be required to invest in retirement funds, they may select them themselves and invest them where they wish—presumably in productive enterprises, not in wars in Vietnam or Iraq or elsewhere.

The pension plan proposed for the moral economy is similar to my own teacher's pension: a fund fully vested in the individual, separate from either government or employer assets, which workers who change employment may carry with them. The government would subsidize the pensions of those with too little income to save. Pensions would be insured by private companies (like houses or automobiles), not by government. In case workers are not believed to have the financial acumen to make investment decisions, then advisory agencies, either private or government, may help them. For those who argue that government social security redistributes income from rich to poor, I would reply first, the case is not proved, and second, redistribution belongs in income tax (see chapter 8) and welfare, not in social security pensions.

Health Care

With automobile, life, accident, and other insurance firmly in the private market, why should health care be singled out to be entrusted to government? I will argue that this is no more appropriate than for the others, but before doing so, we must examine why many think it is. First is the growing sense that goods and services of fundamental importance should be provided by government. Health care is deemed a right belonging to all persons, like water, air, and personal freedom. Unfortunately, this philosophy frequently ignores its other half: that every person's right is another person's obligation. Who is to pay for health care is not clearly stipulated. Second is the eagerness to receive something "free," such as frequent-flyer bonuses, even though intellectually we know we pay for them. Some may believe we want government health care to provide for the poor—including the thirty-seven million Americans who presumably do not have it—but if this were the reason we would simply provide it for them. Instead, our politicians and our vicarious power holders want also to provide it for Bill Gates, Ross Perot, Donald Trump, Michael Milken, Lee Iacocca, other corporate executives, high-paid athletes, and millionaire entertainment stars, financed by taxing people who are, for the most part, not as wealthy as they are.

Suspicion of profit is a third reason. The essential role of profits in promoting economic efficiency, which was outlined in chapter 2, is neither widely known nor much respected beyond economists. Rather, profit is associated with greed—often wrongly, I have argued. Legislate profits away, and greed remains. In November 1993, Hillary Clinton, the president's wife, lambasted health insurance companies for misleading the public in order to guard their profits and said that greed had driven the nation "to the brink of bankruptcy."[43] In fact, insurance profits are no greater than those of other industries; advertisements that deceive the public are legion—insurance should not be singled out—and the nation is far from the brink of bankruptcy.

An enormous rise in health costs is the reason most often heard. In 1960 in the United States, total spending per capita on health care was $143. By 1993, it had risen to $3,299.[44] In 1946, the cost per patient-day in a hospital was about $20 in 1982 dollars; by the 1990s it had risen to over $600.[45] Health expenditures have also increased as a percentage of gross domestic product from 5 percent in 1960 to 14 percent in 1993.[46] But cost increase is a spurious reason to entrust health care to a government that has itself been the cause of much higher cost. Why have costs risen?

Because many employers cover health costs and co-payments are small, medical services become overused. This condition is a direct result of government concession. Hampered by wartime wage controls during World War II, employers looked for new ways to attract workers. Offering health insurance was one, and Congress obliged by excluding the insurance from taxable wages but allowing its cost to be taxdeductible to the company. In addition to the tendency to overuse services, employer insurance led to higher costs in four other ways. Employees could not select health plans tailored to their preferences but had to accept what the employer prescribed; services outside the contract had to be paid for additionally. Employees usually could not carry health plans with them to other jobs—if they contracted "prior conditions," they might not get insurance after moving. Some employers became self-insurers, paying medical bills out of current revenue rather than using insurance companies. If the company failed, workers were left adrift.[47] Finally, small-scale employers and individuals not employed or partially employed could not obtain the same bargains and had to pay higher premiums. Those without employers also do not enjoy tax deductions. All these disadvantages, or cost increases for the employees, were incurred at little or no real effect on profits or wages; hence they were what economists call "deadweight losses" to the economy. Any extra employer costs are passed on either to workers through lower wages or to the consumers through higher prices.[48]

In 1996, a law was approved to make insurance portable by requiring new employers and their insurance companies to accept the policies from a previous employer. Here is an example of how one ill-conceived mandate is "corrected" by yet another. Mostly likely, employers will now bargain with their insurance companies for lower rates if they "voluntarily" do not employ anyone with a prior condition. This defect might be "corrected" by yet another mandate, which would bring the judiciary in to decide whether employment was refused for that reason or because the potential employee was not qualified for the job—a judgment usually beyond the competence of a judge. Also, passing a law and enforcing it are two different matters. In 1998, after I had written this paragraph and this book was already in press, the General Accounting Office, an arm of Congress, reported that "people who exercised their rights under the law were often charged premiums higher than the standard rate [and] some companies discouraged insurance agents from selling policies to people with medical problems, the very people who were supposed to benefit from the law."[49]

For all these reasons, health insurance should be divorced from employment. If payment of premiums were still made tax deductible—though I see no justice in that—the liberal market would cause paychecks to be increased by the amount of the insurance: very soon take-home pay would have the same purchasing power as before. By organizing themselves into larger groups, such as through health maintenance organizations (HMOs) competing with each other, free workers might obtain the same advantages as large-scale employers, just as supermarkets compete with each other to sell bananas to free buyers. However, unions have been so unequivocally opposed to divorcing health care from employment, possibly because of the advantages to their members over outsiders, that this move is politically unlikely—another example of how difficult it is to remove an undeserved benefit once it is awarded to a special group.

All these disadvantages would be avoided if individual insurance were decided upon by individuals; if it were made mandatory to guard against "free riders"—persons who would not join the program but would take advantage of our compassion and presume they would not be allowed to die because of lack of insurance—and if government subsidies were paid for those who could not afford the premiums. This does not happen, however, because political and vicarious power are stronger than market power in this field, at least momentarily.

How might it come about nevertheless? As employees become discontented with employer health programs and employers become disenchanted with controversies over them, the two might strike a bargain: in exchange for an increase in wages, employees might agree to select their own health care programs. The *New York Times* reported a tendency in this direction in 1997: "In response to public fears of restrictions of access to doctors and hospitals, employers have been offering their insured workers and retirees much wider varieties of health care, though sometimes at a higher cost to the workers."[50] Not quite all the way to the moral economy but partly there.

Political and vicarious power are exercised in debates over whether Medicare should direct that colon cancer be detected through colonoscopies or barium

X rays[51]—doctors are divided and Congresspeople have no special expertise—and whether "drive-in" mastectomies should be banned[52]—they are perfectly safe but repugnant to some who do not have to have them anyway. In these and similar cases, government decisions—and forced uniformity for all—invade the privacy of patients who should act with the advice and consultation of their chosen doctors. It would be quite in order, however, for the legislature to rule that insurance policies should specify exactly what is included and what is not, just the way packaged foods must list their ingredients, at least in the United States.

Other reasons for higher health costs include exaggerated malpractice suits, extraordinary technological improvements in health care that we feel should not be sacrificed, and an increase in the human life span, so that we suffer from more expensive illnesses, such as arthritis, emphysema, and cancer instead of dying earlier from smallpox, tetanus, tuberculosis, and diphtheria.[53] In advocating his government health care program, President Clinton pointed to the greater percentage of gross domestic product spent on health care today than twenty years ago. Of course. With rising incomes, we choose to spend a higher proportion on computers, television sets, foreign aid, travel, and health care—among many other things—while not eating much more food or living in more houses. The idea that earlier percentages should be enshrined makes no sense at all, and it never has. Still another reason lies in keeping older, suffering people alive at great cost and often against their will. I would far rather pass on whatever estate I might have for my grandchildren's education, rather than dissipate it keeping me alive a few more months. I believe I should have that choice, which I may not under current law.

The History of Government Health Care

Government provision of universal health started in 1883, when Chancellor Bismarck of Germany yielded to union pressure, much against his political philosophy, and passed the most extensive social security plan in Europe, with sickness insurance, compulsory accident insurance, and old-age pensions. His purpose was to attach workers to the state as a weapon against his opponents, the Social Democrats.[54] Not until after World War II did a surge in government health care come about in Canada, Europe, and Japan. Here are a few newspaper snippets on the results fifty years later, with italics added to emphasize the places:

The *Canadian program,* which provides complete health care to everyone, is much admired by many citizens. However, many cases are reported of a lag in accessibility, particularly of highly sophisticated care, long waiting periods, lack of adequate medical equipment, lack of timely anesthesia for women giving birth, restricted access to advanced technology, unnecessary deaths, patients going to the United States for prompt treatment, and doctors defecting abroad.[55] How does one evaluate such conflicting evidence? I would suppose that the system is praised by those Canadians—by far the majority—who have not had serious illnesses, while I am moved by the abundance of anecdotes of failure where the system is most needed.

In the *British National Health System,* care is free to all comers, and primary care is deemed "brilliant." Cancer treatment, however, is seen by many as "too little, too late,"[56] while elective surgery is long postponed. However, those with money can buy it in private hospitals.[57] A study by "Healthcare 2000, a cross-party research group, points to the widening gap between the demand for health care and the resources available to pay for it [which make it] impossible for the NHS to fulfill its original mandate of providing a comprehensive free service for everyone."[58] A report from London, 1997: "At times as many as 30 patients have been sprawled on gurneys outside [the] emergency room, waiting for treatment for things like pneumonia, heart attacks, stabbings and injuries from car accidents. . . . The problems are mirrored across Britain, where a cold snap and budget crisis have forced the cancellation of non-emergency treatment, sent some of the sickest patients on long odysseys in search of beds and wreaked havoc on a system that has run on a shoestring even in the best of times."[59]

"Everyone agrees that *France's* welfare system is a mess. Its spending of nearly FFr 2 trillion a year—more than the entire state budget—has been spiraling out of control. . . . France has the fourth highest level of health care spending in the world (after America, Canada, and Switzerland), gobbling up nearly a tenth of GDP, but its standard of health care is not outstandingly good."[60]

In *Denmark* "waiting-lists for routine hospital operations are irritatingly long, and the newspapers detail many horror stories about the state of the country's hospitals."[61]

"All of *Italy's* 57 million people are guaranteed access to low-cost public health care, financed by their taxes and employer contributions" for all ailments. However, reports abound of insufficient care, misdiagnoses, unnecessary deaths, and unsanitary conditions. Protests in Naples centered on "fleas in the bed, fecal traces in fish."[62] "Italy's health sector has produced some of the most spectacular cases in the massive bribery and kickback scandal . . . Former health minister [name omitted] has been accused of taking kickbacks worth millions of dollars from pharmaceutical companies to keep prices pegged at artificially high levels. . . . Contracts to build new hospitals became a notorious prize . . . even if the facilities were not needed or did not get built."[63]

"The public health system in *Poland* in theory guarantees universal access to all citizens. In practice, however, the system has suffered from underfunding. . . . Waiting periods are very long: drugs, equipment, and facilities are inadequate; there are not enough hospital beds and specialist services; and patient relations with physicians and other health care workers are poor."[64]

"All over the *formerly Communist region,* financially strapped governments have neglected health care and now face what experts are calling an unprecedented crisis."[65]

"All national health insurance plans, in *all of the Western democracies,* are in acute financial crisis."[66]

The *Japanese* system covers everyone with no frills, but clinics are crowded, with long waiting periods.[67] A Japanese friend tells me that the sheets were not changed during the week she spent in the hospital for a minor ear operation.

The force of all these examples makes a major point: that government-managed health care is neither efficient nor fair and that it is more expensive than taxpayers are willing to finance. Only when recipients pay out of their own pockets will rational choices be made and waste reduced. They will have the means to do so if their taxes are reduced by the amount that the government earlier paid for their care and if they insure themselves privately, paying premiums high enough to support full cost of care in the liberal market. There remains, of course, the possibility that if the government subsidized the poor with cash or vouchers, it would not do so adequately. That is a battle yet to be fought between the poor and their advocates on the one hand and the less compassionate voters on the other.

Private health care is not always a satisfactory alternative. Health maintenance organizations (HMOs) sometimes achieve their lower costs at the expense of the rest of the market. Suppose a hospital has variable costs—those that increase with each patient—of $250 per patient-day and fixed costs—those that do not vary, such as building and equipment maintenance, salaries of permanent staff including the basic number of doctors needed—of $750, for a total of $1,000 per patient-day. An HMO may offer to pay only $400 for a new patient instead of the full $1,000. To prevent the HMO from seeking a competitor hospital, the first hospital may accept the offer, because the variable cost would be covered, plus a contribution of $150 toward the fixed costs, which have to be paid whether the patient is received or not. The remaining share of fixed cost ($600) would be borne by non-HMO patients, who thus have to pay more than their fair share. This is one reason why many HMO patients pay less than non-HMO patients. They would lose this advantage, however, if all patients belonged to HMOs, because then there would be no one else to pay the remaining fixed costs.

Herzlinger has suggested that much dissatisfaction with HMOs comes from their presenting a minimal, cost-effective solution as they compete for private-company or government contracts. If instead they were to compete on quality of service, at different prices for different customers (luxury, basic, or minimal), just like most consumer goods, then purchasers might be satisfied with the level they choose and pay for. She also believes the liberal market might bring about specialization, or "focused factories," each of which would do one thing well, such as treatment of heart problems or eye care.[68]

As national health care seemed more probable in the United States in 1995-6, doctors defended themselves by combining their medical practices or by becoming employees of hospitals.[69] These moves were not always in the interests of patients. Some hospitals are accused of paying their employed doctors bonuses for not recommending advanced care, even when it may be appropriate. Where doctors have combined their practices, they may also own outside services, such as laboratories with catscans, to which they recommend their patients, when other suppliers would be less expensive.

The Economist sums up the situation on health care in the United States as follows:

> Americans spend roughly twice as much on doctors, drugs, and snazzy brain scanners as Europeans, but they live no longer. In contrast to the all-inclusiveness of other countries' socialized medical services, 40 million Americans have no coverage at all. Chinese children are more likely to be vaccinated against disease than Americans, despite the fact that health spending per head in the United States is 150 times higher.[70]

Health Care in the Moral Economy

A reasonable program to overcome the difficulties cited previously might embody the following principles:

Every individual would be required to purchase health insurance from the moment of birth, that would pay medical expenses up to an amount equal to the minimum that the people—through the president or prime minister and the legislature—decide ought to be provided for everyone. This minimum might be very high, including nursing homes for Alzheimer's patients, or very low, covering only minimum medical and hospitalization fees, or probably somewhere in between.

The government would subsidize with cash or vouchers those with incomes too low to buy the minimum insurance. A sliding scale might be established, so that as income increases, the individual contributes more to the cost of insurance, but never so much that net income after insurance premiums fails to increase along with gross income.

To create equity between employed persons, independent workers and contractors, and the unemployed, no employer should be required to supply health insurance for an employee, and those that do so should count the premiums as taxable income of the employee.

Any person should have the right to buy as much health insurance as he or she wishes, above the minimum.

So long as it covers the minimum care specified by law, a policy may be offered by any insurance company that meets certain requirements for financial competence. These requirements might be enforced by a government agency, but they might alternatively be enforced by private overseers similar to the regional accrediting agencies for universities in the United States. Unlike in these universities, however, the overseers should come from outside the profession, to guard against conflict of interest. The insurance companies should be required by law to provide enough information on their financial position for policyholders to make informed decisions.

The requirement that policies should be taken out at birth would override most prior condition exceptions, for no prior conditions would exist other than birth defects. Those with birth defects requiring medical attention might be given government subsidies for their more costly insurance, which might either be scaled to their income or be made regardless of income if the society wishes all its members to share responsibility for birth defects with the innocent parents that encounter them. Alternatively, parents might be required by law, upon conception, to take out insurance against birth defects, but this requirement would be difficult to enforce.

Competition—not laws—would force insurance companies to offer noncancelable policies and HMOs to offer services of differing qualities according to consumer preference and pocketbook.

Private review boards would be set up to establish criteria for treatment of most illnesses. So long as a doctor conformed to these criteria, he or she would be protected from malpractice liability. The criteria would also minimize the time-consuming audits and mounds of paperwork required of doctors by insurance companies, as well as arguments over necessary treatments. Insurers might audit doctors' decisions on a random-sample basis instead of all decisions, much the same way a CPA audits the accounts of a commercial firm. Special cases not fitting the criteria might be handled on an *ad hoc* basis. These procedures would be established informally, in a free market in institutions as defined in chapter 1.

How Can Classic Liberal Arrangements Be Adopted?

My guess on why classic liberal arrangements are not adopted is first, that these changes come slowly, piece by piece, and, second, that social groupings have become so interlinked that making any one change unravels valued relationships, threatens vested interests, and creates uncertainties—"better the devil you know." Power and vicarious power are also among the ingredients. Rather than analyze all possible interconnections and foci of power, I turn to the question What will induce a virtual consensus favoring classic liberal arrangements?

One possibility would be a tax revolt, as has been threatened in European countries, or demands for reduced taxes as in the United States. The electorate is unwilling to pay for all the services it has demanded, and the conflict will be messy. There is, however, a less obvious and more suitable possibility, that Western government will go the way of the company town.

Company towns appeared in Western societies and Japan with industrialization. The locations of mills, mines, and timber cutting were prescribed by waterfalls, minerals, and forests, respectively. To attract laborers, entrepreneurs created whole towns. While many houses were shacks and the only social centers were pubs, eventually owners competed to build attractive housing, restaurants, food stores, parks and gardens, concert halls, art galleries, libraries, and schools, which of course they—not the workers—owned and managed. Some of this paternalism was based on religion—Cadbury, Lever, and Rowntree were Quakers—some on egotism, some on idealism, and some on self-interest: well-treated workers would perform better.[71] Some towns had feudal characteristics: the patron would live in a mansion on a hill, overlooking the humble homes of his workers and requiring that they go to church and not drink alcohol. More than an entrepreneur, in the nineteenth century Robert Owen created several new towns—New Lanark, Scotland, and New Harmony, Indiana, are the most famous—that he hoped would serve as social models. Believing that a wholesome environment would mold a wholesome character, and the opposite for a slum environment, Owen intended his towns to create good citizens out of the workers. He hoped the movement would spread and reform the total society.

It failed. "It is said that, when Ralph Waldo Emerson asked Owen in his old age, 'Who is your disciple? How many men possessed of your views, who will remain after you, are going to put them into practice?' Owen candidly replied, 'Not one.'"[72]Although company towns still exist, technology has changed their faces, and a higher standard of living enables workers to own their own homes and manage communal facilities. "The underlying reasons for the decline of the company town are not hard to spot. To workers, the towns are based on a denial of two principles, individual autonomy and consumer sovereignty. To managers, they contradict new management orthodoxy, because they espouse the notion that employers and employees are bound together by a life-long bond."[73]

Perhaps in another century the same may happen in the relationship of citizens to their government. The principles of individual autonomy and consumer sovereignty may spread to encompass entire countries, not just company towns, and the power-diffusion process may be resumed. The inefficiencies, waste, and corruption of governments may cause citizens to break their bonds. The tide may be turned by pensioners who find government social security not enough for a comfortable retirement, patients who prefer to arrange their own health care and pay for it in amounts they decide, and compassionate people who refuse to paternalize the poor but would rather pay them cash or vouchers for their subsistence and allow them the dignity to decide for themselves how and where to live and, if pertinent, how to solve their drug problems. Only when lobbies represent these forces will vicarious power erode, and with it political power. In losing their power, the president, prime minister, parliament, and congress would become *minister* in the original sense of the word: "one who waits upon; a servant," in contrast to *magister,* "a master, chief, superior." This is not a prediction, just a possibility.

PART TWO
Institutions of the Moral Economy

The Argument So Far

In the millennium just past, the peoples of northwestern Europe and Japan wrested power over economic matters from their rulers and established mainly liberal societies, substituting the market instead of sovereign dispensation. Late in the nineteenth century these same peoples began handing back to the rulers powers similar to the ones they had taken away before. This time, however, the "rulers" are democracies, and the people themselves are sovereign. Nevertheless, they have adopted many of the traits of earlier sovereigns, in that—now using vicarious instead of military power—they direct the choices of their fellow citizens over matters that go beyond the legitimate objectives of security, care for the poor, and preservation of the environment into areas where privacy and choice are invaded.

These attempts at welfare states have run into four obstacles: first, citizens always demand more from their governments than they are willing to pay for; second, without the discipline of the market, governments produce services inefficiently, not only wasting resources but losing them through corruption; third, private groups with political power take more than their fair share and do not pay the full cost of their environmental abuse; and finally, individuals object to the paternalism that forces them into common molds. These four obstacles explain the failure of socialism, the twilight of the welfare state, and the current attempts to limit government and turn the world back toward classic liberalism.

Suppose classic liberalism triumphs in the third millennium. How will the world handle our major social problems? In part 1 we selected seven such problems—environmental abuse, population growth, inequality, poverty, welfare, social security, and health care—to show how they might be resolved through a restoration of classic liberalism. There are more problems, but these serve as examples. We invented a hypothetical world—the moral economy—in which all these problems are treated by classic liberal methods.

In part 2, we turn to the institutions implied by these solutions. How are resources managed in the moral economy? Who is accountable to whom? What about property rights and fiscal and monetary policy? What kind of law is needed? How is corruption contained? What educational system does this society engender? What kinds of religion, morality, and values? While these institutions seem to wander away from the economic, we soon see that they all impinge on how the economy is driven. While at first blush the moral economy

101

seems impossibly distant, in chapter 1 we showed that many of its features are already incipient.

Underlying forces, listed in chapter 2, determine the economic nature of a society, including real market prices and the distribution of income and wealth. This book argues that the collective intelligence of the people understands the nature of these forces more thoroughly than the collective intelligence of elites, such as feudal lords, military junta, clergy, or democratic government, and that attempts by elites to twist a society away from that nature, whether in a "good" or "bad" direction, through contrived prices or excessive regulation, yield inefficiencies and tension that cause a people to digress from consensual solutions. In past centuries, problems similar to those mentioned here have been solved only as almost universal consensus was achieved on how to change the underlying forces, and there is every reason to believe the same will be so in the future. Durable socioeconomic change occurs only as underlying forces change, which they do, but slowly.

The argument continues in part 2 with the proposition that whether the power-diffusion process will be resumed and whether classic liberal markets are chosen depend not on the traditional factors of production—land, labor, and capital—nor on independent action by strong leaders, such as president and legislature, nor on the passage of laws, nor on pressure from outside the society, such as international organizations or the advanced nations, but on our moral systems, or *the kind of people we are,* and the kinds of institutions we create, in ways to be explained.

Chapter 6
Accountability, Trust, and the Management of Resources

Would the moral economy achieve anything more than the efficiency that economists, from Smith (1776) to Marshall (1890), have attributed to classic liberalism? Yes. Over centuries, classic liberal societies have created greater *accountability* on the part of the individual, greater *trust* among individuals, and a clearer perception of the need for good *management,* including conservation of resources, than have interventionist societies. Each person has tended to take more responsibility for his or her actions, reaping the rewards or suffering the penalties, than in any other system. To examine these potential differences, let us first define three types of accountability:

Vertical accountability consists in each person responding to a superior in authority. In pure feudalism, serf accounted to lord, lord to king, king sometimes to emperor, and emperor to God. All these ranks had subdivisions, so the chain was usually longer. In less developed areas—both today and earlier—accountability is also largely vertical, though not necessarily so neat. The top authority may be an elite, including a military, that often is riven by internal disputes, making for an unstable society.

Mutual accountability occurs when there is either no social hierarchy or a mutual one. Citizens are accountable to the law, and the law is accountable to citizens. In theory, democracy illustrates mutual accountability, but the bundling of issues—vote for Candidate A's whole platform, not for ideas one by one—dilutes the accountability of the candidate for the many nondominant themes. By contrast, in the classic liberal market, where the choice for one product can be made independently of the choices for others, the provider of a service is accountable for each item separately.

Accountability to the market implies that a customer may buy products separately—they are not bundled—while a producer who fails in price or quality or in choosing the correct product loses business.

Each type of accountability may be *weak* or *strong.* If CEOs are awarded large salaries because the price of company stock has risen in the market, it may not be known whether they are responsible for that success —whether they "earned" the salaries—or whether it arose out of market forces beyond their control. Accountability is therefore weak. Accountability is weak wherever *moral hazard* is present, such as where a contractor or an employer relies on the behavior of others who have incentive and opportunity to cheat but where monitoring costs are high, for example charging the company for personal phone calls. (Do reporting and verifying personal phone calls cost more than the losses if they went unreported?) Measurements of accountability tend to be subjective, depending on examples rather than mathematical demonstrations.

Mutual accountability is a value to all democratic societies, whether interventionist or classic liberal. How does it come about, historically?

From Vertical to Mutual Accountability

Williamson[1] has written a masterpiece on the economics of accountability. He reports ways in which contracts may be violated, through *holdup* by agents who prove to be less than fully reliable after the principal is already committed, and moral hazard. Like moral hazard, holdup also implies weak accountability. Williamson asserts, correctly, that because accountability has a cost, it becomes built in to the system only if the cost of violating trust is greater. His analysis would apply to vertical accountability at any time—since rulers have spied on their servants since time immemorial—but to mutual accountability mainly in more developed areas, where the necessary constraints have been internalized by society and built into laws and customs. Moral behavior, as understood in a specific society, is one of the constraints upon persons. Instruments of accountability include external audits by CPA firms and internal audits by management, internal control systems that divide responsibilities so that dishonesty would be obvious to fellow workers, separation of administrative staff from ownership of assets, and financial and other reporting. It appears—though I know of no research to prove it—that these methods are far more used in the more developed than in the less developed world.

I hypothesize that the shift from vertical to mutual accountability occurred gradually, first in northwestern Europe and Japan because of the many interest groups that negotiated with each other on economic transactions, in which they held each other accountable for the fulfillment of contracts. The shift occurred on two fronts. First, over centuries the rulers became more accountable to their constituents. Second, traders and financiers became more accountable to each other for the proper quantity and quality of their goods, for payment of obligations, and for other promises. Thus mutual accountability comes about, historically, through trading. These judgments remain subjective, however, because accountability cannot be measured and we may not agree on whether a given instance qualifies as accountability.

Accountability of Rulers to Constituents

Ancient monarchs tended to use crude, draconian controls, with duplicate sources of information that could be cross-checked and torture or death for violations. "Kautilya's words to a wise king illustrate the method. '. . . having encouraged . . . a spy with honor and money rewards, the minister shall tell him . . . Thou shalt inform us of whatever wickedness thou findest in others.'"[2] Chinese emperors sent spies to report on their underlings, and spies to report on spies; they themselves were "subject to no higher law or constitutional checks,"[3] although they might be assassinated. These methods are accepted as the normal course of business in the less developed world. Although they are analogous to the Federal Bureau of Investigation maintaining files on citizens of the United States, they do not induce public outrage when uncovered.

Early stages of mutual accountability may be found in Athens and Rome, where governors used two systems to control expenditures of public funds. "One was personal, internal to the system, and based on voluntary compliance. . . [In the other] councils administered state finances through specialized finance officials appointed from the governing classes and responsible to the entire community . . . [In Athens they] served without payment, for the Greeks believed that salaries would corrupt public officials."[4] This mutuality, however, applied mainly to the upper classes. To the extent that audits were intended to demonstrate the honesty of public officials to their superior officers, accountability was vertical. To the extent that they demonstrated the honesty of public officials to the general public, it was mutual. Common citizens and slaves were at the lower end of vertical accountability only.

The move toward mutual accountability in England dates at least to the thirteenth century, when the barons—aping earlier methods of the vertical variety—began to hold the monarch accountable for the spending of their taxes. British rulers had employed systems of vertical accountability before the Norman Conquest,[5] and returns submitted by feudal lords to the Crown were audited at least as early as the twelfth century.[6] The Exchequer met annually from at least 1116 to audit government accounts. But the first major shift in the direction of mutual accountability probably occurred with Magna Carta (1215) and the ensuing struggles of the thirteenth century, in which English barons wrested power from the king. The Provisions of Oxford (1258) provided that officers of the Crown "were to be appointed for the term of one year, and each was to account for his office at the end of that term."[7] Although the provisions were annulled in 1261, they set the tone for accountability in the future. Audits of royal funds were well established by the end of the thirteenth century.[8] The king could tax only with the consent of Parliament and was required to account to Parliament for his use of tax receipts. Even so, full accountability by the Crown was still centuries away. James I (r. 1603-25) "often told his ministers to find ways of curbing his extravagance, only to circumvent the restrictions to which he had agreed."[9] Greater accountability was a requisite for the restoration of the monarchy after the Civil War and the Protectorate. The House of Commons insisted "on a committee to investigate the national finances . . . The Parliament of 1661 was fast developing a much more questioning stance towards the royal government."[10] By the end of the eighteenth century, the British budget was submitted to Parliament annually, and government borrowing was far more "public" than it was in France.[11]

Kings in Europe became accountable to the law just as they did to the legislature. "From medieval times on, European kings might make law but they also had to obey it, at least in principal and often in practice."[12] The historical events strengthening this accountability occurred over centuries.

Like the king of England, the princes of Germany were forced into accountability to the Estates (parliamentary bodies) over centuries—later than in England and earlier than in France—as constituents were well enough organized to withhold their taxes unless the prince complied with certain conditions, such as spending the receipts "wisely," according to the dictates of the Estates, and not engaging foolishly in war. Carsten is the definitive historian of these events from the fifteenth to the eighteenth centuries.[13]

In mutual accountability, France was the laggard of northwestern Europe. Vertical accountability to the monarch was established by the twelfth century. Kings sent bailiffs to the north and seneschals to the south "as their representatives in the provinces to check on the *prévôts*."[14] However, the royal family itself was notorious for its lack of accountability. In his *Political Testament,* written at various times and intended for the king only after his own death, in 1638, Richelieu wrote to Louis XIII: "While everyone knows there has never been a king who has advanced the prestige of the state as much as Your Majesty has, it also cannot be denied that no one has ever allowed the reputation of the household to sink so low. . . . everything is in confusion from the kitchen to your private quarters."[15] Colbert, minister of finance to Louis XIV, brought high standards of efficiency to the royal finances and "wished to stop members of town governments and provincial estates abusing their power to enrich themselves at the expense of their fellow citizens,"[16] but in 1680 he wrote to the king, "I beg Your Majesty to permit me only to say to him, that in war as in peace he has never consulted the amount of money available, in determining his expenditures."[17] Such extravagance of the monarchy was a factor in the Revolution of 1789 and in the Declaration of the Rights of Man.[18]

Evidence of mutual accountability is found in Japan as far back as the seventh century, when peasants had rights *(shiki)* to land on communal farms *(sho)*. How they happened to have them is something of a mystery, since everywhere else in the world serfs and slaves held no such rights. I have hypothesized[19] that these rights may have evolved because of a system of "alternative power," where "if a lower class could not obtain satisfaction from one [overlord] it might go to another."[20] Competition among overlords may have forced them to make concessions to peasants, in an example of the power-diffusion process.

Despite these beginnings, by the thirteenth century "local governors were not responsible to any persons, cared for nothing, but always hunted after their own interests."[21] Takekoshi believes the country was saved from this disorderly state by feudalism, "which was formed by local powerful families [*daimyo*] who rose in all districts, obeyed no orders from the Central Government, and possessed the lands and the people." From that time on, village governments forming on the *han* (fiefs) of the daimyo negotiated, rebelled, and cajoled the daimyo into granting them land and other rights, as well as the ability to govern themselves, in exchange for protection and taxes. An operating balance of power arose among the farmers, merchants, daimyo, shogun, and emperor, in which each recognized the rights of the other, thus bringing accountability to ever-lower orders.

Mutual Accountability in the Private Sector

In the private sector, the evolution of mutual accountability can be seen only through proxies, of which I select two: accounting and contract.

Accounting. In 1950, I was sent by the International Monetary Fund (IMF) to Caracas to prepare the Venezuelan balance of payments. The Venezuelan government had been unable to do so because the oil companies would not release their data on international transactions, and petroleum was so important that a balance of payments without it would make no sense. The government was either unwilling or unable at that time to demand the information from the companies.

I called separately on executive officers of the major petroleum companies and suggested that they release their accounting information to me, on my personal promise not to reveal it, company by company, to their competitors, the government or central bank, the IMF, or anyone else. Instead, I would prepare a consolidated statement for all the oil companies, which would be published. Would they themselves not be interested in seeing such a statement, I asked? Yes, they would. They trusted me because I was a CPA, a former senior accountant with Price Waterhouse, a worldwide accounting firm, and I carried the credibility of the profession—they had not known me personally. With the data of the companies, plus other information from the government and the central bank, I returned to Washington carrying the first balance of payments statement for Venezuela, which was published in the IMF *Balance of Payments Yearbook.* All parties benefited—the oil companies, the government and central bank, the IMF, researchers, the general public, and not the least, me.

The following year, Price Waterhouse—which audited the accounts of all the major companies—itself performed that task, and some time thereafter the government began requiring the petroleum companies to submit their information to the central bank. Only after they had discovered that confidences were not violated did they accede—how willingly I do not know.

The next year the IMF asked me to do the same for Saudi Arabia. The corporate accountant of the Arabian-American Oil Company (Aramco), then a private enterprise, spread the information I wanted out on the desk in my presence in New York but would neither turn it to face me nor release it, saying that doing so would violate the confidence of the king. Aramco was the only major company in the country; its accounting statements would reveal how much the king was earning, and, I surmised, the king did not want the world or his family to know of his extravagances. In later years, the IMF required balance of payments and other information as a condition of membership; petroleum companies were nationalized the world over, Venezuela and Saudi Arabia included; and data on the balance of payments were published.

In millions of instances such as these—dating back to ancient times in Babylon, Greece, Rome, and elsewhere—commercial transactors informed each other and held each other accountable for their use of assets. Nevertheless, accounting was poorly developed in Europe until the late Middle Ages. "The repeated, almost puerile, instructions which abound in the estate ordinances of the ninth century . . . show us how hard it was for the great men to make their subordinates apply the most elementary rules of book-keeping."[22] As trade increasingly required cooperation among investors and lenders, shipowners and agents, accounting became a means of assuring that each upheld his own side of the contract. Double-entry accounting, although available to the ancient Egyptians, was first used in Genoa at least in 1340, and in 1498 Pacioli wrote the first definitive text. By relating income and expenses to assets and liabilities, this accounting facilitated the monitoring of contracts.

Accounting became a routine part of the economic life of the Italian city-states in the fourteenth and fifteenth centuries. Business accounts became distinct from those of the household. "The most complete commercial and financial records were kept first in the cities of central and northern Italy and then, from the end of the fourteenth century, in Germany as well."[23] The Hanseatic League, in northern Europe from the thirteenth to the fifteenth centuries, and the Medici and Fugger banking families all used double-entry bookkeeping. Mutual accountability is therefore a product of economic transactions, which were more highly developed through extensive trading than through farming. It grew faster in mercantile and manufacturing areas than in agrarian and illiterate societies.

In the eighth century in Japan, a decree of the Emperor ordered the accounts of temple lands to be consolidated by cooperation of local officials and priestly agents and recorded in the public register. Officials of the *sho* (farming community) were required to report to the church on the financial condition of the sho, giving an inventory of all appurtenances and movable properties. By 766, settled managers reported on their activities to the church.[24] Such advanced accountability was far ahead of Europe, where farm accounting was nonexistent or primitive at that time. As the period of warring states ended in the sixteenth century, the daimyo of the various landed estates usually had representatives in Osaka to sell their rice, with credit, warehousing, forward purchases and delivery, all of which required specialized accounting records.[25]

"From the beginning of the Tokugawa period [1603] merchants kept reasonably complete business records. Records of purchases and sales, order and delivery books, cash books, receipt books, stock books, records of wages and salaries and operating expenses were regularly kept by larger firms."[26] Official data for the Tokugawa shogunate extend back to 1722, apparently initiated to avoid corruption among the contractors who undertook services for the shogun. Hatamoto, the direct retainers of the Tokugawa family,[27] were trained in accounting.[28] By the Meiji restoration (1868), modern accounting was known throughout commercial Japan.

We have not reached the ultimate in accountability through accounting, however, and in the more developed areas we may even face reverses. Today, CPA firms, in addition to auditing, have become consultants for their clients, an event that, according to critics, causes a conflict of interest. I agree. After bank failures, CPA firms have been faulted for improper audits and have been held accountable in court.[29] One of the largest firms, Ernst and Ernst, paid a judgment of $400 million in 1992.[30] In 1992 also, management guru Peter Drucker wrote that "few executives yet know how to ask: What information do I need to do my job? When do I need it? And from whom should I be getting it?" [31] In 1996, Abelson wrote of how senior executives manipulate a company's reports in order to mislead investors, with—he maintains—"a remarkable tolerance for such shenanigans"[32] on the part of the investors. who appear to be buoyed by reports of profits, whether they are true or not.

Finally, standard procedures do not account for the "damage caused by mining, fishing, and forestry to the air, water, and soil, as well as the environmental costs."[33] "Green accounting," which would register these costs, was recommended by the United Nations Conference on Environment and Development at Rio de Janeiro in 1992. In the following year President Clinton called upon the U.S. Department of Commerce to produce "green GDP measures."[34] The Central Bank of Chile has undertaken a study of green accounts, intending to include them in the national accounts of the country. However, we cannot expect that the costs of environmental damage will be entered into the accounts of businesses until they are required to pay them in full, in ways suggested in chapter 4.

Contract. Although contracts have been known since the dawn of history, Japan and northwestern Europe led the way in two types. First, *contract feudalism* constituted an agreement between "superiors" (*potentes* in Europe) and "inferiors" (*humiliores*) in which the former granted the latter land and military protection in exchange for services. The "inferiors" received certain contractual rights, of which usufruct of land was the signal one, but also including others such as hunting and fishing on the lord's domain and the use of the lord's mills. These rights were enforceable in the manorial courts in Europe or the *han* (feudal fief) courts in Japan. They were not always honored, but they were taken more seriously than in the feudalisms of the rest of the world. Defining feudalism as only the contractual type, Coulborn finds only two proven cases of feudalism in the world: western Europe and Japan.[35]

Second, and probably of greater consequence, were contracts freely negotiated by independent parties, enforceable at law by the state, which facilitated trade. Rules of contract—validity, acceptance, protection of all interests, damages, cancellation, fulfillment, and settlement of disputes—were all worked out by guilds, producers, merchants, and others, with accounting records as testimony. These contracts were advanced in the High and late Middle Ages, first by towns and guilds and second by overseas trading ventures. "Many cities and towns were founded by a solemn collective oath, or series of oaths, made by the entire citizenry to adhere to a charter that had been publicly read aloud to them."[36] Guilds gave rise to notaries, in the thirteenth century or earlier, who supplied sample forms of agreements that could be adapted according to circumstance.[37] Written contracts between producers, shippers, and agents on overseas ventures were developed by the Italian city-states. The concept of contract, which was held in common by both feudal estate and the world of commerce, therefore helped smooth the transition from one to the other.[38]

Trust

We who live at the turn of the twenty-first century can hardly grasp the degree of mistrust in which the world was submerged ten centuries ago. There were exceptions. Lycurgus of Athens in the fourth century BCE was deemed "so honest that Athenian citizens deposited their private funds with him for safekeeping."[39] Such characters, however, are noteworthy only by contrast. By the same token, those who lived in the year 1000 CE, anywhere in the world, would be astounded at the degree of trust that accounting, contract, and other trading methods have brought about in Japan and the West today.

The early medieval world swam in a sea of distrust. Individuals in one city feared that another might silt their rivers, destroy their roads, or damage their commerce in other ways. Neighbor feared neighbor. Rulers were on guard against usurpers. Kublai Khan preferred foreigners as his civil servants because they were less likely to overthrow him. The Ottomans recruited Christian slaves (janissaries) for the same purpose. Endemic warfare and piracy were such hindrances to trade that it is surprising that any took place at all—but it did.

Trade Engenders Trust

Northwestern Europe was the first world area in which trade began to transcend the power of rulers, and it was private trading—less than the agreements among rulers—that brought about the high degree of trust prevalent today. In the cattle market at Wedel, near Hamburg, in the Middle Ages, "a bargain was concluded when buyer and seller had noted its outcome on their slates. . . . Good faith was the rule in the transactions themselves. The bargain would be sealed with a drink in one of the thirty inns fringing the market place. . . . The rich lowland farmers . . . left their purses in the inn, where the landlord looked after them in a wooden chest in his bedroom. Nobody doubted that its contents would be intact."[40] "In the long history of human morality there is no landmark more significant than the appearance of the man who can be trusted to keep his promises. . . . [Although] conscience and promise-keeping emerged in human history . . . long before capitalism. . . . it was not until the eighteenth century, in Western Europe, England, and North America, that societies first appeared whose economic systems depended on the expectation that most people, most of the time, were sufficiently conscience-ridden (and certain of retribution) that they could be trusted to keep their promises."[41] Haskell, the author of this quotation, may not have taken into account the slow buildup of this degree of trust, but he is correct in the geography and the approximate century. Of course, there are those who will cheat if they can, but the social structure of more developed areas is not designed around cheating and confiscation as major economic forces, as it is in many less developed areas.

We are led to another hypothesis: *In northwestern Europe and its descendants, and in Japan, trade has over centuries been replacing family, tribe, religion, and nation as the dominant basis for trust. This trust is engendered only to the extent that society becomes increasingly classic liberal.*

People trust others who are like themselves. But in what way? In earlier societies, tribe, clan, and family were the major bastions of trust. Bloch writes of the general assumption, c. 1200, that "there was no real friendship save between persons united by blood."[42] Later, religion amplified the basis. Christians trusted Christians—still later, Protestants trusted Protestants and Catholics Catholics—while Jews trusted Jews and Muslims Muslims, and so on. During the wars of religion of the sixteenth century—in France at least—it was assumed that national unity and stability depended on everyone holding the same religious faith. Many assume the same today in Northern Ireland, the Middle East, and Bosnia. Trust may also be based on race: people who are "black like me" or "white like me" may be more trusted than others, even though they are total strangers. Hutus trust Hutus but not Tutsis and vice versa.

As economic enterprise expanded from Europe to the New World and to east Asia, trade came to replace religion and family as foci of trust. People began to trust others who were "like themselves," not necessarily in religion but in the ways they made contracts, paid their bills, and gave receipts. In the twentieth century, the deep suspicions of the cold war lay in the belief that those whose economies were organized differently from one's own were not to be trusted militarily. Logically, there was no foundation for such a belief except that the other side believed it too and might act on its belief. Attempts to bring Africa, Latin America, and Asia into the communist or the free-enterprise camp were founded on this notion. Why otherwise, from the time of Peter the Great (c. 1700), to the opening of Japan, to the present—with the end of the cold war—have Western nations tried so intensely to spread our own modes of production to the rest of the world? Possible reasons are (1) altruism, that everyone should lead the good life that "we" do; (2) trade; and (3) trust: the West and Japan will not be militarily secure until stable, "capitalist" societies—like ours—exist everywhere. While the second reason carries some weight, the third probably is decisive.

Our hypothesis therefore has a corollary: *Trade, carried out over long periods, becomes a new basis of trust, making obsolete the previous bases such as race and religion. The classic liberal society, in which virtually all persons trade, has spread trust more than any other kind of society and will continue to do so if it is allowed to flourish.* Therefore, trade sanctions against China, Cuba, Iran, Libya, or other countries today are counterproductive, for they delay the establishment of trust.

Trade through Kings or Government

In earlier times, and in less developed areas today, where it has been necessary to trade through the king or government, such trust has not evolved. In many African states before colonialism, any trader was required to deliver his product to the king or tribal chief, who would transmit it to another king or tribal chief, receive the payment, take his cut, and give the rest to the producer. Although private trading existed, and local goods were freely sold in local markets, "for the most part, the state was governor, producer, trader, executive officer, and judge, with no separation of powers."[43] When an economic transactor has only one person or one bureaucracy to deal with, and is under the power of that person or bureaucracy, he or she does not develop much trust for other transactors, and the institutions of trust do not evolve. Even today in more developed areas, interventionists believe businesspeople are motivated mainly by "greed"; businesspeople believe interventionists are "irresponsible" and the scant communication between the two fails to counteract these stereotypes and this deficit in trust.

Today, the governments of China and the United States deeply mistrust each other. Chinese who have been interviewed overwhelmingly express their belief that intellectual property violations, human rights abuses, and the defense of Taiwan are mere pretexts for the real intention of the government of the United States, which is to marginalize China as a trading principal.[44] To most Americans, including myself, this idea is absurd. So, if Americans and Chinese were free to trade with each other under few or no government restrictions, would they not, over time, work out agreements on human rights and intellectual property protection more quickly and thoroughly than their governments are able to do through threats and sanctions? Would not the political status of Taiwan become irrelevant, just as the boundary between Germany and France is becoming irrelevant only one-half century after an intense and bitter war? Would not Chinese and Americans come to trust each other on the basis of mutual trading practices? The history of Europe would tell us Yes.

Our hypothesis and its corollary are supported by two other findings. First, the accountability of rulers to their citizens, or citizens to each other, is not nearly so well advanced in less developed as in more developed areas. A very large proportion of African countries is ruled by usurpers, dictators for life, or one-party presidents, who insist that economic enterprise be guided by the state, so that entrepreneurs have little ability to negotiate with their counterparts in other countries and often not in the same country either. Some of these rulers are accountable to no one. Both accounting principles and contract law are weak, and the participation of citizens in drawing them up is negligible or nil. Therefore, trust as the foundation of economic activity does not flourish.

The other finding is that with the rise of the welfare state in northwestern Europe, North America, Australia, and New Zealand, citizens have become less responsible for their own economic affairs and more dependent on their governments. Increasingly, they consider themselves victims instead of masters of their fate.[45] Often they are not allowed to choose their health insurance or unemployment policies, their pensions, or the education of their children but must take whatever the state offers them. To that extent, they do not negotiate among themselves, so trust and the institutions of trust erode. Citizens sue tobacco companies and breast-implant companies instead of shouldering the personal responsibilities and risks of having smoked or having decided on breast implants of their own free will. Proposed government health plans would require nonsmokers and non–drug addicts to help assume the bills of smokers and drug addicts. In this way government contributes to the irresponsible behavior of individuals by shielding them from some of the adverse consequences.

Fukuyama posits that only Japan, northern Europe, Germany, North America, Australia, and New Zealand have built large-scale enterprises in the private sector because only they have extended trust beyond the family.[46] By contrast, in France, southern and eastern Europe, China, and less developed areas, only government could initiate larger-than-family enterprises. Their economic systems have depended on laws and punishment, which are less efficient than market cooperation. Hence economic development is slow. Fukuyama's thesis complements my own, in that the power-diffusion process, and the institutions of economic development formed through it are the mechanisms for the greater trust that Fukuyama finds.

Management of Resources

Mutual accountability for the use of resources implies a standard of management. As eastern Europe and the Third World liberalize their economies, management skills come primarily from foreign training of local staffs or through multinational corporations investing in the countries concerned. Will these new skills permeate the economy, including small-scale producers in the backwoods and farms of all sizes? Or will they be confined to the subsidiaries of multinationals and the large local companies that could afford foreign training? If the latter, will the newly liberalizing economies become divided into a trained elite and a large mass of small-scale enterprises unable to compete in the modern world? This section argues that a high level of management skills is more likely to permeate the economy in a classic liberal than in an interventionist society.

Management skills include the ability to understand the market and select the right product; to design the right size factory or farm or retail store, with a cost-minimizing flow of resources through it; to organize the factors of production and finance so as to minimize costs; to present, advertise, and display the product so that exposure to potential customers will be maximized and the product understood; and to organize delivery in the manner most satisfactory to customers. Managers must read and interpret financial statements, quickly identifying real problems out of sheets of figures. They must get along with labor, know how to bargain, when to hold the line, when to compromise, and when to yield. They must know the world in which they work, how others will react to their moves, and how to assess the market. They must troubleshoot, quickly picking up problems of all kinds and correcting them.

Management must be orderly, so that decision-making levels are clearly defined, rules implemented, flows of information unimpeded horizontally and vertically, and authority roughly in line with responsibility. But it must not be so rigid that it does not mold itself to a changing environment nor so formal that it impedes spontaneity. Achieving this golden mean is a sign of a good manager. Managers must also keep track of the law, to make sure they comply with it, and must learn how to bargain with legislators to shape and interpret the law. In a large enterprise, where different persons perform these functions, top management must understand them all and coordinate them, because ultimate accountability to owners, stockholders, and creditors lies with them. These are no mean skills, often inadequately appreciated in an environment that thinks, wrongly, that physical and financial resources are sufficient for economic development.

Because quality of management is difficult or impossible to measure, economists are accustomed to considering it as part of a residual. In regression models of output on factors of production (land, labor, and capital), economists enter a residual (or error) factor, which is assumed to be improvements in technology or management. In studying Latin American countries, Bruton confirmed his hypothesis that increases in productivity resulted from this residual factor more than from inputs (labor and capital).[47]

Can management skills be imparted by governments or international agencies? For the most part, No. Although instances of good management are found in governments and international lending agencies, mostly these agencies seek political position rather than economic gain. They often appoint favorites, not selected for their management aptitudes, who are accountable only to their patrons and not to the market. They fund projects for reasons of political power rather than sound economic rationale. The failure of socialism worldwide, especially in the Soviet Union, is testimony to this statement. The liberalization currently undertaken in eastern Europe and the Third World often disposes of government assets to political supporters at bargain prices, an event that concentrates the national wealth in a few people while also squandering it. Poor managers cannot impart good management skills.

In 1967, I was contracted by the Inter-American Development Bank to analyze its loan-making process. Because the Bank was a political arm of its Latin American "customers," it made at least one loan in every country each year, whether a promising project was available or not. The result was that many loans were either nonperforming or not the best use of money lent. The president of the Bank suppressed my report, but one of his political adversaries leaked a copy to the *Washington Post,* which featured it in a two-page centerfold (12/14/69). It was then taken up by Jack Anderson, a muckraking columnist, who excoriated the Bank president (2/3/70) for performing the political duty expected of him and later by *Barron's Financial Weekly* in a front-page "exposé" (10/26/70). I was called before a senatorial committee considering U.S. financial contributions to international organizations, where I suggested that if analyses of lending procedures jeopardized funding, no agency would examine its own projects critically. The Bank received its funds, but the implied adverse appraisal of its management remained valid.

History of Management

To understand how management skills become spread, we must look at history, in which three simple—perhaps obvious—lessons assume great moment. The first is that when surrounded by political turbulence and disorder, no productive unit shows great management skills, and as these conditions continue, earlier skills are forgotten. From the fifth to the tenth century Italy experienced "conditions of unparalleled waste and depopulation, [in which] production declined to a miserable level and wealth was confined to few hands."[48] This condition applies today in Rwanda, Burundi, Angola, Nigeria, Sri Lanka, Chechnya, and other places. The second is that efficiency in management responds to objectives. If the object is political power rather than economic gain, management may be inefficient in economic terms but efficient politically. This lesson applies to most feudal estates of the Middle Ages in Europe and Japan and in much of the Third World today. "Land [in seventeenth-century Spain] was a social rather than an economic investment. Nobles were not normally improving farmers and it would need exceptionally favourable conditions to persuade them to invest in extensions of farmland."[49] One writer suggests that in seventeenth-century India, the British wanted land to increase output, while the Indians wanted it to enhance their power over people.[50] The third is that inappropriate macroeconomic policies give wrong signals to business and farm managers, so that they produce the wrong product, in the wrong way, at the wrong prices, and so forth, all being results equivalent to those of poor management on the private level. In short, poor public management leads to poor private management.

Improved management abilities grew in Italian, British, and Japanese firms when the owners became aware that they could no longer achieve top political power themselves but that by serving those in power they could gain the next best: economic advantage. As the pope and Holy Roman Emperor fought for jurisdiction over Italian city-states in the twelfth century, Italian financiers learned how to increase their incomes supplying loans demanded by the pope. "The group of Italian firms used as the papal cameral merchants acquired the means to render to the papacy every financial service that might be demanded of them."[51] Similar firms learned to serve their masters in the city-states through "steady progress in business management. . . . [Surviving letters of these merchants] are models of business-like procedure, matter-of-fact and to the point, without any of the verbiage so characteristic of the notarial contracts."[52] Japanese merchants learned to gain economic advantage by lending to the daimyo and shogun in the seventeenth and eighteenth centuries.[53]

Stockholders and Stakeholders

Traditionally, management has been accountable to stockholders. Increasingly, it is proposed that accountability should instead be to stakeholders—those who hold stakes in the enterprise—who would include not only stockholders but also employees and customers.[54] There is nothing inconsistent with being accountable to customers for quality product, to workers for adequate salaries and good working conditions, and to stockholders for profits, all at the same time. Ridley finds that this cooperation/conflict syndrome extends into many spheres of human cooperation, for example, the fetus both competes and cooperates with the mother in sharing nutrition.[55] Tension occurs in the most cooperative of relationships. Higher salaries and better working conditions may increase both profits and quality of product, but beyond a certain point they may diminish one or the other. How to strike a balance?

As a firm grows beyond the size of sole proprietorship or small partnership, good management requires a clear distinction between managers and workers. While all stakeholders desire the success of the firm, individual stakes are in tension. In tracing this tension back to the fourteenth century, Berman puts it into the context of a developing legal morality that accepted reciprocity of rights of all parties to a transaction.[56] Value is given for equal value in any transaction. But these rights can be honored only if clear boundaries are established among parties, such as stockholders, employees, customers, clients, and the like. "It is a function of management *as management* to seek efficiency in the form of greater productivity and lower operating costs. It is a function of labor *as labor* to seek adequate compensation, conditions of health and safety, and workers' welfare in general"[57] (italics in original).

In the nineteenth century, John Stuart Mill advocated worker ownership of enterprise as a desirable way to live. While this is possible in small enterprises such as Moosewood Restaurant in Ithaca, New York, nevertheless hazards abound. Must an employee risk combining savings and job in the same business, such that if it fails everything is lost? Does an employee who changes jobs lose his or her investment in the earlier company? Will employees act like managers, in conserving the firm's resources, or like workers, in wanting them to be paid out? In the former Yugoslavia, workers milked the very enterprises they presumably owned. According to a 1986 report:

> Inefficiency and apathy have reached astonishing proportions. According to Western estimates, more than a quarter million workers in the public sector are unnecessary. On any given day, 700,000 workers are on "sick leave" and 600,000 more "on vacation." Those who show up work an average of 3.5 hours a day; despite new machinery, it takes, for example, 1,500 man-hours to build a railway car that in 1970 took 1,000.[58]

In the United States, on the other hand, where employees own majority shares in approximately two thousand corporations, management operates mostly just the way it does in other corporations: workers have votes as shareholders but do not *as workers* direct company policy. For example, worker-owned corporations downsized and laid off employees in the restructuring of the 1990s just as did other firms. "It is managers at employee-owned companies who make the decisions, acting independently of their worker owners, just as managers do elsewhere."[59] The Yugoslavia citation reflects not so much worker ownership per se as it does poor management in a socialist state dominated by worker interests.

Compared to the American system, European management "tends to blur distinctions of ownership through a complex system of cross-holdings and encourages long-term relations between the suppliers and managers of capital. It also gives more power to 'stakeholders,' especially workers, than in America."[60] Workers often sit on supervisory boards, help choose managers, or may participate in some management decisions. Capital is raised largely from banks whose officers belong to an "old boys' club," having been to the same schools as corporate managers, whereas in the United States capital comes primarily from arm's-length transactions in financial markets. The productivity of capital in Europe is significantly lower than in the United States, and global competition is driving many large European corporations to shift over to American principles. In Japan also, firms are moving away from the old boys' club of the *keiretsu* (groups of enterprises) and into a more liberal market for finance, supplies, and labor. The old ways in Europe and Japan involved mutual accountability in a small circle, the "club" of friends. In the new moves, with tendency toward American principles, wider mutual accountability, *to the market,* is strengthened.

Management in the Moral Economy

The historical experience of more developed areas shows that a wide spread of efficient management principles, and knowledge of management skills and ability to apply them, develops more extensively in a classic liberal than in an interventionist society. In any society, the same groups may simultaneously have both interests in common and interests in tension, such as workers and managers united for the survival of the firm but at odds over how the proceeds shall be divided. Only in the classic liberal society, however, are the common interests clearly distinguished from those in tension, and only in such a society can commonality and tension coexist peacefully. This is so especially in worker-owned companies. The differing experiences of these companies in the United States and Yugoslavia stem from the historic difference between classic liberal and interventionist philosophy, not from supposed differences between worker-owned and other companies. Mutual accountability is far stronger in the United States than it was in the former Yugoslavia.

The Wildest Hypothesis

We come to the wildest hypothesis in this book: that *the world passes through three stages: power, material greed, and trust.* Since all three exist in all societies, the shift is relative: not which is present but which dominates. Until approximately the twelfth century, all societies were dominated by the need for power over territory, either to aggrandize themselves or to protect themselves from enemies. With the power-diffusion process from the Middle Ages until the nineteenth century, material greed gradually supplanted power as a chief motivating force in northwestern Europe and Japan. Major dilemmas today stem from failure of those in the material-greed phase to understand those still in the power phase, and vice versa. To the West, it is incomprehensible that the Chinese want to hold Tibet, which has little economic advantage for them or (a bit less so) that the Israelis want to settle Palestine out of religious fervor and fear. The potential gains from economic cooperation are eclipsed among power- or fear-motivated peoples.

In the centuries-long perspective of social history, the third phase is barely beginning: we learn *so slowly* that greed is better satisfied by covenants of trust than by dominating others with "trade follows the flag." Yet we do have glimpses that as our basic human needs are satisfied, we become less greedy and pay more attention to protecting the environment and sharing our resources. We begin to question whether *ordering* others to behave well—as through affirmative action and minimum wages— changes their hearts and minds. Or is "proper" behavior more durable if it comes about through power diffusion, which teaches us that "improper" behavior does not work well? The moral economy will evolve—if it does—only in the third phase, when and if we learn to trust from experience that power from below works better than power from above.

Chapter 7
Property, Inflation, and Money

Property

Who would own property in the moral economy? How is it—or how should it be—divided among rich, poor, and other classes of people? Should it be public, as in socialist states, or private, as in a liberal-market society?

Little evidence is found that intellectuals or writers were much concerned about the ethics of property distribution before the sixteenth century, when Thomas More's *Utopia* argued the virtues of communitarian sharing. In the seventeenth century a Parliamentary Committee on Free Trade in England "perceived that the uncontrolled accumulation of property in unequal proportions could be damaging to the Commonwealth."[1] In 1656, James Harrington wrote *The Commonwealth of Oceana* about an ideal state in which no one would be allowed to hold more than £2,000 of assets, and land should be divided among children at the owner's death instead of being bequeathed by law to the oldest son. But the ethos favored inheritance by primogeniture to keep estates intact, a theme in Jane Austen's novels, and membership in Parliament was limited to property holders until the nineteenth century.

In classic liberal societies of today, unlimited accumulation remains legally possible, but three forces mitigate it. One is altruism, which reflects the kind of people we are; another is the inheritance tax; and the third is embodied in the phrase "rags to riches to rags in three generations." Landes has shown that many fortunes accumulated in England were dissipated by grandchildren.[2] Jean-Jacques Rousseau (1712-78) believed that property "should be distributed as equally as possible, . . . but once constituted on that basis, respect for property rights was essential."[3] (How, then, would he have kept it equal?)

Land Tenure

In early, agrarian societies, land was the principal property. By what right do we "own" land, when land is originally given to us free? By what right do we own the fox that runs across the land, when the fox is a creature of God or Nature as much as we? By what right does a soprano own her beautiful voice, when only in part did she train it herself—another part was bestowed upon her at birth? We bear a relationship to what we call "property"—the physical resources, natural or created, that exist around us or are a part of us. What are called "property rights" are the agreements among members of a society on how we will interact with each other and with all items of value external to ourselves, and how accountable we are —and to whom—for their use and preservation.

Inscribed above the entrance to the Secretariat of Education in Mexico City are these words:[4] "Land is for everyone, like air, water, light, and the heat of the sun." Socialists and communists have argued that the land belongs to everyone. Yet someone must plant the crop on a given piece, someone must reap and harvest, and when the food is in, the whole world does not sit at a table and eat it. Some people do these things, and others may not. Land ownership is nothing more than a bundle of rights, agreed upon by people, which for any given piece of land may be held by a single person or divided among many: the right to live on it, to pass over it, not to have it used in a threatening or disagreeable manner, and to invite others onto it or to keep them off. The only land that can be owned by "everyone" is land that is used by no one.

Two to three thousand years ago, when population was small relative to land, the first person to occupy a piece of land claimed the rights upon it, though they were frequently taken away by violence. In the ensuing two to three millennia, people have by agreement and by force determined the rights and obligations pertaining to any piece of land. In communal-land societies, usually a tribal chief or council of elders allocates land rights among the people. In the socialist or communist state, a small group of rulers would arrogate these rights and the product to itself, although in the name of "the people." They would appoint "collective leaders" who would see that tenants carried out the wishes of the rulers.

Theory of Property Rights

Using the prisoner's dilemma game as a basis, Buchanan has outlined a theory of how property rights began.[5] As population grows and land with certain characteristics, such as good hunting, becomes scarce, two or more tribes may fight over it. Because fighting is costly, in human suffering and resources wasted, they agree to divide the property in such a way that each is better off than fighting. Either party would gain an advantage if it violated the agreement and the other did not, but when each discovers that the other replies in kind, they both voluntarily comply. Property rights have been born. However, Buchanan's theory is valid only if power is somewhat evenly divided. It exemplifies how the power-diffusion process leads to efficient institutions. But when one group holds inordinate power, such as in the Roman Empire, property rights are confined to the elites, as in the Roman Empire.

Demsetz has developed a theory of property rights as a way to "internalize externalities."[6] Externalities are costs not paid, or benefits not received, by the property owner; internalization means the owner comes to pay the costs and receive the benefits. He illustrates this theory with reference to Leacock's work on the Montagne Indians of the Labradoran Peninsula.[7] Leacock found that property rights had been established, contrary to the traditions of most

Indians elsewhere, because the value of fur had increased in the international market. Property rights enabled Indians to invest in increasing the stock of game and to avoid overhunting. The situation is similar to that of the sour cherry tree in my back yard. Long having given up the tedious task of baking cherry pies, my wife and I have left that tree to the birds. However, the birds always eat unripe cherries, and by the time they would have become ripe the cherries are all gone. Lacking property rights, each bird has no incentive to conserve. Its choice is between an unripe cherry and no cherry at all.

Early Land Rights

In all societies, early land rights were vested in the tribe or the community, but ultimately levels of ownership emerged. In the Vedic culture of India (c. 2000-400 BCE), land might be owned on three levels: one, that of the overlord, usually *brahmanas* (priests), who collected taxes; two, that of the village, whose elders allocated the lots and collected taxes to pass on to the overlord; and three, that of the individual, who farmed the lot and paid taxes. By the Mauryan period (325-150 BCE), it was well established that "the land belonged to the one who had cleared it, just as the deer belongs to the one who shot it."[8] In China, land appears to have been free up until the Chou dynasty, c.1028 BCE, after which a rigid feudal system was formed. In a typical village, land was divided into plots in a 3x3 matrix, with eight plotholders who jointly farmed the center plot for the benefit of the overlord.[9]

Probably the Romans were the first major civilization to allocate land to families, though not to individual members, without any overlord other than the state as sovereign. Landownership, the upper class believed, was the tie that held society together. "The idea that what belongs to a person . . . cannot be snatched from him without undermining the social bond itself was already contained in Cicero's *On Duties* (*De Officiis* III, v. 21)."[10] This in a slaveholding society! Property "underpinned the whole complex of commercial transactions in [Roman Egypt], buying and selling, speculation and investment, credit, loan and mortgage—all except the smallest daily transactions were founded ultimately on the security of property."[11]

Feudalism

Cicero's writings, which were widely read in the Middle Ages, helped form the basis of feudal land law in Europe. Under contract feudalism, each tenant—serf, villein, freeman—had well-defined rights to land that differed according to the person's status.[12] Japan was the only other world area in which lower-level tenants had legal rights at that time. These rights, called *shiki,* might be bought and sold. Shiki can be traced to the seventh century, when lands originally belonged only to the village, but "with the purification by drinking the sacred saké . . . and the sowing of the seed, there arose for the first time the idea of [private] rights, and some punishment was customarily imposed upon those who interfered with others' cultivation."[13] Everywhere else in the medieval world—outside northwestern Europe and Japan—feudalism, where it existed, was by conquest, and the conquerors had the right to endow the conquered with land in exchange for taxes or services and to dispossess them at will. As feudalism declined in the late Middle Ages in western Europe and in the nineteenth century in eastern Europe and Japan—lords found it advantageous to commute labor services into rents—these rights were converted into fee simple ownership, and private property in land emerged. By the time of the French Revolution, private property rights were highly valued by all classes—by the aristocracy to defend their positions as manorial lords, and by the peasantry to liberate themselves from remaining feudal obligations. The final paragraph of the Declaration of the Rights of Man and Citizen (1789) reads: "Property being an inviolable and sacred right, no one may be deprived of it except for an obvious requirement of public necessity, certified by law, and then on condition of a just compensation in advance."[14] In earlier writings, I have argued that property rights and contracts were essential to the leadership of Japan and northwestern Europe in world economic development.[15] Just as the carpenter builds best if he owns his tools, so also the farmer grows best if she owns her farm.

Other Assets

From land, the concept of property spread in northwestern Europe to other assets, mainly through private contracts and scholarly writings and only secondarily through decisions of the courts and legislative assemblies. In the twelfth and thirteenth centuries, civil law glossators considered *dominium* to be a right *(ius)*, from which they came to the concept of absolute individual ownership *(ius in re)*. Thomas Aquinas "defended individual possession as 'necessary for human life' because it ensured the orderly and peaceful conduct of affairs and made men careful and industrious *(Summa Theologiae)*."[16] Entrepreneurship and innovations are held back unless the innovators have rights over the property involved. For example, the feudal system had to be displaced by individual property rights "before green fallowing and crop rotations became generally accepted."[17] The number of property rights to be protected increased in thirteenth-century England; "property interests not clearly related to feudalism were [also] given protection. Leasehold and other so-called 'chattel interests' in land eventually secured as much protection from the common law as freehold, a property interest of the highest dignity and quite suitable for a feudal class."[18] Later in the same century English courts began to protect all property rights recognized by the royal courts.[19]

In northwestern Europe and Japan, guilds were at the forefront of the movement to define and protect property rights. Lending gave the creditor a lien on the property of the debtor. Legal systems describing agency, laws of delivery (when property changes hands) and debts (the circumstances under which they are paid, and how payment is proved) evolved in northwestern Europe and Japan mainly by private agreements, which were honored over and again, became precedents, and finally laws. In a masterful ten-volume series, Wigmore describes this evolution in Japan during the Tokugawa era (1603-1886): "what constitutes acceptance; how the interests of all parties are protected; when a contract is valid; how its fulfillment is determined; how disputes are settled; damages, discounts, cancellation, and so forth."[20] All this applied to families, because during the Tokugawa period all property belonged to the family, not the individual.[21] The same was happening in China in the nineteenth century,[22] but there the private agreements did not have the same force of law as in northwestern Europe and Japan because the imperial government did not possess a judicial system able to enforce them. Even today, property rights are less respected in less developed areas than they are in the industrial world; foreigners investing there must do their homework, or they are in for surprises. In 1996 in Pavones, Costa Rica, a U.S. citizen bought land legally to start a ranch, but he has been unable to develop it because his property rights have become second to those of armed squatters.[23]

In summary: property rights have arisen in classic liberal societies in the belief that individual autonomy is most advanced if property becomes an arm of the person, who possesses the right to develop it as he or she will, while conforming to community norms such as in zoning and protecting the rights of others. The same, classic liberal thesis that holds that maximum human welfare is achieved through freedom of the individual has a corollary: that property rights are best used when widely distributed among those free individuals.

How widely? Should a classic liberal society prescribe a maximum amount of property that may be held by an individual? My answer is No. It is more important that all individuals have adequate *incomes* than that they have property. In chapter 5 I suggested a welfare system to provide incomes for the poor; chapter 8 will propose income redistribution through negative income taxes; and chapter 12 will summarize the breadth of possible redistributions in the moral economy. While some rich people have enormous amounts of property, nevertheless they are so few in number that if their property were entirely confiscated and divided among the world's poor, of whom there are many, the gains for each of the latter would be inconsequential. Therefore, let us concern ourselves with comforting the afflicted and not—as some have suggested—

afflicting the comfortable, for in that we would be wasting efforts in political battles whose victories, if any, would be hollow.

Takings

Shall the Congress of the United States—or the government of any country—have the right to limit the use of private property for the protection of the environment? The "Takings Clause" of the U.S. Constitution (Amendment 5)—"nor shall private property be taken for public use, without just compensation"—is invoked by those who believe full compensation should be made if the productive use of property is limited to promote the common good. Here we have a dilemma, in that property rights may be construed as "taken" when their value is diminished by any public action. For example, an interstate highway bypassing a town diminishes the value of motels within that town. But owners of these motels took business risks when they bought them, which included the probability that at some time they would become obsolete. The liberal market thrives on "creative destruction." No public compensation is required.

One example is being debated as this book is prepared for press. New technology has brought cheaper ways of producing electricity by generating it in bulk and transmitting it over high-voltage lines, then distributing it in lower-voltage lines to local customers. When fully effected, these ways will make obsolete many investments by local utilities that earlier held monopolies over their markets. They will also make nuclear power uneconomic. Investors in the old methods are now demanding compensation for "stranded costs."[24] By the principle of creative destruction, this compensation should not be allowed, any more than it is made to thousands of other producers whose methods become obsolete. Power companies claiming compensation argue that sometimes they were pressured or required by regulations to build plants now obsolete. They have a point, but it only reveals the instability of government regulation.[25]

A general rule for compensation is the following. If a property owner has complied with all known regulations at the time of purchase, and if subsequently a law is passed, or new finding made that could not have been predicted, as in the case of asbestos walls, that precludes development of that property "in the public interest," the entire public, not just the owner, should pay for the consequences of the public decision.

In the United States, this principle was tested in *Lucas vs. South Carolina Coastal Commission* in 1992. Lucas had bought two beachfront lots for just under $1 million, for which building permits, previously issued, were withdrawn to protect the beaches, thus rendering the land commercially worthless.[26] The Supreme Court decided that Lucas should be compensated. However, not all decisions have favored the property owner, and myriad cases prohibiting the development of wetlands and requiring owners to clean up toxic waste that was not known about when the property was purchased leave this topic in a legal limbo.[27]

Here is an example of when not to compensate. Farmers have an ancient right to fertilize. Suppose the level of fertilizer in the ground in a given area grows so much that neighboring waters are threatened, and the ancient right is restricted. Should farmers be compensated? No, because fertilizing is an action done by them and not to them. It is a cost of their production, and the general rule is that producers should pay all their costs, in a given year or over longer periods.

Compromise is possible, however. On Long Island, east of New York City, towns have forbidden development in an area that supplies them with water, but have compensated the owners with rights for more development than would otherwise be allowed in neighboring areas. A clearinghouse was established through which these owners can sell their rights. This concept has spread to other states.[28]

Intellectual Property Rights

Intellectual property rights (IPRs)—patents, trade marks, copyrights—arose mainly through laws passed by cities and other jurisdictions in medieval Europe—patents for inventions were first known in the Italian city-states in the fifteenth century—and from there they spread outward. Colonial governments in America issued patents as early as 1641, and laws on the protection of IPRs were passed in the United States soon after independence.

Sometimes IPRs appear unjust. In 1986, a U.S. doctor discovered a test that would reveal high probability of the congenital birth defect giving rise to Down's syndrome.[29] He patented his discovery and charges royalties as high as $9 each time it is applied, a prohibitive price for many mothers. Scores of laboratories are angered by his excess of greed over compassion. Suppose the test had been even more serious: patients risking their lives if they did not take it, yet the inventor insisting on prohibitive royalties. In a compassionate, compromising society there is always a solution, which recognizes the rights of both the inventor and the patient. With precedence in antitrust laws, the inventor might be required to share his patent with a certain number of competitors—at a price to be paid by them, which would be all the less because of the potential competition. Alternatively—less favored in the moral economy—would be for the public purse to buy the patent (by eminent domain?) and parcel it out to private competitors.

The enforcement of intellectual property rights is not widely recognized outside the Western world and Japan, probably because other areas have not been so inventive and therefore have not created much intellectual property of their own. Violations of these rights have been a source of much contention and political maneuvering in international diplomacy. For example, it is a sore point in the normalization of relationships between China and the United States. At present, IPRs to computer software are readily violated. Technology is proposed to correct this, by producing software that can be used in only one computer at a time, but some say it will take only two weeks for some hacker to find a technological loophole.

The Trade Act of 1974 in the United States called for special attention to ensure the observance of IPRs in countries with which trade agreements are concluded. By 1994, a special "Watch List" of sixteen countries had been prepared, among them Peru. In response, the National Institute for Defense of Competition and Intellectual Ownership (Indecopi), an organ of the government of free-trade-oriented Peruvian president Fujimori, began a campaign to confiscate pirated videotapes and computer programs. The head of Indecopi appeared on television, driving a steamroller over the pirated material. In an advertisement in the *Washington Post,* the government of China pictured a bulldozer doing the same in Guangzhao, with many persons watching.[30] Amid considerable furor on the part of the "pirates," and charges of undue influence by the United States, Indecopi "is in the eye of the storm of Peruvian economic life."[31] When it took a Peruvian manufacturer to court for registering Reebok sneakers brand as his own, the court decided in favor of the manufacturer. Complaints against Chinese pirating also continue in the United States.

The lack of concern in less developed areas surely reflects the minor role of IPRs in their own societies, just as rights over land were often vague in earlier societies in the now more developed world. Whether IPRs will be honored in the future depends on a balance of pressures from domestic pirates on the one hand and the countries that produce the property on the other. At the moment, the former seem to be winning in most less developed countries. Only when these countries themselves produce intellectual property in larger quantity will the balance swing. In the moral economy, IPRs will be protected by international law, but enforcement may be more difficult than rights over physical property.

Summary of Property Rights

Born in ancient times all over the world as good land became scarce relative to population, property rights have gradually been extended (mostly in the West and in Japan) to cover all kinds of property, including intellectual. These rights have been found essential to the normal conduct of economic enterprise, mainly producing, buying, and selling. Property is an extension of the entrepreneur; without it, one is not motivated and often not able to innovate. Some property rights have been limited by law for reasons of social responsibility, as in zoning and for environmental protection.

Property rights did not evolve in less developed areas as they did in the more developed, and this fact may be both a result and a cause of underdevelopment. Commands on how to use property issued by those who are not close to it do not make for efficient production. Even in the more developed countries, property rights are still evolving, especially as they relate to the environment. Will air, water, light, and the heat of the sun ultimately become subject to private ownership because of their scarcity, as has land? Or will their preservation be assured by community action, in the form of government regulations? Or will they be entrusted to nongovernmental agencies, as we have suggested in chapter 5? How accountable are we to others for the use, misuse, and preservation of property, whether it is held in common or subject to what we call private ownership?

Money and Inflation

Inflation

Inflation serves a purpose: to transfer real resources, without compensation, from those who are caught unawares to those that have initiated the increase in money. It is therefore a violation of property rights. Most citizens, not being economists, are unaware of this and believe that inflation "just happens." Even some economists advise rulers in less developed countries on how to prevent inflation—I have been guilty of that—on the naive supposition that these leaders really want to do so, when in fact killing the goose of their golden eggs is the last thing they want.

Inflation is always associated with an increase in the money supply. Money is created by the banking system or the government or by both in concert. Every time a bank makes a loan, or a government issues new securities bought by a bank, new money is created. If an individual, business, or government borrows newly created money not associated with an increase in production, once that money is spent, prices will rise ("more money chasing the same amount of goods"). The new money holders buy goods starting at the old prices—having taken the market by surprise—but in so doing they bid up the prices of what they buy, and the inflation spreads to other prices. Previous money holders caught unawares must pay higher prices as they make their usual purchases. Thus the new money holders get more and the old money holders get less.

As borrowers gain leverage on the gross domestic product, others try to defend themselves. Suppose—in a simplified model—a society consists of three groups: Government, Business, and Others. Government borrows first, driving prices up, and taking resources away from Business and Others. Business—

more astute than Others—rushes to the banks to defend itself by borrowing, because interest rates have not caught up with inflation. Thus they take resources back from Government and away from Others. If eventually Others catch on, and if they too borrow, theoretically the borrowing of each group may exactly offset that of the other two. From that point on, theoretically no one gains or loses any more, but the inflation rages on. However, equal access to the banks is most unlikely—indeed, it never occurs—so a continuing inflation means that some groups are obtaining advantage over others. As the distribution of output is made more according to access to loans and less according to market prices, to that extent the economy is inefficient. Therefore, with one exception (to be explained in the next section) any economy with any inflation at all—and today this includes virtually the entire world—is not operating at maximum efficiency and is transferring property, without compensation, from some to others. In an earlier work, I have shown with detailed accounting models how this operates.[32]

Even today, money may be privately issued or government issued. Checking accounts are private issue, created by the bank and not by the government. The quantity of money in more developed countries is determined in a delicate balance of private and government decisions—the government does not have complete control. This monetary system is taught in courses in economics and is not a subject of this book.

Commercial Loan Theory

However, new money need not lead to continuous inflation. If loaned to producers who use it in the manufacture of new goods and services, the new money is offset by new goods ("more money chasing more goods"). The manufacturers pay it back when the goods are sold (money is extinguished). The new products may be more costly for awhile, until they are replicated or substitutes invented, but no one has gained or lost from inflation. The money supply may even remain increased as others borrow to buy the new products, however. Thus a long-run increase in output is accompanied by a long-run increase in the money supply but not necessarily by inflation. This sequence is known as the *commercial loan (or real bills) theory of banking.* Under it, the money supply increases only as the production of goods and services increases over time.

In a rapidly innovating economy, the inflationary impact of one innovation may not die down before the next one takes up. Thus the inflation may seem permanent. Such has been the case in Hong Kong, whose consumer price index has risen rapidly in recent years, up to 11.6 percent per year. Because new jobs have been created and real wages and incomes have increased rapidly, however, consumers have not felt deprived.[33] The exchange rate has been protected by Hong Kong's use of a currency board, which is equivalent to a gold standard, and exports have been maintained by the world's willingness to pay higher prices (in dollars) for Hong Kong's products.

Rulers over great trading empires, whose power depended on the success of their merchants, have sometimes favored stable money. Among these are the Aksumite Empire of Ethiopia, from the second to ninth centuries CE; the Arabs from the seventh to the ninth centuries; the British in the fourteenth to nineteenth centuries with a lapse under Henry VIII; and the Americans in the nineteenth and early twentieth centuries. If, however, new money is issued (cash printed or bank deposits created) but not offset by new production, the borrower gains real goods, as explained previously, from others, who "pay" for them by being deprived of the goods they might have bought in a noninflationary environment. This latter activity has been undertaken by rulers for centuries, and it is still practiced by virtually all governments.

To summarize: those with the power to issue money are able to transfer real resources away from the rest, who are caught unawares. If they use those resources to create new goods, they quickly dampen the inflation, often leaving the rest even better off because of higher real incomes. But if they use them only to consume more themselves, or to carry on wars, the less privileged sectors lose from inflation. Before discussing the implications of this power, let us consider, historically, the difference between private and government issues.

Private Money versus Government Money

The dichotomy dates to earliest times. In pre-monetized societies, money consisted of commodities such as metal bars, used by agreement among traders. No government needed to "issue" them. The earliest coins were probably struck by private traders who commanded the confidence of the commercial community. Herodotus writes that the Lydians were the first to strike coins, in the eighth century BCE; probably the king merely stamped small ingots of traders' gold to certify to their quality. Coinage was quickly adopted by the Greeks and assisted in a commercial revolution of the Mediterranean about the seventh century BCE. During the Ptolemaic period in Egypt (323 BCE-30 CE), the export of coin was forbidden, and foreign coins obtained in trade were required to be exchanged for local,[34] so that the government might hold greater control.

Coinage in ancient China was the sole province of the emperor, its primary purpose being for tax collection.[35] The imperial house collected metal from which it made implements; when coins were needed for state expenditures, the implements were melted down. When inflation indicated that too many coins had been spent, they would be collected in taxes and reconverted into implements, so that the value of remaining coin rose.[36] The use of coins in China is traced to the fifth century BCE,[37] but in the third century an increase in minting greatly stimulated trade. Private coins were prohibited in 186 BCE,[38] and from then on coinage was a government monopoly for most of imperial China. The numerous edicts forbidding private coinage, however, indicate that the monopoly was frequently breached.

In Japan, the early money was foreign, but by the eighth century both private and official Japanese coins were in use. The capriciousness of imperial policy is illustrated by the prohibition of private coinage in 709, followed in 750 by award of an official rank to those who produced coins of 1,000 kwan, while in 766 private persons issuing coins would be arrested and enslaved.[39] Muslim gold dinars and silver dirhems were first issued about 700 CE, starting in Arabia and rapidly expanding throughout the whole empire, as a liberal trading zone was established for the first time from Spain to Far East Asia.[40] Russia did not mint coins in the medieval period but used those that came in from Baghdad and Byzantium.[41] Roman coins—in particular, the gold denarius—circulated freely in Europe, but after the fifth century local rulers struck coins with their own images. Traders would bring metals to government or private mints—these popped up everywhere, but they grew rapidly in Lombard Italy after 744 CE—where coins would be officially minted for a small fee, known as seignorage.[42] By the eighth century, the minting of coins was under royal control in England.[43] Charlemagne and his descendants (after 800 CE) began to issue silver pennies, called denarius, with 240 to the pound of silver, which were copied by other monarchs and became a standard European currency.[44] In England, twelve pennies, abbreviated d. for denarius, became a shilling, and twenty shillings weighed a pound of silver. Although weights and metal content were altered as inflation occurred, this system remained in effect until 1971. Scales would be provided at European fairs in the thirteenth century and thereafter, so the weight of coins, both private and government, could be assessed. Milling, or lateral ridges around the circumference, was introduced so that attempts to scrape metal would be detected. Like the human appendix, this vestige of an earlier purpose is still found on some coins in the United States.

Letters of credit and promissory notes—forms of private money—were used by the Arabs of the Abbasid caliphate (750-1258).[45] Issued by reliable merchants, they would be spent as cash; businessmen who maintained networks of traders throughout Dar-es-Islam, the extensive trading area from Europe to the Far East, would use these notes freely.[46] Anyone issuing such a note would, in effect, receive goods—paid for by the note—"free" until the note was redeemed, at which time he would have to pay in some other currency. Such letters of credit and promissory notes became widely circulated in the Italian city-states and fairs of Europe during the thirteenth and succeeding centuries. Naturally, the ability to print cash and spend it for real goods became very attractive, and governments were quick to use it. Paper currency was issued by the Sung dynasty in China in the eleventh century.[47] The Yüan (Mongol) dynasty caught on to the idea and issued its currency—the one known to Marco Polo—in such excess that it rapidly became worthless and was no longer accepted by merchants.

Vicarious Power and Inflation

In the welfare states of western Europe, North America, Australia, and New Zealand, the centuries-old process of inflationary finance continues, but now the sovereign is the people, with vicarious power. Money is created through government deficits to supply goods and services via government rather than the private markets, in amounts greater than the people are willing to pay for in taxes. Any government that refuses to provide them would be voted out of office. The people pay for these goods anyway, but the bill is often paid by the poorest, whose income is spent primarily on consumption of the very goods hit by inflation. Thus the economy is gradually transferred from the private sector to the public, efficiency is converted into inefficiency, and the poor are the main ones to suffer.

In the classic liberal societies of the third millennium, the struggle will continue to be between governments that would generate inflation for the benefit of vicarious power holders and elites, and elements of the private sector—mostly the business community—that wish to preserve the value of money for a sound economy. The battle lines are not rigid. In more developed countries, the central bank may well be on the side of the private sector. For example, the Federal Reserve in the United States surely favors sounder money—not zero inflation however—than does the government, if one judges by its behavior and not by its pronouncements. In many less developed countries the central bank acts in conspiracy with the powerful elite to deprive the citizenry of their wealth through inflation.

Privately Issued Money

With apparent hopelessness, however, comes hope. Many years ago, Nobel laureate Friedrich Hayek suggested privately issued money. "Unlike government," he wrote, "a private issuer must supply the public with a money as good as that of his rivals or go out of business."[48] Technology may now lead us to a return to privately issued money, and the commercial loan theory of banking. Suppose the people, impatient with years of inflation, wish to use an international, stable currency that no government or central bank now creates. Suppose a private firm—call it Techno Inc.—with wealth accumulated from interested stockholders, decides to create such a currency, called (let us say) the techno. It will issue technos to anyone in exchange for any recognized currency at the current exchange rate, plus an insurance fee—Techno would insure itself against inability to meet its contracts. It then guarantees that it will repurchase the technos at any future date for the same value in real purchasing power. For example, suppose the initial rate of purchase is $1 = 1 techno, and later a recognized price index for dollars rises from 100 to 110; Techno Inc. would buy the same technos back for $1.10. Being an astute investor, the company would in the meantime have invested the proceeds in securities that increase in value by more than inflation; hence it would remain in business. Its income would come from insurance fees, plus any capital gains from successful investment, out of which it would pay its costs of administration and yield a profit to its stockholders. Suppose Techno Inc. should fail? There is, of course, no guarantee, but it might invest its proceeds in a wide variety of securities, some safer than others, so that it would retain a sufficient reserve for all who would wish to reconvert their currencies. If it is successful, people would begin to use the techno as their principal currency, acceptable worldwide, so they would not have to reconvert. Whereas governments today gain from inflation, it would be to Techno's advantage to avoid it, in order to maintain the confidence of the public. Therefore, it would issue only the right amount of technos, to prevent an inflation in prices of goods bought by that currency. It could, for example, issue only an annual percentage increase equal to the percentage increase in world gross domestic product (GDP), along lines suggested by Milton Friedman.[49] An alternative way for private money to come about would be through the use of money-market mutual funds as cash, available for transacting business and paying debt. Once again, price stability would be the desirable feature to attract investors/moneyholders.

If Techno is successful, other firms would follow, and eventually the world would possess a number of currencies competing with each other to be the most stable, which is certainly not the case today. Government currencies would either die out because they could not compete, or else they would be forced into stability in order to compete. Consumers will accept the techno when they discover that if the latest-technology car costs 5,000 technos in 2050, then the still-later-technology car will also cost 5,000 technos (or less) in 2060, and 2070, and so on.

Technology would assist in this venture, because the new currencies might be issued on "smart cards," which could be used to transfer amounts from buyer to seller. Each individual might choose a currency in which his or her smart card would be denominated, and the card would "know" the balance in each account. A customer might pay the grocery store in one currency—by presenting a smart card—the grocer would receive payment in another currency on another card, and neither need know which currency the other was using.[50] Exchange rates would be broadcast minute by minute to the machines in which the cards are inserted. (This is not science fiction; it is within the capability of today's technology.) Cash would die out, while Techno and its competitors would replace banks as suppliers of finance to business, on the commercial loan theory, or else they would act like central banks, supplying technos as bank reserves.

How would Techno start? Presumably in a small way, in some country racked by inflation, where a major producer wishes to sell materials to promising producers that cannot buy for lack of a stable currency. So the producer lends technos at interest, promising to redeem them once the borrowers' products are sold. (This is the way money began, centuries ago). After they circulate for awhile, it is discovered that they may be used in other stores as well, and they expand to replace the local currency, which by now has lost its value completely. Technos might serve as the expandable medium in countries where bank loans are restricted by a currency board, but where unrequited possibilities exist for honest business expansion, with increased employment. Replacing unstable currencies in ever-widening circles, and in other countries as well, the techno ultimately becomes a stable currency with worldwide circulation. I do not predict its early appearance, however.

Nor would we envisage large numbers of currencies circulating the world, as they do now, each one with limited geographical area. Instead, perhaps four or five private currencies would compete for public favor, usable anywhere in the world, and instantly exchangeable one for another through smart cards. Any money holder deciding that one currency was not sufficiently stable might change the denomination of the card to another, more stable, by sticking it into a machine, probably a personal computer at home. If all existing currencies became unstable, profit-seeking investors would initiate still another, whose attraction would be its stability.

Of course, there is no need for banks to die; they might merely copy the practices of Techno. Quite possibly other ways will be found by which the private sector can reassert itself into the field of money—Techno is merely an illustration. The requirements would be a public fed up with inflation, governments willing to relinquish their monopoly over currency, entrepreneurs ready to initiate the new system, and investors willing to take the risk. The latter two have never been in short supply; the first two are—for now—the missing elements.

Would not money holders be confused if the price of bananas is quoted in many currencies? No. Some standard of the most stable currency will emerge and prices will be quoted in that currency until such time as its makers err and it becomes less stable than another currency, which will become the standard. In many countries with their own currency, the dollar is now the stable standard.

What about monetary policy? What would be the role of the central bank? None. With inflation kept under control by market forces—people would shift from unstable to stable currencies—and with money supply (in stable currencies) increasing at equal pace with production, there would be no need for a central bank or for the International Monetary Fund. Some economists argue that the central bank should stimulate the economy in a period of recession, along Keynesian lines. Others argue that such stimulation has never really worked. I incline toward the latter view, but the debate—amply argued elsewhere—is not a subject of this book. *The Economist* states: "Since it is (almost) universally accepted that full employment is best achieved in a stable economy, price stability is, in practice, the Federal Reserve's primary concern."[51] At present, the central bank—in the United States, the Fed—tries to stabilize the currency by manipulating the interest rate. Sometimes it is successful and sometimes not; much depends on the skill of the chairman of the board.

In the moral economy, the same goal would be pursued by competition: we assume that money holders prefer stable currencies; therefore they would shift from unstable to stable, with only the latter surviving. Techno and its competitors would set their own interest rates, and the market would balance the prospects of inflation in a given currency against the interest rate. No central action whose success depends on the expertise or frailty of one or a few persons. No more volatile swings of the stock market depending on what the Fed chairman says, since no single interest rate would be governing. No more worry about whether the consumer price index (CPI) adequately represents inflation. No more concern over how much to adjust social security and other government "entitlements" for inflation.

But the main advantage of private money would be to divorce monetary and fiscal policy from exchange rates. In Southeast Asia in 1997-98, risky fiscal and banking ventures induced a domino-effect depreciation of currencies that led in turn to stock markets tumbling the world over. This event focused attention on a consequence of globalized financial markets that had already been recognized by financial experts. No longer can a domestic economy be propped through monetary and fiscal policy while exchange stability is simultaneously maintained. Low interest rates and high government expenditures to propel the domestic economy may induce unwise expansions that jeopardize the exchange rate. On the other hand, high interest rates and low government expenditures to keep the exchange rate intact may slow the domestic economy. In the moral economy, the diffuse role of governments, the increased accountability of both enterprises and banks to the market, and currencies unrelated to national sovereignty would confine the effects of official and banking extravagances to their perpetrators. There is, after all, no good reason why a currency must be associated with a country, and there are many good reasons why money holders of any country should have their choices of currencies.

Following the Mexican monetary crisis of 1995, governments began to rethink ways of supporting each other's currencies, and the International Monetary Fund devised a way "to dole out money quickly to cash-strapped members and began organizing a new special fund . . . to help a country cope with a currency crisis."[52] None of this would have been necessary under the private-money system of the moral economy, for governments would lose their capacity to abuse the currency in the first place.

As this book is being written, European governments debate the Maastricht stability pact, which is considered a precursor to initiation of the euro as a common European currency in 1999. Terms of this pact include not only budget deficits limited to 3 percent of GDP or less but also limits on inflation, long-term interest rates, public debt, and exchange rates. Will the pact prevent governments from following Keynesian stabilization policies? Will the hardness of their currencies condemn them to living out depressions with the austerity of monetary defenders of the 1930s? Possibly both, but the greater probability of economic stability would attenuate these adverse conditions. With private currency such as the techno, governments would no longer be in the money business. They would be reduced to acting like private enterprises—albeit very large ones, probably too large—in their relationship to currency. Their actions would create and destroy currency only to the same extent as do those of nonbanking private institutions. The whole debate over the euro would be resolved by there not being any. Whether the CPI accurately reflects inflation or not—see discussion of the Boskin report in chapter 3—would become a nonquestion.

Wayne Angell, former governor of the Federal Reserve, argues that the Fed's monetary policy during the 1920s actually brought on the 1929 stock market crash and the ensuing depression of the 1930s. Whether it could do so all by itself is questionable, but his argument lends support for the belief that stable money is the prime requisite for smoothening the business cycle. Angell proposes that the Fed's deflationary policy of the 1920s—consumer prices trended downward[53] while wholesale prices rose until 1926 and then declined[54] because the monetary base could not expand—caused real interest rates to rise while money rates fell, thus causing a shortage of investment capital. The Fed thought money was plentiful when actually it was in short supply.[55] This and other experience with monetary policy—which is not part of this book—lead to the stable-money hypothesis, as well as to the proposition that competition among privately issued currencies, for customers who want stable money, will probably be the most satisfactory way to bring it about.

Would governments stand for having their power over money eclipsed? Maybe. European governments seem ready to give up national currencies in favor of the euro. But they are moving toward ever more concentrated power in money, not away from it, as the moral economy advocates. A turnaround in thinking will be necessary before private money becomes culturally acceptable: this may require a century or two, replete with crises in major currencies such as the euro. Before that happens, governments are likely to outlaw the techno and its competitive currencies, for numerous, spurious reasons, but really to preserve their power. Only an enraged public would supplant such a government. How long will that take? I don't know, but the moral economy is open-ended. Like the horizon, it can only be approached, never reached.

In the United States, controversy continues over the Glass-Steagall Act of 1933, which prohibits commercial banks from brokering securities. The Act was born in a day when concentrated money power was mistrusted, and today technology has made the distinction useless. The struggle is a political one for the preservation of economic territory. The classic liberal society demands that the act be repealed, but insurance company lobbies have so far been powerful enough to prevent that. Greater diffusion of power is needed.

In the monetary system proposed for the moral economy, banks—or firms like Techno—might be rated according to risk. Those that invest in government securities or cash instruments only (Class A banks) would be deemed the lowest risk. Depositors might have to pay monthly fees or at least receive no interest on deposits. Those that invested in nothing riskier than mortgages (Class B banks) would be the next rank, perhaps paying some interest to depositors; those that invested in other securities (Class C, D, E, etc.) would pose greater risks and pay higher interest rates. A depositor who wished a secure deposit would choose Class A. Those willing to take greater risks would choose accordingly. While banks might insure their deposits with private insurance companies, it would not be fair for the government to spend taxpayer money to insure any deposits at all, for doing so requires the public at large to subsidize private persons or businesses that should be responsible for their own risks—especially when given the option to assume none. Different kinds of cash might command premiums or discounts similar to bank interest, positive or negative, depending on the class of the issuing bank. Had this classic liberal society been in effect, there would have been no savings and loan crisis in the United States, and taxpayers would not have been charged the millions of bailout money.

Chapter 8
Law, Corruption,
Government Regulation, and Taxes

Law

Law has always been both part of the classic liberal system and exception to it. As part of the system, it codifies and interprets social rules, making the system function more smoothly but not itself acting as instrument of change. As exception, it modifies the intent of the contracting parties and substitutes judicial verdicts in the light of some social goal. When disagreements arise on contracts, the traditional intent of law is to surmise how the contracting parties would have resolved their issue had they foreseen it at the time of making the contract. Increasingly, however, lawyers and judges enforce contracts in the light of a social justice that transcends the original intents of the parties. In this action, legists are becoming an interest group—with the interest to bring about social change.

To those who feel that "social justice"—however it may be defined— is so important that all institutions of society should be dedicated to achieving it, law among them, this is a desirable outcome. Others feel—as I do—that although "social justice" is important—however I define it—it is best achieved when the proper institutions work on it, the way criminal justice is best achieved through the justice department and not through mob rule. Furthermore, institutions work best when dedicated to their assigned tasks. The law ought to be the impartial adjudicator, dealing out social justice when the law calls for it but leaving social change to institutions more adept at shaping it.

In northwestern Europe and Japan, the law was created, over centuries, primarily by midlevel negotiation. The king or emperor tried to capture the law but was usually unable to do so completely. Legal scholars, merchants, bankers, guildmasters, and others who created the law built into it checks and balances that represented the balance of power among them. In the rest of the world, by contrast, the law was directed primarily by the sovereign, who preserved his prerogatives in a way that confounded liberalism. This distinction, I have proposed, is one of the many causes of the economic development in northwestern Europe and Japan and of the underdevelopment of the rest of the world.

Lawyers and Judges as an Interest Group

In *Centuries of Economic Endeavor,* I pictured law in northwestern Europe and Japan as gradually attaining a power of its own, apart from that of any interest group. It was the creation of groups negotiating from a certain balance of power, and it was held in place by the continuing power balance among them. Lawyers and judges were becoming legal scholars with a professional purpose to safeguard the balanced law.[1] Since publication of that book, I have become persuaded that these lawyers and judges are interest groups after all, and like other interest groups they respond to rule number 1 from chapter 2: *Power expands until other power stops it.* Judges have moved far toward capturing product liability law in the United States, for example, using it as an instrument to bring about their concept of social justice.

Why does this happen now and not in the nineteenth century or earlier? This capture is part of a wider movement in Western culture, in which the guilt feelings of mainstream society have motivated political and judicial moves in favor of poorer people and those that have been discriminated against—call them "social victims." This culture change, along with the failure of legislatures to take corrective actions, has opened up a new power space for lawyers and judges, and they have stepped right into it. They are no longer limited to ruling impartially on the contracts of others.

The question is one of degree. When the judiciary interprets business agreements in terms of the original intent of the parties, the law is a reinforcer of the classic liberal society. When it awards punitive damages that the original parties would never have thought of, the judiciary modifies their intents into a social purpose. Thus it acts as exception to the classic liberal society. The latter role is found in the many legal actions that appear to be biased in favor of the social victim. This shift is also reflected in resolutions of the American Bar Association, which in recent years "has adopted formal policy positions on abortion, affirmative action, AIDS, funding for the arts, gun control, homelessness, nuclear proliferation, parental leave, sexual orientation, health care, and a wide variety of other social issues."[2] It is not whether these are worthy issues. It is whether the bar association is a *bar* association, dealing with legal process—how to secure fair verdicts for all parties. As individuals, its members may join many other interest groups dealing with these nonbar issues. Instead, the concept of an independent judiciary is becoming compromised.

A second reflection lies in punitive damages. To the extent that an action is criminal beyond the civil loss of the plaintiff, it should be a crime against the state, like murder. Centuries ago, murder was a crime against the relatives of the victim, who were the ones to be compensated. Now it is a crime against the state, since the social order is violated when someone is murdered. Furthermore, recent punitive damages have been excessive, as if taken in vengeance rather than retribution. "In New Mexico, a jury returned a $2.7 million punitive damage verdict against McDonald's [later reduced to $400,000] . . . because a woman in a car spilled very hot coffee on herself. . . . A San Francisco jury assessed a $6.9 million fine against a law firm for 'failing to do more' to discipline a former partner in a sexual harassment case. . . . A Chicago jury slapped a pharmaceutical company for $125 million because its product was misadministered by a doctor resulting in the loss of an eye. In Texas . . . a wrongful employee termination resulted in an $80 million punitive damage verdict."[3] A customer sued BMW because a car he had bought had been damaged and repainted. The court awarded him $4,000 because of the lower value of the car, plus $4 million in punitive damages, later reduced to $2 million and finally struck down completely by the U.S. Supreme Court.[4] It is not that we do not sympathize with the victims, except for the woman who spilled coffee. (Those of us who have never spilled coffee may cast the first lump of sugar.) Rather, these verdicts are a capricious order by judges, for Party A to pay Party B, in a judgment whose ramifications were never intended by the original transactors.

A third reflection lies in the transfer of risk from shallow pockets to presumed deep pockets. When a producer complies with all laws and guards against all known hazards, a responsible consumer in a classic liberal society takes the risks of one's choices. Harking back to an age when tobacco addiction was normal for many people, a cigarette maker should not be punished for not disclosing the possibility of addiction to a customer. One who enlarges her breasts should take the risk of that procedure, the same for one who built with asbestos before its dangers were appreciated. Even today, strong evidence suggests that silicone breast implants, and asbestos once inside a wall, are not harmful, but whether this is true or not is immaterial.

What if a producer maliciously withholds known evidence of danger? Tobacco companies have aimed at creating addicts, particularly among the young. By contrast, however, fast food companies are not hauled into court for producing foods that drip with artery-clogging fat, nor are television producers who incite young audiences to violence and murder. The tobacco action is serious because today's culture in the United States has made it so. In the culture of two decades ago, when today's addictions were formed, it was no more serious than the fast foods and television examples are today.

It often turns out that deep pockets were not so deep after all, when legal judgments are passed on to customers through price increases and to pension funds and other stockholders through decreased dividends, but this too is immaterial. Right or wrong does not depend on depth of pockets.

A two-year inquiry by the top civil justice of the United Kingdom, Lord Woolf, revealed that "legal costs generally exceed the value of compensation awards when claims are less than £20,000 [and] such abuses occur in part because lawyers have an interest in keeping cases going as long as they can."[5] The deepest pockets perhaps belong to lawyers.

Private Adjudication

What to do? First is to publicize the issue. Two recent books have exposed the problems in the United States,[6] one of them arguing that lawyers "have been weighed in the balance and found wanting."[7] Second, laws to reduce product liability and to cap torts actions have been proposed in the United States, but they have been spurned by legislators who find there are more votes from social victims than there are from corporations. Third, Lord Woolf's proposed solution would be to put cases on a "fast track," requiring that they be tried and settled within a given period.

But fourth, and most promising for a classic liberal society, is a suggestion made by Stephen Williams, to hark back to the Middle Ages, when the law merchant was one of the great successes of European trade fairs.[8] Individual fairs, in competition with each other, had every incentive to adopt legal systems that would attract merchants to use the fairs by reducing the costs of adjudicating and making judgments widely known to be just. I have not found any literature that says they actually did this, but it seems reasonable. As in medieval times, the interests of both parties today, at the time of signing a contract, include fulfillment and avoiding legal hassles. All parties might agree in advance on a private adjudicator who would make those judgments that the contractors would have made *ex ante* had they anticipated the issues. They would select the adjudicator behind a veil of ignorance, having no idea what issues would come up. Adjudicators would have every incentive to be expeditious and fair, since those with reputations for these qualities would be most sought after—therefore, a liberal market in adjudicators. Today's lawyers gain their reputations by winning cases; the adjudicators proposed here would gain them by being expeditious and fair. Whereas today's lawyers have every incentive to string out cases, to "earn" greater fees, the liberal-market adjudicators would have incentive to resolve the cases as quickly and fairly as possible.

The private adjudication proposed by Williams resembles arbitration but is stronger and more public. Arbitration clauses are often included in purchase and other contracts in the United States, facilitated by the 1925 Federal Arbitration Act, about which Supreme Court decisions have held "consistently in recent years that Government policy favors arbitration over litigation as long as the process is fair."[9] Those who oppose arbitration argue that the clauses requiring it are usually inserted by the supposedly "stronger party" (the seller) in fine print and the arbitrator is selected by that party, thereby putting the consumer, who does not read fine print, at a disadvantage. In the moral economy, private adjudicators would be well-known equivalents of courts, widely advertised and available, selected and actively agreed upon by both parties to a contract. The designation of a well-known, impartial adjudicator would enhance the reputation of a seller for honesty.

Corruption

In 1960, while on a one-year appointment as economic advisor to a presidential-level commission in Bolivia, I read in the newspaper that the Central Bank had sold its gold reserves to the political party in power, the Movimiento Nacional Revolucionario, which had deposited them in accounts in Switzerland, to be available to defend the Revolution in case of attempted coup. When I asked the minister of finance about the legality of this transaction, he defended it on grounds that the Central Bank had been paid equivalent value in national currency. He and I both knew that the currency at the day's exchange rate—subject to further devaluation—had less real value than gold, but he considered the explanation final, and I—as his advisor—had no standing for complaint. The next day, looking for an outcry in the newspapers, I saw only silence. The country considered the transaction "normal," and I had had my introduction to politics in Latin America.

Political offices that hold access to public funds or that command bribes are often treated like property rights, bought and sold. In an earlier era in the now more developed areas, and in most less developed countries still today, little or no distinction was/is made between public and private assets and rights. A holder of rights obtained by inheritance, military coup, or other violence commands the associated income, spending much or all of it as he pleases. In this section, we review the history of mixing public and private prerogatives, from an earlier era in which such mixing was accepted worldwide and therefore was not "corrupt." We show how, as the power-diffusion process progressed, the mixing became unpopular and eventually illegal, though far from stopped. Then we show how it persists today, legitimately though illegally, in most less developed countries. We predict that it will be a principal inhibitor of economic development in those areas that are now privatizing state enterprises.

How Corruption Was Lessened, but Not Eliminated, in Northwestern Europe

Historically, a clear separation of public and private prerogatives of office-holders is a necessary but insufficient condition for containing corruption, as I will hereafter call it. When power is concentrated in one or a few focal points, corruption pays off for the powerful, since no one can check them. As rival political figures arise with the power-diffusion process, however, each one sees an advantage to curbing the corruption of the others. When any given power holder is but one of many, one's gain from one's own corruption is small relative to the loss from the corruption of the many others. Since all are in roughly the same position—power is by now diffuse—they agree to suppress the corruption. As in prisoner's dilemma, each plays the game because if one does not the others will retaliate. With further diffusion of power into the lower ranks, protests against corruption also arise from below: the main thrust comes from the middle classes. Finally, containment of corruption has been part of wider electoral reform. Particularly in England, it came about on the coattails of the movement for greater enfranchisement. This model has roughly been the history of northwestern Europe, where it ran its course from medieval times to about the nineteenth century. But corruption has not yet been conquered, and it may even be accelerating as more social programs are entrusted to government.

> Long since an extravagant mother, the welfare state has given rise to a culture of corruption, tragic in its consequences. The tangle of bureaucratic regulations offers all sorts of opportunities for graft on the part of officials, and fraud on the part of would-be beneficiaries, in search of a handout with or without entitlement to it. Special interest groups mobilize in order to oblige the state to buy them off. Fraudulent claims may be as much as twenty percent of budgets.[10]

Corruption in the Less Developed Areas

Nor has the model run significantly in the less developed areas, where most of the world's corruption resides. Although public and private powers are legally separate where governments have copied the laws from more developed areas, culturally the separation is not widely accepted. Both national figures and local bosses still command allegiance to their private persons. In one-party states— of which there are many in Africa; Indonesia and China are Asian examples— no opposition figure, corrupt or not, threatens. Even in multiparty states, one elite group often dominates. Anticorruption laws are selectively enforced to rid oneself of some opponent whose sins are no greater than one's own, but there is little opposition powerful enough for a ruler to be forced to bargain away his own corruption.

Democracy, by which a corrupt official might be voted out of office, offers the best opportunity for the future, but to date the bundled platforms of candidates—one has to vote for the whole platform or none of it—plus the corruption of virtually all candidates, has weakened the choices of voters and therefore the corruption-containment potential of democracy.

The wider reform movements in less developed countries (in favor of classic liberalism and privatization) are being urged by international agencies and industrial powers, to be implemented by the very persons whose perquisites are prejudiced—the fox guarding the chicken coop. If they propose anticorruption campaigns, as did the Lopez Portillo and Salinas administrations in Mexico, they do so for show, with no intention of carrying them out. There are no coattails. For example, President Zedillo of Mexico found few allies when he fought an almost one-person battle against corruption.

In 1990, the *New York Times* wrote of social services bogged down by corruption in the face of great poverty in Latin America. "Underneath lies an ingrained system of winks, nods, kickbacks, bribes and outright corruption that will take many years to root out."[11] In 1991, the U.S. ambassador to Argentina, having received no satisfaction from the president, complained to the press (contrary to usual diplomatic protocol) about government officials demanding payoffs to give licenses to U.S. firms.[12] In Brazil, President Collor was impeached and removed from office for widespread corruption in 1992.[13] In 1993, the *New York Times* also wrote of powerful clans holding local areas in their grip in much of Latin America; the Bulhoes clan in Alagoas State, Brazil, was cited as an example.[14] In 1994, a report by a Brazilian congressional committee recommended that eighteen members of the Congress be expelled for corruption.[15] It is not yet clear whether these cases mark an incipient public rage against corruption or whether they are moves to eliminate political opponents.

A History of Corruption

Max Weber pointed out that "in patrimonial systems . . . all governmental authority and corresponding economic rights tend to be treated as privately appropriated economic advantages."[16] Early societies often had a vague understanding of the separation of private and public powers; complaints against corruption occurred from time to time; and occasional reforms were tried. For example, John of Cappadocia "began a long series of reforms directed against pervasive corruption and the consequent purchase of offices" in Byzantium in the sixth century.[17] But such reforms were short-lived and did not catch the attention of anyone with the power to implement them.

Before the twelfth century in Dar-es-Islam, "merchants often secured the right to farm taxes under conditions that allowed them to use in private business, money that in fact belonged to the state." Before the twelfth century in Europe, the concept of a public authority, with public responsibilities, assets, liabilities, and power apart from the private prerogatives of the king, lord, or other officeholder, lay beyond the horizon.[18] Bribes to sway the outcome of lawsuits were common.[19] "Machiavelli and his generation . . . argued that men should realize their potential for heroic excellence *(virtu)* by . . . establishing the republic in a hostile environment dominated by corruption and despotism."[20] In Europe "before the eighteenth century public and private sectors are difficult to distinguish, and the earlier the period in question, the more artificial and antihistoric the distinction becomes."[21]

In England, the separation of the king's official and personal prerogatives probably began under Henry II in the twelfth century,[22] continued gradually thereafter, and was finally cemented by Thomas Cromwell in the sixteenth, but its purpose was to enhance the efficiency of government, not to deny the king his absolute rights. Challenges to members who had amassed fortunes were made in Parliament in the seventeenth century,[23] but they appear to have been motivated more to bring down an adversary than to question the legitimacy of corruption per se. Such charges also protected the king from his subordinates, as when Pepys, in the seventeenth century, prosecuted those who stole from the navy. Gregg describes how Prince Charles (later Charles I), in reading Guicciardini's *Aphorisms,* was intrigued by the notion that there could be a line between public and private conduct.[24] Charles's statesman, the Earl of Strafford, "lost no opportunity of enriching himself, and his immense fortune laid him open to criticism."[25] Parliament complained of judicial corruption during the civil war,[26] and cases were prosecuted by Edward Coke, but these appear to have been politically selected and again, not an indictment of the concept of corruption. During Anne's reign (1702-14), "public and private matters were mixed even more completely than usual."[27]

More so in France. In the thirteenth century, "profitable offices, already held as private property, could be sold with the patron's approval and bequeathed to heirs."[28] "Allegiance in the fourteenth century was still given to a person, not a nation, and the great territorial lords of duchies and counties felt themselves free to make alliances as if almost autonomous."[29] In the fifteenth century, "Jacques Coeur conducted a thriving export business. . . . [He] raised large sums for the crown, but as partial compensation for this, used crown revenue to finance his own trading."[30] In the seventeenth century, "far more people made far more money out of the royal finances in France than in England."[31] Under Henry IV, "the jurists deduced from the idea of 'mariage mystique' between the King and the Crown, that his personal possessions were united with those of the Crown."[32] But when Louis XIV died leaving an enormous debt from his wars, jurists considered whether this was his personal debt or that of the state; they decided for the state.[33] In the eighteenth century, "each receiver [of taxes] had his own set of accounts, his own treasury *(caisse),* and the freedom to mix his private business affairs with those of the state."[34]

In Japan, as far back as the seventh century, territorial governors were forbidden to accept bribes;[35] a similar prohibition is included in the Kemmu Formulary laws of 1336.[36] Nevertheless, references to what would today be called corruption are as numerous for Japan as they are for western Europe. In the fourteenth century, guild monopolies were recognized in return for gratuities to authorities,[37] while those who wanted lands bribed the emperor Go-Daigo's favorite lady, Renko, "who interfered at will with the decisions of the registry office."[38] In the seventeenth century, "the dependence of the Edo [now

Tokyo] trade on the patronage of the nobility led to flattery, fawning, and bribery."[39] In the eighteenth century, to prevent "increases in their rice tributes, [villagers] often bribed local officials,"[40] while bribe-taking senior counselors strengthened the shogunate's powers at the expense of daimyo.[41] In 1826, Mizuno Tadakuni wanted to stamp out corruption and curtail unnecessary expenses of the shogunate, but the power of the shogunate still supported extravagant and corrupt officials.[42] Half a century later the early Meiji governments provided "private enterprises with aid and privileges of a sort that would be considered corrupt favoritism today."[43]

During the eighteenth century, politicians in both England and France began to discover that refusing to feed from the public trough brought them acclaim from the voters. William Pitt the Elder, appointed paymaster general of the forces, ostentatiously refused to accept more than the £4,000 allotment for this task, although it had earlier been customary to receive commissions on official purchases for the armed forces.[44] In France, Lafayette gained popularity by refusing compensation offered him by the municipal council.[45] The coming of democracy, by which such popularity might be translated into votes, diminished corruption.

Only in the nineteenth century did politicians in northwestern Europe begin to forgo their own corruption specifically to outlaw that of others. The same point came in the twentieth century for Japan. The British reform movement, begun toward the end of the eighteenth century, led to the Great Reform Act of 1832, which expanded the voting franchise and initiated a vast array of other social reforms, including the Corrupt Practices Act of 1854, with a precise definition of bribery, the Education Act of 1870, the secret ballot of 1872, the Judicature Act of 1873, the Employers and Workmen Act of 1875, the Public Health Act of 1875, the Factory Act of 1878, and finally the Corrupt and Illegal Practices Prevention Act of 1883. One reform had bred another, so that the success of one cannot be evaluated in isolation.

The Napoleonic code, followed by the Orléans government of 1830 and the constitutions of 1852 and 1875 in France, clearly established the distinction between the private and public affairs of political officers, such that in 1887 President Grévy was forced to resign because he had defended his son-in-law in a corruption scandal.[46] With the liquidation of a Panama Canal company in 1889 and losses from a succession of loans, corruption in high places was charged. The novelist Emile Zola sensitized the electorate to high-level deceit by publicizing the Dreyfus case (1894-1906), in which high military officers covered up their own treason by sending an innocent Jew to Devil's Island.

In Japan, the theory that "the emperor is an organ of the state rather than the state itself"[47] was put forth by a professor in 1911. That country is undergoing a series of corruption scandals even as this book is written. A former prime minister was convicted of taking bribes in 1987.[48] In 1989 two prime ministers were forced to resign for receiving money illicitly,[49] and in 1992 a top politician resigned after admitting that he had received an improper contribution.[50] The *Washington Post* wrote that "despite the law, politicians are expected to hand out cash to constituents . . . [and] almost nobody is seriously trying to change things,"[51] but the *New York Times* reported that the scandal stirred atypical anger in the Japanese, who are usually very tolerant. But "this time some unseen line seems to have been crossed."[52]

In each case, a crescendo of feeling, first about particular cases and then against corruption in general, led to court cases and then to legislation. Corruption is far from obliterated in the more developed areas, but at least it is unpopular, illegal, and illegitimate. Anyone who undertakes it does so at his or her political peril, as Senator Packwood found out in the United States in 1995.[53] Nevertheless, the power of governments in more developed areas to regulate, to grant subsidies, and to play political favorites is still a strong force for corruption in both Europe and the United States. Only a further continuation in the power-diffusion process will alleviate that.

In China, Creel writes of bribery of judges as far back as the eleventh century BCE and of rampant bribery in the sixth century BCE.[54] The ruler's private wealth and the public exchequer were in principle distinct as far back as the Qin (220-206 BCE) and Han (206 BCE-9 CE and 23-220 CE) dynasties, but thereafter the separation ended.[55] The Qing dynasty tried to stamp out corruption in its own interests, from its inception (1644) until the mid–eighteenth century, but thereafter its efforts declined.[56] Other historians supply examples of continuous mixing of public and private funds and prerogatives all the way up to modern times.[57] Almost without a break, newspapers in the twentieth century take up where historians leave off: abuses of privileges by children of government cadres;[58] the growth of official corruption along with the economy;[59] "running China has become a family affair" with rampant nepotism.[60] By exception, Liu Shaoqi, Chinese head of state in 1959, "was meticulous about not receiving gifts or salary beyond what he merited;"[61] he was later expelled from the party and died in prison. From time to time the official press calls for an end to corruption, or the government announces a campaign against it.[62] But the children of the party elite continue to receive favored places in education, in jobs, and in permissions to start businesses.[63] Considering the penalty for doing so, no organized political group has sufficient interest in stopping this favoritism.

Elsewhere in the less developed areas, no historic turning point is found similar to that of northwestern Europe and Japan. In 1977, American firms became forbidden by U.S. law to pay bribes, even abroad. The U.S. government "documented almost 100 cases between April 1994 and May 1995 in which American firms lost contracts [in Asia] to foreign firms that pay bribes."[64] After much pressure by the Americans, in November, 1997, twenty-nine industrial nations signed a treaty to outlaw bribing of foreign officials by their nationals. However, the borderline between legitimate transactions and bribery is not clear, so the ability to enforce such an agreement is dubious. Nowhere in the less developed areas is power sufficiently diffuse that each political group would have more to gain than to lose by containing corruption. While any particular case is difficult to confirm—corruption by its nature is not put on record—nevertheless the massive number of reports, from all over the less developed countries, must have substance behind them. I have collected hundreds of such reports, which I have recorded in my computer; only a sample of the more interesting ones is listed in this footnote.[65] Some of these reports reflect government concern to contain corruption; some reflect protests from the general public or from opposition figures; but most show the stubborn continuation of corruption, which would indicate that affirmations against it are usually for show. President Zedillo of Mexico may be an exception, because he does not belong to the traditional "political family," and he appears to have a conscience of his own. But he is up against tremendous odds, and charges of corruption have been leveled against him.[66]

Government Regulation

Classic liberals and interventionists have vastly different views of government regulation. To interventionists, known popularly in the United States as "liberals," regulation is necessary to assure justice, fairness, environmental protection, and safety. To them, abuses of power by regulators are rare. Naturally they occur once in a while, they say, since regulators are human. To classic liberals, known popularly but incorrectly as "conservatives," on the other hand, regulations are a source of pervasive corruption, favoring one producer over another, destroying business activity like a growing cancer, diminishing entrepreneurship and employment, and dragging down economic welfare. To examine to what extent either is correct, let us consider three types of regulations.

First are regulations to which all are agreed, such as traffic controls, airport safety checks, and the privacy of the home. I will say no more about these.

Second are regulations to prevent persons from harming themselves. These include laws forbidding drugs and assisted suicide. For classic liberals, these should be matters for persuasion, not for law. For some, the government should keep out completely. For me, the government is a legitimate researcher, such as on the effects of smoking and drugs, and a legitimate persuader, such as through announcements by the U.S. surgeon general about smoking. Indeed, I believe these efforts have been more effective than attempts to eradicate habits by coercion, pressure on other governments, lawsuit, or punishment. "There has been a tendency . . . to absolve adult smokers of the responsibility they took on when they chose freely to smoke. Many of those suing tobacco companies knew full well from the beginning that their habit was dangerous."[67] This tendency would be reversed in the moral economy. The use of pharmaceuticals that can harm no others, such as "quack" cancer cures, should be allowed, to preserve individual choice and to allow terminal patients to feel they are not helpless. Antipornographic laws and abortion have arguments for and against, on which I offer no opinion here. The moral economy will just have to decide on them.

The third group, regulation of economic activities, requires more detailed attention. In earlier chapters, I have argued that many social goals, such as affirmative action, will best be achieved by the classic liberal market and not by government regulation. I have also argued that environmental protection is best achieved by requiring individuals to purchase their abuse of air, water, forests, and the like from nongovernmental agencies dedicated to their preservation and to pay full price. Here I turn instead to other kinds of regulation.

Zoning and Building Restrictions

Zoning and building restrictions recognize that neighbors have property rights over neighbors' land. Often, however, these "rights" have been exaggerated, in that they reflect the power of the regulators rather than what the neighbors would have agreed among themselves. For example, they may restrict the ability to remodel the interior of one's own home or garage in ways that are invisible to the neighborhood and will not provoke a nuisance. My neighbor built a totally-fireproof house but was still required to put in sprinklers and create an extra-wide driveway, passable to a fire truck, that defaced his beautiful hillside. He should have been allowed to take residual risks himself, such as that his furniture and papers might burn. "Pioneers" who wish to live on farms with outhouses, far enough from neighbors so as not to disturb them, should not be required to put in plumbing. Regulators of these activities exemplify rule number 1 from chapter 2: *power expands until other power stops it.* In the moral economy, zoning controls limiting harmless activity might be appealed to an impartial officer with decision power, who does not require legal training, thus not to burden the courts. Other zoning controls are legitimate, and the classic liberal society should work out ways of distinguishing which is which.

Airlines

Regulation of airlines often occurs to provide service to outlying regions that could otherwise not afford them. Suppose, for example, service from Denver to Mudville, a mythical town two hundred miles to the west, would cost on average $100 per passenger, but passengers cannot afford to pay more than $80. Regulators might require Great Airlines, a mythical major line, to provide the service as a condition for permission to fly the more lucrative route from Denver to Chicago, on which passage costs (say) $400 per passenger on average but for which passengers could afford to pay more, say $420. In effect, Denver-Chicago passengers subsidize Denver-Mudville passengers. With deregulation, competitors for the Denver-Chicago route bid the average rate down to $400, and Great Airlines, with no one to subsidize the Mudville route, drops it. This is roughly what happened with deregulation in the United States. Opponents of deregulation argue that the outlying regions should not have been abandoned to the benefit of richer travelers and the enrichment of major airlines.

Let us suggest a classic liberal alternative. Start with the illiberal idea that all air passengers should subsidize the Mudville passengers, in order to promote wholesome life in the countryside. Let us now apply the mind of an economist, so that noneconomist readers may see how we think. Once the subsidy is agreed, why should Mudvillians spend it on a flight to Denver? Perhaps they would prefer clothing or anything else. If the subsidy is limited to an airline ticket, the welfare of Mudvillians is restored to its level before deregulation. If however it may be spent on anything, their welfare is increased all the more, at no extra cost to those who finance the subsidy. So much for economic thinking. At that point, some might argue that the subsidy, even if available for any expenditure, should be given only to those who would have flown to Denver anyway; others will say it is not fair to single them out for benefit as opposed to all Mudvillians; still others will say that citizens of Leadville, Fairplay, and Buena Vista should be similarly subsidized. Now the situation becomes ludicrous.

So we are led instead to the classic liberal principle. People have a choice of where to live within their means. Those who choose faraway places do so with the expectation of certain advantages and disadvantages. It is not fair for other air passengers to be forced to subsidize them. Indeed, doing so will attract more people to live in these places, increasing the gross subsidy and possibly offsetting the advantages of the peaceful countryside. In the classic liberal society, "you pay for what you get."

Transportation, Telecommunications, Gas, and Electricity

Deregulation in the United States has reduced rates for these four activities by over 40 percent within ten years, according to a study by the Brookings Institution. Earlier, regulators had required customers of services in greater demand to subsidize those in lesser demand, as in the case of Great Airlines for Mudville. Shippers and passengers in areas of heavy railroad traffic subsidized those in less heavy areas; long distance telephone customers subsidized local service, while customers of local electrical monopolies paid rates high enough to preserve the profitability of those enterprises. In 1997, sixty-two countries agreed to open their communications markets to foreign competition, ending local monopolies.[68] With new competition and new technology—communications can be wireless, electricity can be produced in bulk and transmitted greater distances—prices fall, and local monopolies lose out. It is no more necessary to own the high-voltage line to "ship" electricity than it is to own the railroad to ship a product. The line can become a common carrier, usable by many producers. The local electrical monopolies and subsidized customers lose out; after deregulation these consumers pay higher prices, just like the Mudvillians. So we call on the classic liberal principle that each subscriber pays full cost of his or her own consumption. Competition in the globalized economy is already enforcing this principle, whether we like it or not.

Insurance

In the moral economy, the government undertakes no insurance for its citizens. If instead it should provide flood insurance, it would encourage individuals to live close to the Mississippi River, for if their farms were flooded the government would pay. Free earthquake insurance would encourage construction in earthquake-prone areas because government would cover damages. The government may offer information on the likelihood of disasters and urge persons to protect themselves with private insurance or else to live elsewhere, but once again: in the classic liberal society people accept the consequences of choices freely made. That said, a compassionate citizenry should step in with rescue squads and ambulances to alleviate pain and to comfort those who suffer, but ultimately those who have voluntarily taken risks should cover their losses, just as those who drive cars should insure themselves. However, a government might provide assistance where disasters could not be foreseen, such as the sudden appearance of a deadly disease or a meteor. The rule should be: provide help wherever there is emergency and pain, regardless of fault or improvidence. However, if disasters can be reasonably foreseen, citizens should take their potential into account in determining their locations and their insurance. A person suffering a heart attack should be taken to a hospital with no prior inquiry on health insurance, but if afterwards that person is discovered to have neglected the law requiring universal insurance, he or she should pay the bills, with all legal methods of collection applied.

The Power of Regulators

Both western Europe and North America have become overregulated societies. Presidents, prime ministers, parliaments, congresses and other legislatures and regulatory agencies illustrate rule number 1 of chapter 2: *power expands until other power stops it.* Regulations initiated with all good intent—for safety, environmental protection, and equal opportunity—have gone beyond reasonable limits, to invade the decision-making privileges of private individuals and companies. They are supplanting unions, which used to negotiate conditions of employment; they encourage parents to leave children by requiring professional child care; they mandate that in certain ways we all behave alike. For example, "the Family and Medical Leave Act of 1993 . . . requires employers to give 12 weeks of unpaid leave to new parents."[69]That sounds good, but its pernicious effect is to dissuade employers from hiring women younger than menopause, or even to drive out of business employers who could not afford the cost of locating temporary replacement help or of hiring and training less experienced workers. It is well to require unpolluted air and water and machinery that will not kill or maim, but to extend regulations much beyond the requisites of safety and environmental protection not only usurps personal autonomy and individual agreements but it drives firms out of business and causes unemployment. "The best estimate of the regulatory burden, compiled by Thomas Hopkins of the Rochester Institute of Technology, puts the cost of complying with federal rules [in the United States] at $668 billion in 1995, compared with $1.5 trillion in federal spending. Mr. Hopkins's figures are conservative. They include only the burden of complying with rules for which cost studies have been done. Some costs, such as the loss of productivity caused when new regulation forces firms to adjust, are left out altogether."[70] The same study shows that "in 1995 federal regulation cost the American household $7,000 (more than the average income-tax bill, which was $6,000 per household last year)."[71] Economist Milton Friedman shows that if the depression of the1930s is omitted, real income in the United States grew at an average rate of about 4 percent per year from 1869 to 1969, compared to only about 2.5 percent today. "The explosion of government regulation of the economy since the mid-1960s might well be the major factor explaining our poor performance."[72] While most regulatory demands are merely excessive, a few are outrageous, such as a bank in Kansas City being "ordered to put a Braille keypad on a drive-through cash machine" presumably for blind customers who drive automobiles, and the "man who cleared 7,000 tyres from his property [being] prosecuted for destroying a wetland; the tyres had trapped water from a nearby stream, creating several pools which the regulators deemed worthy of protection." *The Economist* goes on:

> Multiple levels of authority produce endless reels of red tape, from the state, county and city governments to semi-autonomous local agencies charged with controlling pollution and other evils. All produce rules which overlap, replicate, and on occasion, contradict one another. [73]

Bovard refers to regulators as a "fourth branch of government," citing how the EEOC "is suing United Parcel Service for refusing to hire one-eyed truck drivers,"[74] though of course UPS would be responsible in case of accident. Another example: "The floors at the sausage plant in Baltimore were wet and possibly slippery, and the worker safety inspector from OSHA did not hesitate to enforce the law. . . . [But] Agriculture Department rules, for obvious sanitary reasons, require meatpackers to keep the floors hosed down."[75]

What power will stop the relentless expansion of the regulators? Citizens *like* what the government is mandating for them—social security, unemployment benefits, parental leave, and so on—but they have not calculated the costs. The result, as in Europe, is governments that have to be conscious of costs because they disburse them, but a citizenship that has lost the moral constraint of paying one's own way—hence, strikes and protests demanding the impossible. Three long-term outcomes appear possible before a reasonable move is made toward the moral economy, if it ever is. One is a 180-degree swing, with a general revulsion against regulation per se, so that even beneficial regulation will be abandoned, a victim of the overzealous demands of regulators and the vicarious power of their citizen-supporters. Another is social breakdown, to wreak havoc upon the distributional coalitions that Olson has written about. The third is that businesspeople will ignore regulations and produce on the informal, or shadow, economy. For example, "on the streets of the Sentier district [in Paris], a thriving labour exchange has sprung up. Employers hire workers when they need them, without obligations, for about Ffr50 ($9) an hour."[76] Friedrich Schneider, an Austrian professor, has estimated that one-fifth of gross domestic product in Belgium, Italy, and Spain, and one-seventh in Germany, is produced in the shadow economy. As this continues, greater compromises may be worked out and new institutions formed, so that the world may swing peacefully and democratically into the moral economy, or something like it. As consumers become increasingly aware of the advantages to them of deregulation, political pressure in favor of it will be increasingly exerted on any country's legislative body—one more step toward the moral economy.

Taxes

In most of the world, throughout most of history, the rich and powerful have taxed the poor and weak of whatever they have produced above the minimum necessary for subsistence, and the proceeds have been spent primarily for the extravagance of the elite and for war. The poor thought of taxes more as robbery than as sums paid willingly for services rendered by governments. This principle has not much changed in the less developed countries—most of the world today—where tax evasion and loopholes for the rich combine with corruption and where "essential" services such as telephones, roads, safety, and public order—scantily supplied and poorly maintained—are treated as second-ary to filling the pockets of politicians and maintaining an extravagant military machine. The four principles of taxation cited universally by economists—fairness, clarity and certainty, convenience, and efficiency—were enunciated by Adam Smith in 1776.[77] They arose out of the diffusion of power in the West, which occurred also in Japan, but not much in the rest of the world.

Taxes in History

In the seventeenth century in France, Jean-Baptiste Colbert described the art of taxation as "plucking the goose so as to obtain the largest amount of feathers with the least possible amount of hissing."[78] Some snapshots from history illus-trate this principle: in the first millennia BCE and CE in China, direct taxation, mainly in kind, was imposed so severely on the peasantry[79] that in 44 BCE, Gong Yu, imperial counsellor, said that taxes "drove parents to infanticide."[80] He also wrote that taxes caused "people [to] abandon primary production and chase after secondary occupations."[81] "Up to very recent times the peasant who rented his land paid 40-50 percent of the produce to the landowner, who was responsible for payment of the normal land tax."[82]As late as 1993, WuDunn wrote of local tax collectors in China who took more than they were authorized by law: "Whatever the peasants have, they take…excessive tax burdens have led peasants to commit suicide, according to Government documents and news reports."[83]

Centuries earlier, taxes levied by Septimius Severus (emperor, 193-211 CE) to supply the Roman army "caused lasting hardship to the taxpayers and in the end . . . virtually wiped out the middle class of society."[84] During the Byz-antine rule in Italy in the sixth century CE, "the crushing weight of direct taxa-tion . . . finally destroyed the class of smaller owners and favoured once again the concentration of estates in very few hands."[85] In the Ilkhan Empire of Per-sia (1256-95), "taxes were levied 20 to 30 times a year, [and the collectors] by using the basinado and torture . . . collected abundant wealth."[86] "Such was the extortion practiced by officials that on the approach of the tax-collectors the peasants would leave their villages."[87] In all the Mongol conquests, taxes were "simply the maximum conceivable degree of exploitation. There was little pre-tence that in Mongol eyes their subjects had any justification for their existence except as producers of revenue."[88] During the reign of Ivan IV ("The Terrible") in Russia (1533-84), the chief magistrates "'fed' off, or derived their income from their locales by retaining a portion of the court fees and taxes they col-lected. . . . it was . . . incipiently predatory, for appointees were more or less expected to recoup whatever losses they had occurred elsewhere in the service

of the grand prince."[89] In the early seventeenth century in Russia, "the asses-
sors realized that if they entered the amount of land really under cultivation,
the peasants, already impoverished, . . . would be completely ruined by the
taxes they would have to pay. So they deliberately falsified their returns by
reporting much land actually under cultivation as empty."[90] Peter the Great
(tsar, 1682-1725) "was prepared to accept any suggestion which seemed likely
to bring in extra money...until experience taught him that ruined peasants pay
no taxes."[91] In the Ottoman Empire in the sixteenth century, the needs of war
increased the tax burden "so that the lot of the peasant population became quite
unbearable."[92] In the eighteenth century, only in towns "does the cultivator
seem to have produced a surplus not wholly absorbed by forced sales or payments in commutation thereof, taxes, dues, and gratuities."[93] In nineteenth-
century India, "high tax rates on precarious tank-irrigated land prevented re-
pairs from being done . . . because rebuilding a broken tank . . . would trigger
exorbitant tax hikes [and] tax rates discouraged farmers from digging wells."[94]

Power Diffusion and Taxes in Northwestern Europe and Japan

In northwestern Europe, by contrast, the power-diffusion process enabled the
middle classes to hold the king and nobility increasingly in check, over centuries, beginning with Magna Carta in England (1215), or perhaps earlier, continuing as the Estates gained power vis-à-vis the princes in Germany, and cul-
minating in the French Revolution in 1789. As in Europe, peasants in Japan
rebelled and bargained their way up from crushing taxes. In the seventh century they "groaned under the heavy burden of taxation."[95] Shogun and daimyo
of later years reserved lands of church and nobility free from taxes, but armed
uprisings put some limits upon peasant taxes.[96] In the nineteenth century, the
Japanese tax system was rationalized and modernized in ways similar to the
European.[97]

   The great cultural shift, from the concept of taxing as much as the citizens
can bear, for the benefit of the rulers, to the concept of taxing according to the
means of each, for the benefit of the total society, is virtually confined to the
more developed areas. Little if any discussion of the Smithian principles is
heard in less developed countries or of any analogous principles arising out of
their cultures. So, we turn now to more developed areas and the concept of
fairness. Taxation according to means would imply only income taxes and/or
property taxes, but even the more developed areas are riddled with sales taxes,
excise taxes, value-added taxes, social security taxes, unemployment taxes,
and many others, mostly regressive, in that the poor pay more in proportion to
income than the rich, and mostly "hidden," in that they become embedded in
prices, and consumers are unaware of them.

Capital Gains Taxes

Should capital gains be taxed just like other income? The argument in favor is that investors conceive of capital gains and income similarly: they decide between investments on the basis of how much they will gain, whether by interest and dividends or by capital gains. Henry Simons, a well-known professor and tax authority at the University of Chicago six decades ago, argued that capital gains and ordinary income were similar; both should be taxed.[98]

The argument against is that a capital gains tax is unfair. Fairness requires that persons in the same position with respect to income (or some other reasonable quality) should be taxed similarly. Capital gains arise mainly from two causes: (1) inflation, and (2) undistributed profits. (1) For inflation: Suppose John Smith buys a house for $100,000; all prices rise by 100 percent, so he sells the house for $200,000. He has gained nothing in real terms, for he will have to pay $200,000 for another house or indeed for anything that would have cost $100,000 at the time he originally bought the house. (A minor exception: relative prices may have changed.) He should not pay a tax on what he has not gained. (2) For undistributed profits: the corporation has already paid a tax on the profits; therefore, the capital gains tax, effectively a second tax on the same profits, is unfair. (So also are taxes on dividends, for the same reason.)

Some argue that capital gains should not be taxed because they are not ordinary income. Rather, gross domestic income (GDI) is identical to gross domestic product (GDP); they are opposite sides of the coin. Employees and investors earn an aggregate money income (GDI) equal to the aggregate money value of their product (GDP). Capital gains, by contrast, are increases in property value arising out of trades. If Mary Jones sells her house to John Smith for $100, then a year later Smith sells it back to Jones for $200, then a year later it is resold to Smith for $300, then a year later back to Jones for $400, in each year a capital gain of $100 accrues to the seller; yet it is the same house. The same is so for securities. Smith buys a security for $100 and later sells it to Jones for $500; Smith has a capital gain of $400, but it is the same security. No new product has been created. If one argues that only real income from real products should be taxed, there is no room for a capital gains tax.

Yet this argument may be spurious. Suppose a machine is built for $1,000. For ten years it depreciates at a rate of $100 a year and then is replaced, not by an identical machine but by one five times as productive. (It differs from the Smith-Jones deals, in which the house each year is no more productive than the last.) During each of these ten years the company charges $100 to capital consumption allowance (depreciation), which is deductible from profits though it is not a cash cost in that year. Based on the greater productivity of the machine ten years later, the company has a more valuable asset, for which it has paid no greater cost than that of the first machine. The incremental value might be construed as "product" even though it has never appeared in the national product accounts and has cost the company nothing more than the $1,000 (spread over ten years) paid for the old machine. The increment is nevertheless reflected in the company stock, which shows a capital gain. That capital gain might reasonably be deemed "income," on which a tax would be as fair as any other income tax.

To me, the principal argument against a capital gains tax is none of the above—neither that they are similar to other income and hence fair nor that they are different and hence unfair. Rather, a capital gains tax distorts investment. The tax is levied only at the time an investment is sold. (There is no other way). In order to postpone the tax, investors tend to hold on to assets longer than they should. An efficient economy requires a smooth flow of investments from less profitable to more profitable opportunities. This flow is hampered if investors are reluctant to shift because they will have to pay a tax. In the United States, if an investment is held until death, it is passed on to the heir with no capital gains tax, and the heir is presumed to acquire it, for later capital gains purposes, at its value at that time, known as the "tax basis." It might be subject to inheritance tax, but only if the total estate exceeds a certain amount. If the would-be inheritance tax is lower than the would-be capital gains tax—as it often is for persons of moderate wealth—investors are encouraged to hold investments for the rest of their lives, when efficiency would call for shifting them, in response to profitability, from one asset to another.

To summarize: capital gains taxes should be repealed not because they are unfair but because they create inefficiency in investment. An increase in personal income taxes, to cover the government's needs, would be the fairest way to compensate the government for the loss of revenue from capital gains taxes. The undistributed profits of corporations should be included in stockholders' taxable personal income.

Property Taxes

Like income taxes, property taxes are based on ability to pay. Presumably, the rich person—with more property—is taxed more. Usually, however, only real property is covered. Since real estate is taxed but financial assets are not, the investor is encouraged to buy the latter more than the former, and once again the choices are distorted. Taxation of financial assets, however, fails the test of convenience: reporting and enforcement would be costly and open to loopholes.

Taxes in the Moral Economy

All the above considered, the moral economy will probably choose some combination of income and sales taxes. Set these as high as may be necessary to cover justified government expenditures. If the capital gains tax is repealed, the personal income tax may be increased to replace it. Corporate profits would be imputed to stockholders, who would pay personal income tax on it whether it is distributed or not.

Some have argued for a flat income tax, with a high exemption. Say the first $40,000, or other amount, of income is untaxed, so the poor are exempt. Income above that amount would be taxed at a flat rate—17 percent to 23 percent has been proposed, with no deductions. This kind of tax makes sense, for its simplicity and effectiveness, but there is no reason why it may not alternatively be graduated, say 10 percent on the first $20,000 above the exemption; 20 percent on the next tranche, and so on. Some have argued that higher taxes on the very rich deter the investment that brings prosperity, while others argue that higher taxes for the rich are more fair.

All taxes distort the economy in one way or another. The income tax biases taxpayers toward leisure and away from work; the sales tax biases them toward saving and away from consumption. The sales tax is regressive, in that it hits the poor more harshly than the rich, relative to their income. (The poor spend a greater percentage of their income on consumption than the rich). Which is chosen depends on one's biases, for the condition of no bias is impossible. *The Economist* and the Cato Institute favor value-added and/or sales taxes to encourage saving, which would not be taxed. These classic liberal organizations are, however, interventionist in their willingness to override public preferences by official action to promote saving over consumption. My own bias is toward income taxes on grounds of fairness and the regressiveness of sales taxes, but the moral economy might make a different choice.

The income tax may have negative brackets, for redistribution of income. Poorer people may receive money from the government (negative income taxes), while richer people pay taxes. Negative income taxes should be sufficient to keep poorer people housed, clothed, and fed but not great enough to discourage work. They might eliminate the need for subsidized housing and food stamps. The negative tax should diminish in absolute quantity as recipients earn other income, but never so much that the net income after tax is lower than before. Always, the tax system should reinforce the market in encouraging work.

Reforming the tax system in the United States is a merry-go-round. Changes of the mid-1980s were intended to delete complexities and remove special privileges. In the 1997 tax reform bill, many were back. Robert Samuelson writes that that tax bill "drowns the income tax system in added complexity. For poorer families, the combination of a new child tax credit ($500 in 1999) and the earned-income credit may prove baffling. There will be five special rates on capital gains (28, 20, 18, 10, and 8 percent) and four different holding periods (one year, 18 months, and two separate periods of five years). The bill creates at least three types of new tax-free savings accounts."

A Theory on Why Tax Reform Occurs Every Few Years

Surely the public does not like facing a new tax law every year. Surely they do not like to support a whole industry (tax accountants) that alone understands the rules and changes. Surely they do not like to fill out new types of forms annually. Why, in a democratic society, do taxpayers put up with this? Why do they not vote for representatives who will simplify the tax structure, and maintain it that way once for all? I propose a theory in four parts.

First, in the bundled agenda of democracies, citizens vote on issues that mean most to them, such as tax *rates*, women's rights, environment controls, health care, and "family values." Compared to these, a simplified tax *structure* does not swing many votes.

Second, for legislators, filling out tax returns is free (except their own). They can make them as complex as they like, and the taxpayer—not the legislator—pays for reorganizing accounting systems and compiling the data.

Third, Parkinson's law applies to legislative bodies: work expands to fill the time available. Unlike competitive businesses, the number of parliamentarians is determined by "fair representation," not by the smallest number needed for a task. Although Congresspeople always appear busy, their number depends not on the tasks they must perform but on the number of states and Congressional districts.

Fourth, legislators enjoy their power. They make changes of little social value—such as many different capital gains rates and holding periods—the way a chess master moves pawns across the board, enjoying the same thrill and challenge.

Until these conditions change, we will suffer tax reforms every few years. In the moral economy, on the other hand, power will be divested to nongovernmental agencies, while corruption and regulations are curtailed. Consumers will make choices that government now makes for them. Then tax rates may be cut, and representatives will experience less thrill in playing their games.

The main virtue of the moral economy lies in its cultural acceptance that neither power nor wealth may be concentrated anywhere, either in government or in private corporations. Billions of positive-sum moves, decided on by millions of people who take responsibility for their actions and who insist on their autonomy, while also caring for the less fortunate through welfare agencies and income redistributions, mean a *better* society.

Chapter 9
Education and Religion

Both education and religion in the West are, or at one time were, dominated by the state. Religion broke its bonds in approximately the eighteenth century; education will probably do so, for much the same reasons, in the twenty-first. In the late Middle Ages, it was widely believed that all persons in a given society should have the same religion. Today, it is widely believed that a single way to teach reading, writing, and arithmetic in the public schools is "best" for everyone. Which way—phonics or whole language, mathematics by rote or by problem-solving, creationism or evolution, own history or other history, native language or national language—is much debated, just as the choice of a uniform religion was much debated earlier. In each case—religion in the Middle Ages and education today—it was/is physically possible for some persons to choose one way and others another. Yet in each case a dominant elite believed/ believes that it possessed/possesses the ideal way for all, which all should be required to adopt.

The kinds of knowledge and morality, and the manner of teaching them, lie at the crux of the debate on education, just as they did with religion three centuries ago. This chapter projects that by the end of the twenty-first century, citizens of the West will see no more reason for uniformity in these ways of public education—subjects taught, manner of teaching, required achievement, and the like—than they do for religion—Protestantism, Catholicism, Judaism, Islam, Buddhism, or other. If the history of education follows that of religion, school will be separated from state just as church has been in the West, and with that separation individuals will choose their schools according to their beliefs, just as they do their churches. In the classic liberal tradition, truth in education—like other truths—evolves in the market place of ideas and not through decisions of the local school board or a ministry of education.

Education

In the moral economy, "public" and "private" schools are merged, and schools may be for profit or nonprofit. Any student will have access to any school or university for which he or she qualifies, and some school or university will always exist for students regardless of qualifications. How these principles will be implemented and financed is explained in this chapter.

Education and Culture

Like religion before three centuries ago, education has always been directed toward creating or preserving the culture that the dominant society wants. In a military society, education is for war; in a religious society, it is for church or monastery; in a medieval society, it is mainly for the nobility, who learn war, falconry, and chivalry. In a male-oriented society, women learn needlework and home economics. In a politically minded or nationalistic society, education teaches the current political fads or nationalism. Only in a society that values science and human creativeness is education founded on universality, open-mindedness, unbiased research, and factual truth.

The education department of each government tends to demand a history that puts one's own nation into a heroic or at least laudable perspective; few governments are willing or able objectively to confront the sorry elements of their countries' pasts. They may also demand a history that will bring more votes for the party in power, as when George Pataki, governor of New York, passed legislation to introduce the Irish potato famine of the 1840s into the city's school curriculums.[1] Why not the many famines in India and Africa?

History supports these propositions. In the early Han period in China (206 BCE-9 CE) the bulk of the people were to be kept uneducated, but state schools were created for the sons of officials; mathematics courses were designed to measure the sizes of fields and facilitate taxpaying.[2] Secondary education in Rome in the third century CE "was directed toward the elimination of all causes of discontent that might prevent the maximum exploitation of all classes to serve the state and pay its enormous taxes."[3] St. Augustine of Hippo (354-430 CE) believed that the Roman system ought "to be preserved to maintain a literate church."[4] As the Roman schools collapsed with the empire, Benedictine communities established schools, libraries, and *scriptoria.* "Their attitude toward learning was almost entirely functional . . . [for] the dissemination of the Biblical-patristic tradition . . . Such an attitude precluded the monastic church from becoming a center of creative thought."[5] King Alfred (r. 871-899) improved education in England so that the people could read his pronouncements.[6] Medieval scholasticism began in Europe as an attempt to organize, sort, and classify existing knowledge so that "barbarians" might better become Christian. It led to endless controversy on whether the dialectic method—arriving at "truth" by reconciling opposing arguments—would lead to the same "truth" pronounced by the Scriptures. Thomas Aquinas (1225-74) taught that the truths of faith and those of experience as presented by Aristotle were consistent with each other. In Turkey of the fifteenth century guilds and dervish orders enunciated rules of behavior by which learning was "to be acquired through service and through prolonged association with the master rather than as a rationally ordered body of knowledge that could or should be propagated through a pedagogical process."[7] Peter the Great (r. 1682-1725) trained Russians "so that commerce and industry would contribute to the military and political strength of the nation."[8] For Frederick the Great of Prussia (r. 1740-86), education "was to make people better fit for the performance of their work and was not designed to carry them beyond their station in life."[9] In nineteenth-century Russia, education was directed toward skills, as a means to industrialize the country,[10] rather than toward independent thinking. In Iran, the overthrow of the shah in 1979 shifted education abruptly from the western style favored by the shah to the Islamic favored by the imams.[11] Before black government in South Africa, students of all colors were taught that history began in 1652. Nelson Mandela and the fight against apartheid were not formally mentioned.[12] In Turkey today, Ataturk's "philosophy of statehood, Kemalism, is required reading in schools, universities, and military academies."[13] These are but a small number of observations found universally in history, that education is designed to serve the religious, political, military, or scientific thought of those in power.

Even today, when people are sovereign in the West and Japan, their vicarious power is directed toward a uniform educational model to which all students are expected to subscribe—with universal standards—instead of a liberal market in which students and parents may follow the education of their choice. This principle reflects the belief that only an elite will set optimal standards, which will not emerge from the free choices of the citizenry—exactly the opposite of the classic liberal view.

Humanism and Education

With the advent of humanism and dominance of science, in northwestern Europe and Japan of the eighteenth and nineteenth centuries, education became increasingly directed toward discovery, creativity, open mindedness, and academic freedom. The change in Europe came partly from the Reformation, where liberal education was called on to create doubt of the Catholic Church, through "humanist educational forms, which encouraged critical scholarship and a degree of independent judgment in Protestant schools."[14] "The humanists exercised particular influence in Germany through educational reforms carried out in cities under Protestant auspices."[15] But the movement was not confined to Protestants. Jesuits taught "philosophies which emphasized human reason and ethical freedom in contrast to divine omnipotence."[16] The French Revolution stressed freedom of thought in opposition to royal dominance. The Institut National promoted "the philosophe's idea of a rational social science grounded on the analysis of sensations and ideas."[17] Humanism took a different form in Japan, where "the samurai kept alive the ideal of training in *both* the military and civil arts. He thereby remained true to his calling and his sense of cultural identity as a Japanese." This in turn led to "a diversity of intellectual inquiries within the realm of moral philosophy, political economics, and history."[18] Whether northwest European or Japanese, the humanist model was both old and new—old in the sense that it followed the universal rule that education conforms to the social mode proclaimed by leaders and new in that that mode was new. This is the model to which Western education still aspires today.

But it is under challenge. Educational institutions throughout the centuries have been battlegrounds for rival cultures. The struggle in our century is between those who favor academic freedom, creativity, and unbiased research and those who see education as a tool to sensitize students in favor of desired goals such as "multiculturalism," preservation of environment, redistribution of income and care for the poor, religious dogma, armed revolution, or peace. Political infiltration is far greater in less developed areas—where the humanist movement has been bypassed—than in the more developed. Children learned revolution in the Sandinista schools of Nicaragua;[19] in Peru the guerrilla organization "Shining Path" (Sendero Luminoso) infiltrated schools, making them a "decisive battlefield."[20] The political philosophy of the Inkatha movement has become part of the curriculum in Zulu territory in South Africa.[21] My own students at the University of San Andres (La Paz, Bolivia, 1960) participated eagerly when we talked about social revolution but became listless as I lectured on national income accounting.

In the United States, accrediting agencies have delayed recognition of universities, not always on the basis of inadequate libraries or poor scholarship but also for insufficient affirmative action or "incorrect" political positions.[22] American universities have been rightly criticized for overemphasizing national culture compared to others, but the movement known as multiculturalism has overstepped scholarly bounds to depreciate American culture and to praise other cultures by teaching "facts" known to be historically untrue, such as that Greek culture originated in Egypt and that Cleopatra was black.[23] D'Souza argues in favor of high-grade multicultural literature, including both Western classics and the Upanishads, Confucius, the Koran, Tales of the Genji, and others of similar quality. Instead, he says "multiculturalists" have emphasized bad literature with shaky political content.[24]

Bloom has attacked universities for turning from constant or universal truths to emphasize trivial ones and popular culture.[25] The editor of the *Stanford Review* ridiculed a Stanford course on "Black Hair in History";[26] another such course is "The Madonna Phenomenon" at the University of Colorado.[27] A professor in Dennison University wrote that she will look at student papers that disagree with her with a more critical eye than she will those she agrees with.[28] When I asked students in my course at the University of Colorado in 1998 whether they had ever written on an examination something they did not believe, in order to receive a better grade, sixteen out of twenty-two raised their hands. Windschuttle has attacked the popular idea that "objective truth is an illusion and that history is nothing more than a fancy kind of literature: a sort of fiction with footnotes."[29] William Bennett, secretary of education, has denounced campus radicals for tending to see the university as a "fortress at war with society."[30] The National Academy of Scholars and the American Academy of Liberal Education resist politicization of the universities, wanting to return them to creative thinking and unbiased research.[31]

When a state-appointed panel recommended that New York schools should place greater relative emphasis on the roles of nonwhite cultures in American history and life, two historians—Arthur Schlesinger and Kenneth Jackson—objected that "the report encourages students to identify more with their specific racial and ethnic backgrounds than with the themes and influences that unite Americans."[32] Neither side was advocating choice for its own sake.

In 1997, it was reported that Japanese thirteen-year-olds outperformed children all over the world in mathematics and science except those in Singapore, South Korea, and the Czech Republic.[33] At the same time, Japanese educators were concerned that American schools surpassed their own in their attention to superior students, thus encouraging creativity and individualism. Which is right? Why not allow this question to be answered by individual choice of schools?

Choice in Education

In the moral economy, parents and students who do not like modes of teaching in one school will choose another. The "best" methods of education (if there are any) will be the ones that survive, not those that school boards or education departments decree.

The debate on choice in the United States focuses on five issues. The first is benefit/cost: whether choice in education—through a voucher system, magnet or charter schools, or other means—will improve the academic achievements of students more, per dollar spent, than the present system. The second is whether public funds (taxes) should be paid for private education, especially if it overrides the boundaries between church and state. The third is whether choice will divide the nation, with an elite attending private schools and the remainder left to decay in public schools. The fourth is whether students and their parents do indeed favor choice—polls are divided on this. Finally, persons with vested interests, such as teachers' unions, try to defend their positions, while others try to enhance theirs.

The moral economy will take a different perspective, that choice itself possesses intrinsic value. The elite should no more define the education that the public consumes than they should specify baskets of food that their neighbors will eat. All five issues have their counterpart in the grocery store. Will the citizenry have more healthy food if the government decides what they should eat? Should public funds be paid for food for the nonpoor as well as the poor? Will the nation become divisive, between healthy people who eat their vegetables and unhealthy ones who prefer junk food? Does the public at large *want* to choose its food? Should the vested interests of the junk food union be protected? These questions are ridiculous for food—which is more important to life than education—but they assume great moment when applied to education.

Complaints increase against public schools in large cities. In an editorial whose message is echoed in Washington, DC, Chicago, Los Angeles, and other large cities, the *New York Times* wrote about local conditions: "The city has known for years that it had too few classrooms and that too many schools were actually losing space because of leaky roofs, crumbling walls and antique heating systems."[34] In Compton, California, parents filed a lawsuit in 1997 "asserting that classrooms in the state-run district are so dilapidated and school management so inept that the students are being deprived of a basic education and are at an increased risk of injury."[35]

Other complaints include low-quality instruction, violence in schools, lack of discipline, and truancy. "Employers say that one-fifth of American workers are not fully proficient in their jobs, and they express a lack of confidence in the ability of schools and colleges to prepare young people for the workplace, according to the first national survey ever done by the Census Bureau of hiring, training, and management practices in American businesses."[36] The National Committee on Teaching and America's Future, a nonpartisan panel of governors, educators, and business leaders reported that "more than a quarter of newly-hired teachers enter their classrooms with inadequate teaching skills or training in their subjects."[37] "Business executives say about 37% of their work forces lack math and writing skills, according to a poll by Olsten Staffing Services, Melville, New York."[38] In an age of the highest gross domestic product per capita ever, when expenditures on education have grown yearly, in real terms, many public schools have been unable to use them effectively.

Curiously in a "free" society, the main theme is still to decide which of many models is "correct" and to apply it to all schools, possibly with national standards specified. Increasingly, however, parents are seeking alternatives, such as home schooling, vouchers, and magnet and charter schools.

Two studies were done of elementary school pupils in the first school-voucher program in Milwaukee. The first showed that they did no better than public school students. The second study, criticizing the first for not using comparable subjects in the control group, found that pupils using vouchers scored higher in mathematics and reading than those in public schools.[39] A Harvard study of vouchers in Cleveland, issued to low-income students, found both that students and parents were pleased with the system and that the scholastic achievement of students was greater than in the public schools.[40] Charter schools, such as Noah Webster Academy in Michigan, established under state laws to allow schools formed by individuals or groups outside the school bureaucracy, are advancing in several states,[41] although it is too early to show with what success. As of January 1996, 246 charter schools had been established in the previous five years nationwide.[42] In Uxbridge, Massachusetts, vouchers are paid to parents to buy books and supplies for home teaching. In Baltimore, a public elementary school that scrapped the citywide teaching curriculum in favor of the privately generated Calvert system, reported that students "routinely performed up to 40 percentage points higher than their predecessors in reading, mathematics, and language tests."[43] Baltimore also contracted with a private agency, Education Alternatives Inc. (EAI), to manage its schools, but the contract was ended when a University of Maryland study showed that although EAI schools were cleaner and better managed, they cost 11 percent more per pupil than public schools, while students scored no higher.[44] However, the Edison Project, based on for-profit schools, is reported doing well. At one such school, with 320 on the waiting list, students are "excited by extras like computers in each student's home, Spanish classes that start in kindergarten and the availability of extra tutoring,"[45] all at the same per-pupil cost as in the public schools.

Strangely, one powerful agency that ought to be advocating choice has opposed it. The American Civil Liberties Union (ACLU) blocked funding of charter schools in Michigan, arguing in court that the state constitution prohibits aid to private or religious schools.[46] Apparently, the ACLU believes "liberty" is defined by how government budgets are spent, not by whether people have liberty of choice. It forgets that "public funds" were taken from citizens under duress—that is what taxes are—and that the constitutional question is up for interpretation. The other side argues that parents who send their children to private or parochial schools are discriminated against, for they pay for public schools as well. Ohio has given vouchers to parents to send children to religious schools.[47]

Suppose the moral economy does initiate diversified schools and citizen choice. How many, how large, what size classrooms, and above all, how will they be financed?

Financing Education

In the moral economy, those who receive education in one generation pay for that of the next. Competing loan funds, privately established and lending at market interest rates, finance any person to attend the school or university of his or her choice and acceptance, from elementary through graduate school. Any student may advance as far as his or her ability allows. Repayment replenishes the fund for the next generation.

Who would invest in educational funds? While no legal source should be precluded, a promising possibility would be "socially-conscious" mutual funds. Such funds already allow for savers wishing to shun tobacco, liquor, or war-related investments. But these funds are negative—where not to invest—and have sometimes yielded less than market returns. What could be more positive, more socially conscious, as well as financially rewarding, than a fund to provide loans at market rates to aspiring students?

Any student of the appropriate age, who is persistently turned down by any school for whatever reason, may bid greater amounts for acceptance at a given school or university.[48] For example, if the normal rate were $10,000 a year, a "difficult" student might bid a higher price, say $15,000. Surely there is some market price at which difficult students would all be accepted by some schools or universities, which would use the extra tuition to finance the extra attention they need. This extra tuition might be payable by the students concerned, borrowing from an education fund, if their difficulties were the results of their own actions, for example, problems resulting from "goofing off" instead of studying or from committing crimes or taking drugs. The possibility of having to pay more for school might deter antisocial activities. Or it might not, but in the moral economy the individual takes responsibility for his or her actions.

On the other hand, for students whose handicap is not their fault, the extra tuition might be financed by the required birth-to-death health insurance or by the government. These matters would be decided democratically by citizens of the moral economy, who are already culturally attuned to seeking ways of private involvement to avoid government power and paternalism. Alternatively, a difficult student might opt for a special school privately established for his or her needs. Therefore, no prospective student is denied an education, and no school or university would accept more difficult students than it believes it could handle. Required attendance and truancy laws may apply up to a certain age, say sixteen.

Educational loans are like home mortgages. Drucker writes that "it would not be difficult to shift paying for a college education from the 'front end,' when students have no money and next-to-no earning power, to a later period when their incomes are already sizable and rising fast."[49] One is not expected fully to pay for one's house at age twenty-five but may pay the mortgage with earnings over the next twenty or so years. The same principle applies to educational mortgages, except that a house can be repossessed if the mortgage is not paid; education cannot. Therefore, educational borrowers may be required to pledge future payroll deductions or to take out insurance against default. Students may elect to repay in equal installments, in lump sums, or as a percentage of lifetime earnings, the election being made at (perhaps) age sixteen. Thus no student is deterred from a life of service at low salary because of the need to repay. Different interest rates may apply to the different commitments.

The Federal Direct Student Loan Program in the United States already allows borrowers the option of repayment according to their income after graduation but bears the flaw that any balance not repaid within twenty-five years is forgiven.[50] This provision might cause the loan program not to pay for itself.

The flaw might be mitigated (if not corrected) by making loans repayable as a percentage of income, continuing until liquidated or during the lifetime of the borrower. Those who take this option but end up with higher than expected earnings, or with windfalls, might have to pay back more principal than they had borrowed.

Since education boosts the earning power of most persons, those who are better educated are more able to repay, and paying for the product they receive, they value it more highly. No student is required to take a loan; those with adequate finances may pay up front. No government funds are needed, not even vouchers, hence no complaints about public money used for private education. Taxes, which no longer include school assessments, are significantly lower than at present, and the tax relief may allow personal investment in the loan funds or in anything else. Some educational loans may require down payments, as do home mortgages, but this up-front expense may be no greater than current tuitions in public universities. Scholarships might still be offered as at present.

In 1997, tens of thousands of German students converged on the capital to complain that "cuts in education have been too deep. Classrooms are crowded, . . . equipment is outmoded, textbooks are scarce, and cuts in government loans and grants that have totaled about one-third since 1992 have left many students without enough money for living costs."[51] The students rejected increased taxes as a way to pay for their education. Needless to say, the means of financing education in the moral economy would have avoided these problems completely.

In the United States today, "zero tolerance" is proposed for students bringing drugs or dangerous weapons to school, a policy that is usually good but not always. The Federal Gun-Free Schools Act of 1994 requires every state receiving aid for primary and secondary education to expel any student carrying a gun to school. Local authorities have passed similar regulations for lesser offenses. Kameryan Lueng, eight years old, was suspended for one month in Alexandria, Louisiana, and required to attend a school for problem pupils because in "show and tell" she had presented a gold-plated pocket watch from her grandfather, with a chain and pocket knife that he had used to clean his fingernails. Knives were prohibited, with zero tolerance.[52] Another pupil was suspended for bringing Advil to class and failing to turn it over to the school nurse. This inflexibility is the product of government finance, which gives governments the power to impose unbendable rules that may do unintended psychological harm in a few cases. Decentralized, nongovernment schools would have been able to make both the rules and the exceptions.

The financing system of the moral economy also helps students who are required by overbearing parents to study (say) religion instead of science, or vice versa, to attend the university of the parents' choice, or to study for the career that parents wish, with family financing being denied if they do not make the "right" choice. Beyond the age of (say) sixteen, the student might take out a loan on his or her own cognizance and be free of parental dominance. Whether and how such rebellious students make peace with their parents is to be worked out personally.

Why has this arrangement not arisen spontaneously in the mainly liberal market of the West, at least for university education? I can think of three reasons. First, up until the past two decades, private loans may not have appeared to be needed as a major source of funding. Higher education for the very poor or for minorities was not highly valued by society at large, and the market for such loans may not have been sufficient to justify them. However, the culture has changed, and the market probably exists now. Second, two decades ago it may have been easier to work one's way through college than it is today. Third, as soon as the market emerged, the government preempted it, with free or subsidized education. Not being able to compete, private funds kept out; mutual funds were not formed. But governments have not been fiscally able to supply the quality and quantity of education they had promised. If this hypothesis is correct, the fact of government loans in the United States and free tuitions in other countries may have prevented the supply of education finance that is truly needed.

Foreign aid for education also presumes that education leads culture, whereas the moral economy presumes the reverse. Whether less developed countries would be better off if foreign-aid resources were directed to higher versus elementary education is widely debated among Western intellectuals and local rulers. Those who favor higher education want to jump-start the culture into becoming scientific, "like us." This will not work, because it reverses cause and effect. Instead, the type of education most demanded is the one that should be supplied. There is ample evidence that in less developed countries, if the choice is presented to all the people and not just the rulers, elementary wins by a wide margin.

Each year Harvard turns down many applicants who—the admissions officers agree—would do quite well at Harvard, but there is not enough room. Some go to colleges they consider equivalent, such as Stanford or MIT or others in the Ivy League. But many find no place at all in the top-tier universities. Why does the market not clear for such universities, as it does for bananas and milk? By the laws of economics, new resources should flow into those activities for which demand exceeds supply. For example, my own University of Colorado could easily be upgraded into another Harvard if resources were available.

They are not, because the state legislature controls them and puts a cap on tuition. Students may not pay for the education they want, even if they have access to funds. Private universities have difficulty upgrading themselves for many reasons, including the competition from subsidized state universities, the prejudice in our society against for-profit schooling, and accrediting agencies that share these prejudices. If education might be for profit, raising funds on the ordinary capital markets, freed from government restrictions, cultural biases, and the prejudices of accrediting agencies; if educational mortgages were available through mutual funds and other sources; and if taxes were lower because government does not support education, then quality education might compete with housing, automobiles, refrigerators, and the like for the consumer dollar. Resources would flow into upgrading universities if that is what consumers prefer, just as they now flow instead into Caribbean cruises. The moral economy is one of free choice. Although limited in total by our means, within that total we should get the choices we are willing to pay for.

Many obstacles stand in the way from education in the present to the moral economy. First, vicarious power asserts itself strongly. Voters want the power to determine—for all persons who cannot afford private schools—the language in which classes are conducted, with or without religion and prayers, whether scientific thinking should be taught instead of intuition and Scripture, the kinds of history and culture presented—one's own or those of other peoples—and more. In the moral economy, no such uniformity is expected. Students and their parents choose schools and universities of different emphases, and the marketplace of ideas rather than vicarious power determines validity.

Second, the public school system is almost sacred in the eyes of many in the West. Belief in the virtue of public education grows out of democratic sentiment of the early nineteenth century in Europe and the United States that schools should be open to all, not just the chosen few. In a society eager to help the poor but unwilling to allow them their choice, the easiest way to universal education was through government mandate, with government choice over curriculum and teaching methods. In the moral economy, the whole concept of public and private schools is changed: private schools have become "public" just as much as "public" have become "private." "For profit" is no longer a damning phrase, but one intended to draw resources to where they are needed. Choice allows competition among schools to provide the education their customers want. Shift to moral-economy concepts requires a shift in deeply ingrained popular attitudes, which will come slowly and only with repeated failures of the public/private system that we now have.

Third, the strongest argument against vouchers and school choice is that the more affluent or industrious would opt for private schools, leaving only poorer students in the public schools. With the merger of public and private and the universal availability of education mortgages, this argument will no longer be valid.

Fourth, in Western society today, education is supplied to some who abuse it by disrupting schools, threatening teachers, or killing their classmates. These students should be required to take out a higher mortgage for their education, perhaps in special schools, until/unless they value education for itself—which some of them may do, as over time they are exposed to educated people and realize what they are losing. (No guarantee, however.) Requiring them to pay directly for their education with loans they will pay back, instead of giving it to them "free," through taxes, will help.

Religion

Religion as a Binding Force

For many centuries in the West—and still today in some other parts—religion has been a force to bind a nation together. It was/is widely believed that only persons of the same religion could/can be trusted to carry on traditions and to cooperate in economic ventures. This feeling is strong in Islamic societies such as Iran and Iraq; it is found in some Christian nations as well, such as Northern Ireland and Serbia; in India between Muslims and Hindus; and to some extent in Israel. It is presumed that the nation would fall apart if too many religions were practiced. In these societies, also, religion has been/is a bastion of power.

Like education, religion follows the culture and does not lead. Protestants were entrepreneurial in Europe not because that was what their new religion taught but because they built into their new religion traits they had already adopted: production, hard work, and trade. Weber to the contrary, Catholics were just as entrepreneurial as Protestants: witness the Fuggers and the Hanseatic League. But the old religion threatened entrepreneurial traits by denying that they were sources of trust and power, which the pope and clergy fought to keep within the church.[53] Just as the Jews—deemed to be moneylenders and economic adventurers—were already anathema to church Inquisitors, so also were Protestant traders and entrepreneurs. As all traders and entrepreneurs (Protestants and Catholics alike) learned to trust each other through trade, and as their wealth brought more power than religion did, they and the old church increasingly fell at odds. This was the climate of the European Reformation, and only after it was long over did diversity of religion become legitimate in the West. This is one reason why freedom of religion is found mainly in economically advanced countries.

Politics and Religion

In societies where religion is free, citizens do not choose their churches at random. Religion often becomes a political statement. Persons belonging to certain churches may tend to support similar political platforms—witness the "religious right" and the "religious left" in the United States, with their opposing positions on abortion, gun control, and other issues. In my own church (unprogrammed Quakers) members are overwhelmingly Democrat. They frequently ask why more African Americans do not come to Quaker meeting, but they never ask why not more Republicans. A visitor from Mars might be astonished at this, if he or she or it had been led to believe that religion on Earth was determined by one's relation to God or to the Spirit of one's choice. Such a visitor might expect that—if Republican and Democrat are equally valid in God's eyes—the membership proportion in any church might reflect the political persuasions of the population at large.

How did the contrary come about?

It began before 1000 CE, when state and religion were closely related if not unified. The Christian emperors did "recognize a boundary—though not a separation—between imperial and priestly functions, between *imperium* and *sacerdotum*."[54] Constantine believed that Christians "alone possessed the universal aims and efficient, coherent organization that, in the long run, could unite the various conflicting peoples and classes of the empire in a single, all-embracing harmony which was 'Catholic.'"[55](The "hol" in "Catholic" has the same derivation as the "hol" in "whole.") "The permanence of the Roman empire was seen no longer as a mere matter of fact, but as an essential part of the divine plan for the salvation of mankind."[56] "The Church in Egypt dominated secular as well as religious institutions and acquired a powerful interest and role in every political issue" in the fourth to seventh centuries.[57] In Muslim teaching, no distinction between *imperium* and *sacerdotum* arose, nor did any "separate ecclesiastical institution, no Church, with its own head and hierarchy. The caliphate was always defined as a religious office."[58] By the fourth century in China, "rulers were appointing 'bishops' to control the church, and the Northern Wei fixed limits on monasteries and their lands."[59] Here, the object was to possess the church's wealth, not to control its beliefs, but the result was the same. In Germany, Christianity "served to raise to a new height the authority of the king—indeed, to transform him from a tribal chief *(dux)* into a king *(rex)* . . . the king no longer represented only the deities of his tribe; he now represented in addition, a universal deity whose authority extended . . . to many tribes."[60] "Never could [the Carolingian Franks] securely hold the Rhine until the Frisians at the lower end of it and the Saxons across it were tamed and Christianized."[61] Tamed, yes, but why Christianized? Because in the eighth century in Europe no ruler could trust a subject of a different religion. What if the subject pretended to adopt the religion but did not truly believe? He or she would be frightened into "knowing" that God's wrath would descend on the untrue. Preambles of early-eleventh-century constitutions carried the words, "He who resists this power resists the Order established by God." The image was that "the social body . . . is the body of Christ. To break its unity is to mutilate Christ."[62]

Separation of Church from State

The first major break between church and state in Europe came, not with the Reformation, but with Gregory VII's reforms beginning about 1050, which were intended to increase the power of the pope vis-à-vis the kings.[63] This Papal Revolution, a struggle of the pope versus the kings, feudal lords, and lay authorities in all countries of the West, brought three major consequences that helped differentiate northwestern Europe from the rest of the world. First, the lower classes—principally peasants and bourgeois—obtained leverage by supporting one or the other side as part of the power-diffusion process[64] that led to a pluralistic society.[65] Second, the settlement of the investiture controversy, in all countries concerned, constituted compromise of a degree rarely seen before the twelfth century. It was one of the earliest notches in northwestern Europe's centuries-long move toward a compromise culture rather than confrontation. Third, it marked the beginning of the secularization of the monarchy, a process that can be traced henceforward, on through the Reformation.

Even so, the identity of church and state died hard in the West and only over centuries. "Never was there a state," wrote Rousseau in the eighteenth century, "that religion did not serve as a foundation." During the French Revolution, Robespierre agreed: "The unique foundation of civil society is morality."[66] In the Concord of 1801, Napoleon converted the Prussian church into an arm of government.[67] Hegel believed that "all turning points or new ages in world history were initiated by a new stage of religious history. . . . Still, the full realization of a new morality could only be achieved in the state, which, therefore, would absorb the Church."[68]

The Humanistic Church

Yet a strangely different concept of the European Church had also been growing from at least the tenth century. Long before the Enlightenment, a portion of the church was becoming humanistic. "The judging, wrathful God of the Old Testament, which predominated in early medieval religiosity, was coming to be replaced by the loving, self-abnegating son of the New Testament, with his weeping and charitable mother."[69] This quality, enhanced by St. Francis of Assisi in the early thirteenth century, established within the church a tradition toward identification with the poor and the outcast, even to taking vows of poverty oneself. The Cathari, Albigenses, Jesuits with their vows of poverty, chastity, and obedience and the mendicant friars are part of this tradition.

The extremes of the European church—on the one hand wealthy landholder, authoritative pope, kings with divine right, lawgiver, and inquisitor, and on the other hand friend of the poor and participant in poverty—easily led into the church as social reformer, first of itself and then of society at large. In

Latin America, while the church defended the king of Spain, the priest Bartolome de Las Casas defended the peasants, launching a campaign against enslaving Native Americans and pointing out the moral turpitude of colonial exploitation. Whereas Luther preached loyalty to the prince—he condemned the German Peasant Rebellion of 1525—Calvinism "emphasized two elements that were subordinated in Lutheranism: first, a belief in the duty of Christians generally, and not merely Christian rulers, to reform the world, and second, belief in the local congregation, under its elected minister and elders, as the seat of truth—a 'fellowship of active believers' higher than any political authority."[70] For Swiss reformer Zwingli, "politics and the Christian life went hand in hand."[71]

The twentieth century ended the identity of church and state in the West and even outlawed the church in some places, as in Portugal, where all religious orders were expelled in 1910[72] and in Mexico, where the legal status of the church and its right to own property were outlawed in the constitution of 1917; this provision was rescinded in 1991.[73]

The Political Component of Religion Today

The political component of religion raises two dilemmas for the modern West, both of which have their origins in the medieval church. First is the dilemma of religious oversight and societal reform, which harks back to the era in which church and state were one, as so presumably were religious and political life. However, persons who claim the same God or who worship in the same manner today may have vastly different beliefs about secular life. Political positions taken in the name of religion have always threatened a divisiveness that might challenge the spiritual realm.

Here we find echoes of the division of the church—no matter in which century—between defender of the *status quo* and transformer of economic and political institutions. While pope and much Catholic clergy today stand for property rights, fulfillment of contracts, and obedience to law, radical priests have supported land confiscations, violation of unjust contracts, and civil disobedience, especially in Latin America. Did the same God guide both the papal Inquisition and St. Francis of Assisi? Does the same God guide the pope and the radical priests today?

Throughout Latin America, thousands of "basic Christian communities" have been formed by Catholic clergy and laity under the banner of "liberation theology," to "raise the consciousness" of the poor on how they have been exploited by the rich—the elites in government and business.[74] These communities, known in Haiti as the Little Church, supported President Aristide, so that after his overthrow in 1991 the military government attempted to shut down their newspapers and to kill their supporters.

Second is the dilemma of revealed truth versus scholarship, which harks back to the medieval debate on scholasticism—truth direct from God, through the priesthood, versus the truth of Aristotelian logic, which St. Thomas Aquinas thought he had resolved. Today "religion can be an obstacle to economic growth, as when clerics rather than the markets establish a just price for goods or declare a certain interest rate to be 'usurious.'"[75] Economists debate the minimum wage, affirmative action, welfare reform, and other issues. If churches take sides on these issues because of a divinely revealed truth that supplants scholarship, they may unthinkingly do harm if they are wrong.

Perhaps the greatest contribution of religion to the social economy is as bastion of a moral behavior that may have been developed in the marketplace but is preached by the church. "Religion provides a means of internalizing the rules of proper market behavior."[76] This role too is at least ten centuries old. In the moral economy religion will probably continue to play this role and to display these controversies and quandaries, just as it has in the past. But citizens will have choices, as they do now in religion and—perhaps—ultimately in education.

I prefer research-based answers challenged by intuition but not formed from intuition alone. I am for academic freedom over "political correctness." I favor a religion founded on spiritual values that welcomes persons of all ethnic origins and all political persuasions. I stand for education that encourages unbiased science, exploration, and creativity. I favor both religion and education that teach honesty, politeness, listening, and respect for the minds and bodies of all persons. However, no one can compel these cultures; they can arise only out of citizen choice.

Chapter 10
Morality and Values

Globalization of the economy will demand a shared sense of morality that is far from agreed upon today. People and organizations the world over must understand each other, communicate with each other, and trust each other much more than they do now. Let us consider three categories of behavior: *morally required, morally neutral* (may be done or not), and *immoral.* Export and capital restrictions, violations of intellectual property protection such as for patents and trademarks, trade in land mines and nuclear weapons, are morally neutral in some societies and immoral in others. Import restrictions are not immoral anywhere today, though in the moral economy they would be. Will economic morality converge the world over and, if so, how? Will all the legislatures of all the different nations pass compatible contract, labor, and other laws, or will these come about by international agreement or not at all?

Economic morality changes over time and is different in different places. Slavery, piracy, executions for minor offenses, flogging and torture, the stocks all are now immoral in societies where they once were morally neutral. Unfortunately, torture is still deemed morally neutral in many societies today. Will changes in world morality take place the same way that changes have in the past?

Economists argue that world prosperity depends on sound economic policy, but usually they do not distinguish between policy achieved democratically or through dictators. I agree with that, but this book goes further: the durability of sound policies depends on their not being imposed from above but on the morality of masses of people and their agreement to abide by rules they themselves have composed, for their own mutual betterment. What creates this morality? What creates a Sue Sumii, who died in 1997? Although not a *burakumin* herself, she spent most of her life defending this little-heard-of group of Japan's untouchables, enough so as to rate an obituary in *The Economist*.[1] What creates a Martin Luther King Jr. or a Mother Theresa? The world does not need to be peopled by saints such as these, but it does require citizens who deal fairly with each other, do not discriminate by ethnic origin, gender, religion, and other traits, and who negotiate and compromise instead of crushing opponents with superior power. Such citizens exist; indeed, they are found in large numbers everywhere. Why everybody is not like them is the main topic sociologists should be studying today. Since the universe of morality is too big for us to contemplate, this chapter confines itself to the economic, or the morality of doing business.

Why do people voluntarily obey rules when each individual would gain by disobeying if he or she is unlikely to be caught? Why do we tip servers even if we will never return to the same restaurant? Why do automobilists dim their lights for approaching vehicles? Upon reviewing the many social scientists who have studied this question, Ridley writes: "Those groups in which cooperation thrived were the ones which flourished and, bit by bit, the habit of human cooperation sank deep into the human psyche."[2] In northwestern Europe and Japan, in medieval times, serfs and landlords cooperated because neither had the power to defect. This is the point I argued in *Centuries of Economic Endeavor.*

Let us pose three theories of economic morality. The *theory of unfettered morality* would argue that economic morality evolves in a free market in institutions. Two or more persons decide to conduct business in a new way, say by electronic transfer. Others observe them and copy them. The idea spreads. Contracts are made on the new basis. The actors—following prisoner's dilemma—behave properly because they expect others to do so. Eventually—at a dividing point no one can identify clearly—respecting these practices becomes morally required. The *theory of activist morality,* which is also consistent with a classic liberal society, accepts the theory of unfettered morality but argues further that as the new morality spreads, regulation is necessary to prevent some from taking advantage of it as "free riders." For example, the new morality might require safety regulations in factories, maximum hours, restrictions on child labor, and the like. While many—even most—employers might accept these principles as moral obligations, they would be at a competitive disadvantage vis-à-vis free riders who kept their costs down by not implementing them. Laws are necessary to bring computer hackers and free riders into line.

Each of these theories contrasts with the *theory of interventionist morality,* which has recently become popular in Western societies. It argues that morality will evolve at a greater speed if an elite part of the population propels the rest along by laws requiring them to behave in some desired way. Courts in the West increasingly have assumed that they are purveyors of new morality. It is presumed that businesses are mainly opposed to the changes and must be forced into them by law, as through affirmative action. This theory is problematical because the laws perceived may not conduce to the morality desired and because that morality may prove wrong in the long run. Economic morality, whether beneficial or not, is probably not advanced in a durable course when a small group (whether an elected legislature, a feudal lord, or an army general by coup) can compel the nation or the world into new ways of doing business that have not been accepted by the society at large.

The nineteenth century was the "age of reform" in Britain and in much of the West. Gregg describes the British reforms in detail: of factory, mine, workshop, health and housing, the end of the poor law, with "a comprehensive Act . . . consolidating existing Acts concerning the relief of the poor," and education.[3] All these reforms conformed to the theory of activist morality. While some businesses opposed them, others supported them, and they certainly did not drag down the economy. By contrast, the welfare state of late-twentieth-century Europe and affirmative action in the United States follow the theory of interventionist morality, in that they reflect the actions of political groups pledged to require others to adopt the reforms and pay the costs, which the reformers themselves usually do not have to pay.

Values

As morality forms in one setting, it spreads to others that are similar. Freedom from dictates of the king in the Middle Ages spread to the idea of freedom of trade and freedom of slaves, finally becoming a loosely-defined *value* called "freedom." The value of "do unto others" implies that actions one would wish for oneself ought to be applied equally to others. Each action is an element of morality; the encompassing idea is a value. Equal treatment for (say) African Americans has become moral in white cultures—at least verbally so; it is often not practiced. The idea spreads to women and minorities other than African Americans, and ultimately "equal treatment" for all citizens becomes a value. With some exceptions, it does not yet include foreigners. Values have vaguer boundaries than morals, but they are essential guidelines to the spread of morality.

In the moral economy, citizens hold freedom as a value. But the liberal market holds no values; it is a tool. Some say that the liberal market holds "profit" or "accumulating wealth" as values. That is not true. The market is like a pencil sharpener, which does not hold the value that pencils ought to be sharpened. Rather, it is a tool, to be used by those who would sharpen pencils. In this book, I argue that the liberal market is the most efficient tool, compared to intervention, socialism, and the welfare state, for achieving whatever kind of society we value, including a compassionate one.

Interventionists and classic liberals often hold stereotypes of each other. "Those who call for environmental protection do not care about the welfare of loggers" is a stereotype held by critics of environmentalism. "Those who value markets do not care about the welfare of the poor" is a stereotype held by many interventionists.

The latter stereotype is expressed in the following statement, which reflects a misunderstanding of economics, if not of values as well:

> Americans do not want market forces to prevail exclusively when it comes to such matters as health care, education, housing for the homeless, food for hungry children, and a helping hand for the blind, the mentally ill, and other Americans who cannot help themselves.[4]

This paragraph suggests that only through sovereign dispensation do health care, education, and the like come about. The moral economy rejects that stereotype, accepting however that the government may have to subsidize these products for the poor, but only for the poor. The willingness to spend large resources on these matters may be a value, but the tools through which to spend them—liberal market or sovereign dispensation—do not hold values.

To understand how morality may evolve in the future—such as the morality of providing a higher quality of education than we now have or of caring for the poor better than we now do—let us consider two elements of morality that have evolved into values in the West and Japan through a free market in institutions: respect for human rights and conflict resolution through negotiation and compromise.

Respect for Human Rights

Over 9,000 Argentine citizens disappeared in the "dirty war" of the 1970s. Two decades later, even as this book is written, the mothers of university students, wanting to know what became of their children, march around the Plaza de Mayo, in front of the presidential palace in Buenos Aires, demanding that the government reveal what they believe it knows. I too walked around that Plaza, though on a different day, because I wanted to tread the same ground as those mothers. In 1995, a retired naval officer, himself an admitted torturer protected by an amnesty law, told the media that he had participated in the mass executions. Weakened by torture, prisoners had to be helped on to an airplane, where they were stripped, drugged, and dumped into the ocean.[5] Shortly thereafter, the military officially admitted they had tortured and killed political prisoners. Hundreds of reports of sadism and torture in this our "enlightened" twentieth century have been reported in verified investigations by Amnesty International. By far the greatest number is in less developed countries.

When—if—social scientists investigate the matter, they will likely discover that human rights become more respected in a liberal market, but not completely and not in orderly fashion. In this section, I abbreviate as "cruelty" the most intense kinds of purposely inflicted suffering, both mental and physical: flaying of bodies, rape and murder, dismembering live people until they gradually expire, cementing prisoners alive in dungeons, the rack, and the whole array of machines we have come to associate with medieval times, especially the Inquisition.

Four Categories of Cruelty

Let me suggest four categories of cruelty. First is the cultural cruelty associated with lesser development. Northwestern Europe, Japan, and the populations descended from them were far more cruel in their less developed centuries than they are today. The greater respect for human rights, and therefore the decline of cruelty, in the West is often associated with the Enlightenment of the seventeenth and eighteenth centuries. However, a similar decline occurred in Japan, whose "Enlightenment" was less dramatic and less heralded. I will argue that the increasing cooperation associated with trade and economic growth is the main cause of this greater respect for human rights.

Second is the cruelty of the individual sadist, out of keeping with the times. Ivan IV "the Terrible" of Russia (r. 1547-84) lived in an age when cruelty was commonplace, but he was exceptionally brutal even by the standards of the time.

Third is the cruelty associated with intense ideology and high authority, which may occur anywhere, regardless of the degree of economic development. Man-made starvation in Russia in the 1930s, in which millions died, the Holocaust in Germany, murder of abortion doctors in the United States, "ethnic cleansing" in Bosnia, and Islamic fundamentalism fit this type.

Fourth is the cruelty associated with modern, impersonal war, in which nuclear explosions and saturation bombing are deemed justifiable to conduct the war more efficiently and save the lives of one's own troops.

In the first three types, the perpetrators often knew their victims as persons. Studies of the Holocaust reveal that the scientists and doctors of the Nazi death camps led double lives: they were educated, family men and loving fathers in one life, cold-blooded torturers in another. This anomaly is explained by their fervently holding a set of beliefs defining the "victims as an evil group who pose a tangible threat to the social order."[6] An exhibit that toured Germany in 1997—"War of Destruction: The Crimes of the German Army, 1941-44"—presented pictorial and written evidence that ordinary German soldiers were proud to have indulged in the killing.[7] In fact, soldiers in all wars are proud of their killing and manifest that pride in some manner, for example by putting emblems on their airplanes to commemorate each enemy plane downed, each human pilot kille

The willingness to obey authority was tested in an experiment in the United States by Stanley Milgram in the early 1960s, which showed that "obedience . . . can lead otherwise ordinary people to inflict pain on innocent victims. Research subjects administered what they believed was a painful shock to another subject, actually an actor, despite his protestations and screams. For most subjects all it took was the authoritative assurance by a white-coated researcher that it was necessary to use ever stronger current."[8]

The second, third, and fourth types of cruelty have changed little with economic development, except for the technology to implement them. In this section I ignore them, not because they are any less cruel or less worthy of concern, but because we direct our attention to the first type: cruelty associated with lesser economic development. Reading the examples that follow, one wonders how people can be so unspeakably cruel to fellow beings whom they encounter face-to-face. Was there—is there today—no sense of morality to mitigate such cruelty?

The Cruelty Associated with Lesser Development

I have collected hundreds of examples of cruelty and violations of human rights in less developed areas, including a number from Europe and Japan of earlier times. This is not the book to publish them, though I hope their causes and relationship to the wider society and economy will some day be studied rigorously. Here are a few examples from my file:

"Farm slaves [in ancient Rome] were to be worked to the limits of their endurance and to be sold when they were no longer productive. . . . Incorrigible slaves were to be prodded to a place of execution, flogged and hoisted and nailed to a beam and left to strangle."[9]

The Spanish Inquisition, with unspeakable horrors in the fifteenth century, was inflicted mainly upon *conversos,* descendants of Jews who, by converting to Christianity earlier, had avoided being expelled from the country. Inquisition documents state that these descendants had confessed to secret practice of Judaism, for which they were tortured. In a meticulous study of the period, Netanyahu argues persuasively that these documents were falsified: the victims were successful holders of public office—administrators, judges, bishops, and noblemen who had created enemies along the way. "Blood purity" *(limpieza de sangre)* was called on to do away with them through torture.[10]

When supplies became short during the siege of Rouen in 1418-19, the French evacuated twelve thousand "useless mouths," hoping the English would let them pass. "But although there were old men and nursing mothers among the groups driven forth from every gate, the king [Henry V] ordered his troops to herd the pathetic exodus back into the ditch, to die slowly from hunger beneath the winter sky and unending downpour. It rained continuously during their weeks of slow death. . . . 'one might see wandering here and there children of two or three years old begging for bread since their parents were dead. Those wretched people had only sodden soil under them and lay there crying for food—some expiring, some unable to open their eyes and not even breathing, others as thin as twigs.'"[11]

The treatment of convicts transported from Britain to Australia in the eighteenth and nineteenth centuries included daily lashings—sometimes one or two hundred to a single prisoner—that lacerated the skin and left the victims bloody, after which salt water would be poured in the wounds to increase the pain. Long hours of difficult physical labor while encumbered by heavy irons, days in frigid water or solitary confinement, and other tortures were designed to make potential criminals fear the terror of transportation. These abuses diminished during the nineteenth century and were abolished by 1860.[12]

In 1976, the Pol Pot regime in Cambodia "launched a massive effort at social change, in the course of which most urban dwellers were forced to relocate in rural areas under conditions of such brutality that upwards of 2 million were estimated to have perished."[13] Torture and sexual abuse of prisoners are reported as routine today in Turkey, Egypt, and Algeria, among others.[14] In Ethiopia, during civil war in 1985, villagers from "the northern highlands [a supposedly hostile area] were forcibly moved to the south," presumably into areas of richer soil, but they were left there without homes, implements, or other means of survival. About 100,000 died.[15] Death squads eradicating those suspected, often without proof, of opposing the government have been active in Brazil, Guatemala, El Salvador, and other countries.

In 1996, Human Rights Watch charged "that thousands of children have died in China's state-run orphanages from deliberate starvation, medical malpractice, and staff abuse."[16] Apparently these were abandoned children, mostly female, that the state did not want to support. The Chinese government assertion that the deaths were accidental is belied by the quantities of official documents, death certificates, and gruesome photographs smuggled out by doctors and older inmates. The proportion of deaths was so high as to make accident an unlikely cause.

We would like to think of this behavior as confined to tyrants, under whom compassionate masses suffer and object. Yet when condemned criminals were tortured under Roman law—healed wounds were torn open and treated by doctors so the torture might continue—fascinated crowds watched.[17] Ancient and medieval warfare was conducted by ordinary soldiers who murdered their prisoners with no second thoughts. "Such practices reveal a signal indifference to human life and suffering," wrote Marc Bloch about Europe.[18] When the Romans destroyed Carthage in 146 BCE, they killed all the men, took the women and children into slavery, and strewed salt on the ground in the belief that so doing would turn it barren. In medieval England, "reports describe travellers being attacked with knives, shot with arrows, struck on the head with pole-axes, dragged into churchyards where their toes were cut off"[19]—sadism far beyond the necessary in an ordinary robbery. Also: "Audiences demanded horror as well as humour. There had to be bladders of blood, severed heads, lambs for sacrifices, fearsome masks, instruments of torture and full-throated cries of anguish."[20] Even persons guilty of petty crimes would be placed in the pillory, where passersby would hurl insults and sometimes fiercer objects at them. In eighteenth-century France, an entire village might participate in a *charivari*—a cruel display of derision for those who had violated community norms. "In all these punishments the public was supposed to serve not as passive onlookers to be edified by example but as active participants."[21] In Aztec Mexico, families disciplined their children by exposing them "to the chill rigors of a mountain night, lying bound naked in a mud puddle."[22] Mass exterminations of tribal foes are common in Rwanda, Burundi, and the Congo Republic (Zaire) today, and horrors committed by common citizens have been recorded in Angola, Mozambique, and Ethiopia, among others. In Afghanistan, when the Taliban government condemned a couple to death by stoning in 1996—they were lowered into pits with only chest and head showing; it took ten minutes to kill the first one, more for the second—"townspeople came by the thousands to witness a spectacle not seen in Kandahar for decades."[23] In Kenya, a European friend of mine screamed when her purse was snatched; the robber was apprehended, and when she went to the police station to identify him, she found him on the floor, being kicked in the head by police. She wished she had not raised the alarm. Amnesty International reports that even in our own century, one-third of nations use torture systematically.[24] More developed areas are not immune to this cruelty, but where it becomes publicized, as on several occasions in the Los Angeles and New York Police Departments, it is widely condemned and investigated.

Human Rights and Morality

As these horrors have taken place, many have pronounced them morally wrong. Most religions urge compassion for the poor and love for enemies. From observing the behavior of children, James Q. Wilson concludes that human beings possess an innate morality—possibly in our genes—causing us to be considerate of each other and empathetic toward the suffering of others.[25] After all the examples of the preceding section, it is hard for me to agree with Wilson, though I do not doubt the possibility.

Following Dawkins,[26] Ridley has a way out of the dilemma. He suggests that genes are selfish—their main objective is to re-create themselves—but that this re-creation requires cooperation among the bodies that they compose. "Our minds have been built by selfish genes, but they have been built to be social, trustworthy, and cooperative."[27] He goes on to point out that animal and early human societies did and do engage in intense cruelty. However, economic interaction through trade is associated with a decline in cruelty.

The greater respect for human rights, found on the path toward the moral economy, may function analogously to the selfish gene. Genes that do not create cooperative bodies cannot re-create themselves. Successful genes discover that only by cooperation, trust, and loyalty of the bodies that they compose do they become preserved for the next generation. Consequently, cooperation, trust, and loyalty among societies promotes their mutual survival.

Power Diffusion and the Rise of Human Rights

In both Japan and northwestern Europe, greater respect for human rights evolved during the same centuries that the power-diffusion process was advancing. "The earliest protests against judicial torture in the modern world came from the Italian jurists of the thirteenth century."[28] By the 1640s the English were backing away from witchcraft; "many already felt that only those witches whose activities resulted in death should be executed." By that time, "torture was not permitted in England."[29] "An unprecedented wave of humanitarian reform sentiment swept through the societies of western Europe, England, and North America in the hundred years following 1750."[30] Private schools in England advertised that they treated their pupils with tenderness. They might be expelled, but they were not caned.[31] New, more compassionate penal codes were written throughout Western Europe. In France, a royal pronouncement of 1788 ordered that those accused should be considered innocent until found guilty.[32] "Burning at the stake was outlawed by the end of the eighteenth century. Thereafter, little by little the ritual punishments were gradually discredited, freeing judges who came upon rites of derision to declare firmly and unequivocally that they were unquestionably illegal."[33]

Human rights also become more respected in Japan in the eighteenth century, though not so much as in Europe. In 1709 Shogun Ienobu abolished penalties of severing ears, noses, and fingers. They were reinstituted by Yoshimune in 1718, but in 1720 they were again discontinued.[34] A new penal law on Kumamoto feudal estate aimed toward "a new system of more varied and more humane penalties to replace the harsh penalties imposed during the political and social chaos of the sixteenth century."[35] New penal rules of 1790 on Aizu feudal estate, which lasted until 1814, abolished banishment, but allowed beating and imprisonment instead. The death penalty was abandoned but severing noses and ears was restored to replace it.[36] Today, however, Japan is on a par with the West in respect for human rights.

Why did all this happen, more so in Europe but also in Japan, in the eighteenth century? Why not the seventeenth? sixteenth? and so on? Why not elsewhere? Ridley believes humaneness evolves as we learn the advantages of reciprocation that come from trade.[37] Haskell concurs, offering the most likely reason for Europe: the thesis "that the crucial links between capitalism and humanitarianism stem not from the rise of the bourgeoisie per se but from its most characteristic institution, the market, and they are bonds created not by class interest but by the subtle isomorphisms and homologies that arise from a cognitive style common to economic affairs, judgments of moral responsibility, and much else."[38] In simpler language, traders found similarities with each other in the liberal market; employers and employees came to depend more on each other: "the humanitarian impulse emerged when and where it did because of its kinship with those social and economic changes that we customarily denominate as 'the rise of capitalism.'"

I would broaden this reason, to assign it as part of the great change known as the Enlightenment, that took place over Europe. Change happened in a different way in Japan, but in both cases the increased humanitarian sentiment is closely linked to the vision of similarity in another person that arises out of shared economic interests, power diffusion, and economic development. Just as trade engenders trust (see chapter 6), so also does it engender humanitarian sentiment. If this reason is accepted, it will by its converse explain why one-on-one cruelty is so much more practiced in the less developed than in the more developed areas today.

The experience of trade in earlier centuries is also a lesson for more developed areas of the twenty-first century. As power has been re-concentrated in the welfare state and as we have transacted relatively less with each other one-on-one, we become a more litigious society, turning to the courts to resolve those conflicts that were earlier answered in a free market for institutions. Some may feel the government and courts are more just than that market, but those who believe this may be the very ones whose interests, often altruistic, are served through their vicarious power. Although the West or Japan will probably not again become as physically cruel as three centuries ago, nevertheless the division of society into social classes whose grievances are answered only by superior power may—unless it is reversed—be a step in that direction.

It seems that persons become more humanitarian, more compromising, and less cruel as they themselves resolve conflicts instead of leaving their conflicts to the authorities or the courts. While the classic liberal society promotes economic efficiency more than any other, to me its humanitarian aspect—entrenched in its history—is the strongest argument in its favor.

Confrontation and Compromise

Start with the proposition made earlier[39] that the economic development of northwestern Europe and Japan is explained, in part, by the historic abilities of these areas to solve their conflicts more and more by negotiation and compromise and less and less by confrontation and violence. One demonstration of this is the fact that Western governments are now called upon as the conciliators in major world conflicts such as in Bosnia, the Middle East, and many African countries. Unfortunately, many situations are mixed—compromise and confrontation together—so that any judgment is subjective. In the absence of objective definitions, only a series of examples will convey the idea. The examples of the following subsections—drawn from hundreds recorded in my computer—are intended to express the contrasting ideas of compromise and negotiation, on the one hand, and confrontation on the other. A middle set contains elements of both extremes.

Compromise and Negotiation

The landholding unit of eighth-century Japan, known as the *sho,* consisted of farms to which a large number of persons held rights of property, rights to income, and rights of use. These rights were part of the moral order. Decisions on who should do the work and how the product was distributed were clearly specified. Many people shared decision making and profits. Rights could be traded from one person to another.[40]

On the feudal manor in medieval Europe, labor services, fees, duties, and rights were regularly negotiated between peasants and village authorities. "From the bottom up, each echelon was able, on occasion, to demand rationality from its superior."[41]

In the Investiture Controversy of the eleventh and twelfth centuries, the king of England and the Holy Roman Emperor challenged the pope over the right to select and invest the clergy of their countries, and over the pope's rights to oversee church lands and taxes. In England in 1107 and Germany in 1122, the rights to select and invest bishops and priests were divided between king and clergy by agreement. "Ultimately compromises were reached on a whole range of issues involving not only the interrelationship of church and state but also the interrelationship of communities within the secular order— the manorial system, the lord-vassal unit, the merchant guilds, the chartered cities and towns, the territorial duchies and kingdoms, the secularized empire."[42]

In Tokugawa Japan (1603-1868): "Continually discussing, communicating and reporting within a small fixed group resulted generally in a village consensus—as a means of governance and a way of life. And, the impression that remains from working with village documents and vicariously experiencing the underlying activities is one of profound social (as opposed to legal) efficacy in the process; village problems were such face-to-face personal matters and their solutions so consensual and agreeable. . ."[43]

A conflict between two Japanese villages over the location of a dam in the eighteenth century was resolved in a contract, of which the following are excerpts: "Kawashima village and Kami-Ichiba village [entered into] their own earnest negotiations . . . and the mediation of twenty-one other villages [and] have settled the dispute so that the land for the dam will become land transferred to their overlord. . . . But if the dam becomes buried [presumably by a flood or by accretion], it will be dredged out . . . by Kawashima village after requesting Kami-Ichiba village to inspect and while its officials are supervising."[44]

Peace treaties in the major European wars over centuries before the mid–nineteenth included many elements of compromise, in which the negotiating powers conceded some points they had fought for. These included the Treaty of Westphalia, which ended the Thirty Years War (1648), the Treaty of Utrecht, which ended the War of the Spanish Succession (1714), the Treaty of Vienna after the War of the Polish Succession (1738), and the Congress of Vienna, which ended the Napoleonic wars (1815). Most of these compromises resulted from exhaustion, when neither side had clearly defeated the other, except in the case of Napoleon, who had clearly been defeated. Later peace treaties were less compromising, possibly because victory was decisive: those that ended the Franco-Prussian War (1871) and the two world wars (1918, 1945).

A twenty-year civil war in Guatemala, with more than 100,000 lives lost, was ended in December 1996 through the efforts of both guerrilla leaders and military officers exhausted by battle and a persistent, compromising president, Alvaro Arzu. "One reason that the Arzu government has succeeded is because it has been able to build an environment of trust after years of cheating on both sides."[45] It is too early to know whether the peace will hold, but its fact alone is an accomplishment.

The Catholic/Protestant peace agreement in northern Ireland of April 1998 is a masterful compromise, if it works. I do not have space to elaborate, because this book is well into press, and for every line I add I must delete another.

Mixed Situations

In the 1990s, negotiations were begun between Israelis and Palestinians, a Palestinian state has been created, and talks between Israel and other Arab countries take place. They are punctuated, however, by instances of confrontation, as in the assassination of Prime Minister Rabin, the violence by Hezbollah and Hamas, retaliation bombings by Israel in southern Lebanon, and Israeli building of settlements in Palestine.

After seventeen years of dictatorship under General Pinochet, democracy was restored in Chile in 1990. With one exception—a murder committed in the United States for political reasons—the new presidents have agreed to an amnesty for the military, which had committed torture, murders, and disappearances, and to continue Pinochet's liberal-market policies. The greater prosperity that followed these compromise policies contributed to the ability to compromise further.[46] However, the military has declared itself the guarantor of "institutionalism," according to the constitution that it created itself. It has put on several demonstrations of its power as threats in case the civilian government steps out of its bounds.[47]

Confrontation

During the Counter Reformation, when Emperor Maximilian imposed a Catholic priest at Natternbach in Upper Austria in 1625, he sent his representative, Adam von Herbersdorf, to conciliate the Protestant peasantry. Herbersdorf "promised mercy to those who complied and threatened forfeiture of properties, family, and life to those who did not. . . . [However, several who had failed to convert to Catholicism escaped.] Herbersdorf asked the estate bailiffs, village councillors, and parish guildmasters to step forward. . . . He berated them severely for allowing such criminal behavior and concluded that, since the perpetrators had escaped, the bailiffs and council [and others] would have to suffer the criminal punishment instead. These men . . . paired off, and were made to roll dice against each other. Those who lost . . . were bound and executed. Their bodies were left to hang for three days and then impaled on pikes."[48]

In the defenestration of Prague (1618), the Assembly of Protestants threw the regents of the emperor out of a window—they were not hurt seriously—to mark the beginning of the Thirty Years' War.

A growing mutual hatred between the president of Ecuador and his predecessor—refusal to shake hands, wars of words—helped tear the nation in two in 1987.[49]

In modern China, accused persons have been taunted at public meetings, in the belief that "dictatorship means masses' dictatorship: 'if we don't finish them, they will finish us.'" The Cultural Revolution of 1967 pitted young revolutionaries against intellectuals, who were tortured, executed, or sent to farms to learn what it was like to be among the proletariat. Mao stressed contradictions. "Contradictions when perceived lead to struggle, eventual polarization, and resolution in a new unity. Thus one struggle only led to another without any end to the process, which Mao aptly called 'continuing revolution.'"[50]

A sense of black and white, right and wrong, with nothing between these extremes, has permeated the rhetoric of Latin American revolutionaries and the governments they have opposed. While obscenities and insults are known the world over, here ordinary political discourse is laced with *Muerte! Asesino!* and *Traidor!* Established governments frequently cannot communicate with guerrillas. This failure has been felt in Bolivia, Cuba, Colombia, Ecuador, and Peru. It dominated the civil wars of the 1970s and 1980s in El Salvador and Nicaragua and still lurks in the background of uneasy peace in those two countries.[51] In Mexico, the government ostentatiously maintains troops in Chiapas, where revolutionaries shout for its overthrow.

In 1960, strikers in the Bolivian National Mining Company (Comibol) negotiated with the government by radio. The strikers were afraid to go to La Paz for fear they would be arrested, and the government negotiators were afraid to go to the mines for fear they would be hanged, which had been the fate of agents earlier.[52]

The armed forces of Myanmar (Burma) have killed dissidents in uncontrolled fashion during the 1980s and 1990s, forcing students to flee to the jungle, from which they cannot easily return.

Unveiled women, secularist intellectuals, artists, journalists, and tourists have been targeted for death by Muslim fundamentalists in Algeria.[53] Leaders of Islamic fundamentalism have also threatened murder and other violence in Libya, Egypt, Iraq, Iran, France, and the United States, among other countries. (However, these confrontations should not be considered as representative of the religion of Islam, which emphasizes peace and conciliation, nor of the many devout.)

A Hypothesis

The following hypothesis is proposed: Compromise, negotiation, and consensus are the dominant themes in more developed areas, while confrontation, intransigence, and violence are more characteristic of less developed areas, although in each area both types of behavior are found. Wars in the successor Soviet states, the former Yugoslavia, the Middle East, and Africa, human-rights abuses in China, Bosnia, and Myanmar (Burma); religious and nationalist violence in India, Sri Lanka, Egypt, and Algeria; and guerrilla action in Latin America, plus the fact that Western powers are called on to mediate many of these disputes, all lend credence to this hypothesis. The categories are fuzzy, however: some more developed areas take on characteristics of less developed, and vice-versa, for example violence in inner cities in the United States and the peace of 1996 in Guatemala. A confrontation ethic, the hypothesis goes on, inhibits the formation of institutions of economic development, such as good management, neutral trade rules, open banking systems, impartial law, and parliamentary democracy.

As theorists and diplomats of more developed areas are gratified by the surge in liberal-market economics and the increase in incomes in less developed areas at the end of the twentieth century, they might be sobered by the following part of the hypothesis, which is supported by histories in earlier centuries: economic development will be more durable as a compromise ethic dominates confrontation.

In the classic liberal society, morality is established mutually and slowly, transaction by transaction. It is more durable than in the interventionist society, where it tends to come by law and punishment, leaving part of the citizenry disgruntled. In the liberal market, a consumer dissatisfied with a product simply walks away from it, and the provider learns a lesson. In the interventionist society, dissatisfaction leads to divisiveness, victory or defeat, and in some areas to escalating lawsuits. The greater the number of economic activities entrusted to the political process and the courts, the greater the potential for confrontation rather than compromise.

Autonomy: A Moral Precept

Let us recast some ideas from earlier chapters into a framework of morality. From the tenth until the nineteenth century, the peoples of the Western world had gradually wrested power from kings and emperors and placed it, more and more, into the hands of citizen groups. Unfettered morality operated to create the new moral order. The powers taken away from the monarch were assumed by private citizens who adjudicated disputes face-to-face with each other. They created and governed the monetary system, composed the laws, established courts, and wrote the rules for corporate enterprise. Decisions about the economic system were made through negotiations among the merchants who issued the money—their promissory notes—the guilds that set up town courts, the legal scholars who wrote the laws, and the trading companies that created their own bylaws. In the twentieth century, these powers were handed back upward, to Parliament or Congress and to government agencies through the collectivization of goods and services in the welfare state. Once again, unfettered morality led to a new moral order.

The changes had to be, or so it seemed, because there were too many groups to negotiate; legislatures had to decide for them. Besides, some groups were deemed so powerful that weaker groups could not stand up to them; the government had to represent them, or so it seemed. Still, a meaningful feature—face-to-face negotiations—had been lost. We do not usually see the Sierra Club sitting down with logging companies over the right to cut timber on national forests. Instead, each side appeals to Congress and the president for decisions, and they rarely talk to each other directly. Even when they do, the result is not usually a contract between them but petitions for a law. Sometimes lawyers serve as intermediaries, to avoid face-to-face contact by adversaries, just as "shuttle diplomacy" was employed by Henry Kissinger in the Middle East.

Not just the Sierra Club and the loggers, but Sierra Club, loggers, and government. Not just minority and majority groups, but minorities, majorities, and government. By the end of the eighteenth century, governments in western Europe and North America were mainly impartial adjudicator, with no interest of their own in any dispute except over how to govern. By the end of the twentieth century they had an overriding interest: preserving their power, even enhancing it, and defeating their opposition. As more and more activities were entrusted to government—defense, education, social security, unemployment insurance, health care, workplace safety, limiting smoking on private property, requiring special toilets and parking places for the handicapped—with each new one the government gained power, or the ability to decide the fates of common citizens, just as the monarch had possessed that power centuries earlier. In many cases, preserving its power assumed a higher priority than adjudicating fairly, as was also the case with earlier monarchs. Furthermore, finding consensus is more difficult with three parties than with two. In a study of small-claims settlements, McEwan and Maiman found that mediation between two parties brought about greater compliance than when settlement was dictated by a judge.[54] With a whole society moving toward third-party-dictated rather than two-party-negotiated settlements, compliance can be expected to be lessened.

In summary, the monarch, or religious leader such as pope or caliph, had been historically the embodiment of truth and justice, which the "lower-level" populace was advised to emulate. The ruler composed the morality and required the people to follow, to their peril if they did not. With the beginning of democracy, the rules began to come from below. By their behavior and popular legislation, the majority patterned the social morality. Beginning with the late nineteenth century in the Western world, however, a re-reversal took place. The creation of morality was increasingly handed back to the legislature, and the theory of interventionist morality was born again. Presumably this legislature would lead the people—as the monarch and pope had done earlier—devising a type of morality "superior" to the morality that the people would have created on their own. However, social security, unemployment insurance, welfare, health care, and affirmative action are all activities that might have been undertaken privately, based on an unfettered or activist morality taught in families, churches, and schools. Instead, they are more and more coerced collectively, on the supposition that the government is more moral than civil society—a strange assumption in a democracy—and the further supposition that coercion works better than persuasion—a strange assumption for Western Enlightenment.

Personal versus Business Morality

Western civilization is not alone in its schizophrenia concerning profit. On the one hand, profit is an essential element in the efficiency of society—efficiency in the sense of avoiding waste—and in determining the right quantity of goods and services to be produced with the proper technology (see chapter 2). On the other hand, profit is associated with materialism and is contrasted with spiritualism, or the deeper meaning of life. According to much Western morality, profit is good, but seeking it is bad. On the "good" side, Cato declared that "a man was to be admired and gloried like a god if the final inventory of his property showed that he had added to it more than he had inherited."[55] On the "bad" side, three of the four major religions discourage—and in some periods have forbidden outright—the lending of money at interest, on two grounds. One was the immorality of converting money into a greater amount without having worked on it. The other was that of seeking "shameful gain" *(turpe lucrum)*[56] from one's fellow creatures. Christian, Jewish, and Islamic religions have all ordered similar proscriptions. Faced with the impracticality of forbidding usury, since the economic system could function well only with the lending of money, Christian nations adopted a euphemism: instead of usury, they reported something that simply "is between" the lender and the borrower: *inter est.*

In the fifty-fifth anniversary report of my college class, a classmate lamented "the emphasis on greed, with grinning, highly paid CEO's rationalizing the abrupt discharge of thousands of employees."[57] In chapter 2, I argued that the high salaries of some CEOs and the downsizing and outsourcing of businesses are caused by underlying forces. Technology and markets change, so the structure of the firm must adapt. Employees may have to move. CEOs who can manage the change are scarce, so some of them command high salaries. Consumers benefit through lower real prices. Those who decry the "immoral" behavior of business executives would act more constructively by seeking ways to create more CEOs, thus bringing down their wage through greater supply, and ways to help employees make the transition to other jobs.

Businesses must earn profits in order to survive, just as persons must breathe. Corporations are neither moral nor immoral, but the people within them are. The morality of people will evolve "when most people learn, as the Japanese and northwestern Europeans did, that it is good business to be just and considerate toward one's neighbors; to solve quarrels peacefully; to be held accountable for the efficient use of resources (both public and private); and to abide by modes of behavior (or institutions) that have been negotiated and agreed by interested parties."[58] Many business schools in the Western world now offer courses in business ethics, which might include easing the adjustment of the workers who are let go.

Economic prosperity and reasonable distributions of income have resulted from the diffusion of power, more so in northwestern Europe and Japan than elsewhere, and this diffusion grew out of the many positive-sum moves available to many interest groups that negotiated and bargained with each other. Moral behavior depended on no interest group, including the government, attaining an "undue" position of power over others. Each group wanted a monopoly in its own market, but when this became impossible—because of the diffusion of power—they settled for the liberal market. The institutions they formed—the financial system, the legal system, corporate enterprise, and the manner of hiring and firing laborers—became efficient because private costs and benefits approximated social costs and benefits respectively, and they became moral because they were widely accepted. Thus the practice of a CEO earning a high salary is not immoral in Western society if the salary reflects the productivity of the CEO, or the ability to make the firm profitable. A high salary for an ineffective CEO is immoral if he or she retains the position because of collusion of the board.

Western society considers an unregulated monopoly to be an immoral act of the people who created it. Witness the many antitrust laws, and the regulation of public utilities and transport. With advances in technology, however, many former monopolies are becoming competitive. Only two decades ago the telephone company in any city was a regulated monopoly because duplicate wiring in the city streets would be wasteful. The same for railroads, water, gas, and electricity. With new technologies of communication and transport, neither telephones nor railroads are natural monopolies, and it is right (moral) that competition should replace regulation.

Olson, whose writings preceded mine, would not accept the notion that interest groups—which he calls distributional coalitions—may have led to a diffusion of power.[59] He points out that the more stable a society, the greater the number of "distributional coalitions" (interest groups) it will foster, which—instead of balancing power—will concentrate it in themselves, obtaining political preferences, as in subsidies, controlled prices, or market limitations, that would violate the liberal market. Small, concentrated coalitions, such as the professional associations of physicians, lawyers, and accountants, do this regularly, since no one of them is large enough to attract voter attention. Larger interest groups, such as consumers and taxpayers, are discouraged from collective action, because those who would undertake it, such as Consumers' Union, pay a high price themselves for benefits extended to many free riders. Because consumers and taxpayers therefore cannot organize themselves as political forces, they do not bother to understand how they are being victimized by the numerically smaller but politically powerful groups. "If the victims of distributional coalitions even had a faint idea of what was really going on," Olson argues, "they would easily put a stop to it."[60] He suggests that distributional coalitions in stable societies bring about a sclerosis that may ultimately cause the society to lose its vitality—hence his title, *The Rise and Decline of Nations.*

My earlier work, *Centuries of Economic Endeavor,* has a different perspective. It shows first, how interest groups—for example, guilds—brought a degree of economic sociability into medieval society that had not existed earlier; second, how they promoted the concept of negotiation and compromise relative to confrontation; and third, how they tended toward a balance of power without necessarily achieving it. None of this would contradict Olson's thesis, which applies primarily to later centuries.

Yet Olson's thesis is incomplete. Using the power of the market, unorganized groups do have ways to offset the distributional coalitions. While powerful coalitions may swing political action to their advantage, actors in the market may respond effectively though they create no lobbies. As telephone companies, banks, insurance companies, and physicians all try to preserve their monopolies or semimonopolies, consumers will dodge around them, through new telephone companies, health maintenance organizations, banks finding extralegal ways to do insurance business, credit card companies doing banking, and the like. Now, at last, they also have the Internet.

Power is far from optimally diffuse in even the most advanced societies, for concentration in both government and private groups is still a force impeding economic development and fair distributions. A major struggle of the next century will be between those who—to preserve their vicarious power—would take power from private concentrations and hand it over to government concentrations and those who would diffuse power further through a classic liberal society. Morality—which condoned regulated monopolies in one era—is changing to fit evolving realities. Whether the morality of vicarious power or the morality of citizen autonomy will prevail is a big question for the next and succeeding centuries.

Chapter 11
Ukraine—A Personal Interlude

Before me sat forty provincial *(oblast)* planning directors, who faced the task of converting urban property in their provinces from government-owned to private. It was late in 1996, five years after the Soviet Union had collapsed. They wanted to know how private property is handled in the United States.

"Guess what I would do," I asked them, "if I were 25 years old, had a good job, and wanted to buy a house, but I had no money?"

A: "You would work hard until you had saved enough to buy the house." But that would take many years. I replied that I want the house now.

A: "You would ask your friends and relatives to lend you the money." But they don't have it either, or their money is invested elsewhere.

A: "You would go to your employer for a loan." But he doesn't know if I will quit next year.

A: "You would go to the bank." Or an insurance company or (I added) other financial institution. But how do they know I will pay back the loan?

A: "You ask your employer to guarantee it." But he still doesn't know if I will quit. Besides, all his money is tied up in the business.

A: "You ask the government to guarantee it." But if the government guaranteed all loans and had to pay off, that would be inflationary.

A: "You pledge some collateral." But I have no money. What other collateral would I have?

A: "You could give the bank the right to take the house if you didn't pay." Right, but what would they do with the house?

A: "Sell it."

It took nine rounds—count them—of the Socratic method to extract the full answer. After that, we discussed how the bank would sell the house. (How does the real estate market work?) What if the bank got a price higher or lower than the outstanding loan? Would I end up in bankruptcy court? (What's that?) "Does a bankruptcy ruling forgive the remaining debt?" I asked. The wrong answer won heavily, though a few guessed right. (Yes, it would.) Some thought I would go to jail if I didn't pay the debt.

Here were mature, thinking civil servants, about to plan property distribution, who had little or no idea of how the private property market works in other countries. They knew virtually nothing about deeds, title search and registration, title insurance, zoning, and so on.

In four cities in Ukraine (Rivne, Kirovohrad, Zaporizzia, and Sumy) I spoke to similar groups of provincial planners. All my lectures were conducted by the Socratic method, with similar questions and similar responses. Students at the Institute of Management in Zaporizzia wanted to know about public services in the United States. I told them about social security and how much it was helping me, but I had to add that the "fund" had no money in it—the government had appropriated all my lifelong payments and blown them up over Vietnam and Iraq. My social security income comes from the current taxes of children ("baby boomers") born in the years immediately following World War II and not from investments, as the income from private insurance would. The boomers' contributions will dry up when they retire, about 2015. I told them about proposals for government health care, and their almost unanimous response was, "Keep it private. In a few generations the government will fail you, and you will have forgotten how to do it yourselves."

"Why did the Soviet Union fail?" was for private conversations, since this was not a seminar topic. Though I had only a small sample, possibly not representing mainstream Ukraine, the overwhelming response of those I met was a combination of political and economic causes.

Political Imperialism

"We have been occupied by the Russian Empire since 1654, when the Ukrainian Cossacks made a deal with the Russian tsar to protect them from invasions by the Poles, Lithuanians, Habsburgs, and Tatars." "We have been in a cage," a professor at the Institute of Languages, University of Kiev, told me. "Now we are glad to be free." Because other republics also let Moscow settle their quarrels, now they do not know how to do it nonviolently. Their court systems do not work well, for example.

Economic Imperialism

"Central planning is inefficient," I heard over and over. The mayor of Sumy told us how his city had been required by the Soviet government to build a central steam-heating plant to provide heat for all houses in the city. (The same was so for cities all over the USSR.) Steam was piped underground to stations where it met cold water, which was heated by the steam and delivered to the houses. "Grossly inefficient," the mayor said, "so much heat was lost in transit." Another Ukrainian told how Khrushchev had returned from the United States, enchanted with maize (corn) production there, and recommended that farmers throughout the Soviet Union plant maize. Though not required to do so, he explained, many farmers followed the suggestion, whether maize was economic or not, because central planning evokes a follow-the-leader mentality.

Although highly touted as scientific, central planning is often by whim, such as in the two cases just mentioned. Multiply these whims by the millions upon millions of decisions ordered by Moscow, to be undertaken in remote areas that the Soviet government was not familiar with, and we see how the Soviet economy lost productivity and could not meet the demands of its people. (It was, however, highly efficient in the space program and advanced weaponry, because it could command resources and the best talent for activities valued by the rulers).

The economy of Ukraine has slipped greatly—disastrously even—since 1991. Gross domestic product is down precipitously, and unemployment is high. No one can be sure why this has happened, but the dominant opinion seems to focus on two points: economic failure and the hostility of Russia.

Economic Failure

The economy is even more inefficient than before, because no one knows who owns what. The land still belongs to the central government. Collective farms were intended to be divided into private property of the farmers. Instead, each farmer has been given a share certificate in the collective farm. This share may be sold to someone else, but the farm continues to function as a collective. Not knowing whether they own the land or not, farmers are reluctant to improve it. The *New York Times* wrote of a Ukrainian couple who did manage to obtain fifty acres privately. "But for the last two years, as the couple have coaxed higher yields of potatoes and carrots and wheat from their earth, they have been blocked at every turn by the state. . . . the local state farm manager refused to sell the family equipment and spread rumors to undermine them. And farm workers refused offers of employment [from them]. . . . Fearful that private farmers will succeed and eventually supplant them, the managers, mostly stalwarts of the old Communist party, are doing everything they can to preserve their power."[1]

"Ordinary Ukrainians . . . have suffered sharp drops in their standard of living since 1991. Ukraine remains bedeviled by a corrupt and backward-looking political elite dominated by former Communists and socialists. The Government has preferred collectivization to privatization, and snail-paced reforms. . . . About 50 percent of the economy is in the black market, largely because of efforts to evade huge taxes. The total tax on some businesses . . . sometimes amounts to 89 percent."[2]

When I asked Ukrainian colleagues whether these examples from the American press were representative, they told me yes, that the bosses of collective farms act like little princes, who rule over not only the farms but also the local schools, government, and public services. Thus it was under the Soviet Union, and thus it still is today. By their control of farm inputs and outputs and by offering or denying services and privileges, these "little princes" can harass those who do succeed in privatizing, thus deterring others from wanting to do the same.

The Hostility of Russia

Because Ukraine has tended to look to the West, for example toying with the idea of joining NATO, the Russian government has been denying Ukrainians the markets they once enjoyed. Traditionally, Ukraine is both the breadbasket of eastern Europe and an industrial region, with coal, iron, and steel. Before the breakup, they exported all of these to the rest of the Soviet Union, principally Russia. The Russians have now been finding ways to keep Ukrainian products out as political reprisal. Even while I was there, they increased the import duties on Ukrainian products by 20 percent. All this has caused further unemployment and a shortage of foreign exchange.

Attitudes toward the Soviet Union

Those who long for the Soviet Union have misplaced their nostalgia, however. The Soviets were living on their capital: mines, railroads, and other infrastructure were all deteriorating. Consumption of the middle class was sustained only by diverting resources from infrastructure, which was not maintained. So the economic collapse was inevitable and would have come even without the political collapse. To go back to Soviet times would be like returning to a sinking ship because the lifeboat was shipping water. Though the Soviet Union had been touted seventy years ago as a republic of workers, nevertheless power was concentrated in several hierarchies: central power (Moscow) and local power (oblasts, collective farms, factory managers). In each case, orders were handed down by superiors, and except for the limited scope of small, private farms, no opportunity existed for innovators or private investors.

Yet we did encounter some who reiterated the Soviet line. At the Sumy seminar, as we discussed economic aid from the G-7 (governments of seven advanced countries) and the International Monetary Fund (IMF), I mentioned that the aid was given in exchange for Russia and Ukraine agreeing to balance their budgets and privatize their state enterprises. But I have long argued that a Western-style liberal economy cannot be imposed from the top, as the G-7 and IMF want to do. "The rulers cannot force all civil servants to banish corruption and privilege; they cannot force local governments to respect the free market; they cannot force bankers to make loans based on probability of profit rather than personal favoritism; they cannot force local elites to promote competition instead of monopoly; they cannot force businesspeople to cooperate in forming corporations for complex economic activity; they cannot force the governments of all regions of Russia to live in peace with each other—and even less so the other successor states."[3] I wanted to make the point that reform had to be done at *their* level (in the provinces and cities), by *them,* not that of the central government. "Do you agree?" I asked.

To my surprise, they not only defended the rulers in imposing policy from on top, but they disagreed with my premise that the IMF and the G-7 were even giving aid in exchange for reform and privatization. (How can they disagree, I thought? It's right in the contract.) "Then why do the IMF and G-7 do it?" I asked. "They're not *giving* aid," one replied. "These are loans that have to be repaid." True in part, but loans at a lower-than-market interest rate have an aid component (the interest they don't have to pay). They wouldn't buy that idea, however. "The loans are made to put us on the side of the West politically, and to force us to give up our arms." Partly true again, I thought, but not part of the contract. They *have* to privatize industry or they won't get the loan. Disarming and political favor may be in the minds of the G-7, but the recipients don't *have* to do it, contractually.

Then it suddenly occurred to me that I was hearing the voice of the Soviet Union, played back as if on a record. This is exactly what the Soviets used to say about loans to the Third World—they were political. I agreed that such loans were political, but I did not agree with ignoring their contractual element. Finally, my basic idea that the G-7 and IMF were bribing the former Soviet states did not get across, because they had not accepted the premise on which it was based.

After that same seminar, one of the participants asked me about the role of the state in property in the United States. "It supplies the ultimate security," I replied, thinking of protection against robbery, zoning violations, and uncertainty of title. "But that means that the state *is* the ultimate power, doesn't it?" I could see he was pushing me toward saying that the state (anywhere) had to play a dominant role in property, just as it did in the Soviet Union. To him, it seemed, "ultimate security" required that the state dictate how property was to be used, who had permission to use it and who did not. To me, on the other hand, "ultimate security" meant only enforcing the law. I felt he could not understand how ordinary citizens might participate in the use of property through ownership, and therefore he thought the state *must* make all the rules and decisions—in the United States and anywhere else.

These were the only instances in which I felt seminar participants would have wanted to return to the Soviet Union. In the other three cities (all except Sumy) I felt the participants were strongly convinced that state-owned property had failed and were eager to learn Western ideas about the rights and responsibilities of owning private property. The same was certainly the sentiment in the Institute of Management at Zaporizzia.

The remark that has most stuck in my mind was made by my professor/interpreter at that Institute of Management: "All our lives the government has taken care of us, and now that it has failed us, we have no idea of how to take care of ourselves." I wondered whether advocates of the welfare state in the West would understand that lesson.

Chapter 12
The Horizon

Dimensions of the Moral Economy

Eschewing the old expressions of "hawks" and "doves," Thomas Friedman has invented a two-dimensional vocabulary for economic disagreement.[1] Those who favor globalization of the economy—called "integrationists"—are placed at one extreme of the horizontal axis, while those who argue against it—called "separatists"—sit at the other. History is against the separatists, says Friedman, and I agree. On the vertical axis he juxtaposes those who favor government intervention to protect the losers—called "safety-netters"— against those who would not—called "let-them-eat-cakers." The Zapatista revolutionaries in Mexico are separatist/safety-netters, President Clinton is an integrationist/safety-netter, Ross Perot is a separatist/let-them-eat-caker, and Newt Gingrich is an integrationist/let-them-eat-caker.

The moral economy sits somewhere in the integrationist/safety-netter quadrant, but it also lies on a third dimension that Friedman ignored. Those who would protect the poor by determining which goods and services they need, buying these for them, and conditioning their gifts on behavioral constraints lie at the interventionist end of the third axis, while those whose safety nets consist in financial instruments that the poor might spend freely lie at the classic liberal end. Though interventionists differ one from another on particular issues, many of them also seek governmental "gifts" for the middle classes and wealthy as well as the poor, and they would prescribe ways of behavior for all members of society, such as how their children shall be taught to read. The moral economy tends toward the other end of this third dimension.

The Moral Economy in History

King Faruk of Egypt is alleged to have said, on his abdication in 1952, that ultimately only five kings would be left in the world: the kings of spades, hearts, diamonds, clubs, and England. I think he was wrong about England, but only time will tell. The main lesson learned by the kings of Europe and the shogun and emperor of Japan, from the Middle Ages to the nineteenth century, is that after so many centuries they could no longer support themselves by commanding resources from their people. That lesson has not yet been imposed on the rulers of the Third World, who extort resources routinely, and certainly it has not been grasped by the new sovereigns in the more developed countries, the people themselves acting through vicarious power. But they will learn it soon.

In More's *Utopia,* individual interests are subordinate to those of the community at large. All have to work, universal education is supplied, all religions are tolerated, and all land is owned in common. More's thesis implies significant intervention. His Utopia is an island; the moral economy is the world. Yet it is also not the world, for it will not come everywhere at once. If it happens at all, it will come slowly, first in some parts, then in others. It will spread gradually, both in territory and in concept. I do not call it utopia, because utopia (from the Greek, *ou,* not any, and *topos,* place) is a final destination. Utopia is *there,* not—like the moral economy—*how-to-go-there.* Instead, the world will not end in two hundred years, or a millennium, and new perspectives will arise. As the horizon of the moral economy is approached, more horizons will be revealed farther away.

The moral economy is the logical extension of the historic power-diffusion process. Whether it will come about depends on whether that process continues and is spread. The principal characteristics of the moral economy are outlined below. I do not urge that any of them be put into place by government power but instead by agreement among all peoples to honor the rights and feelings of each other and of other societies. Gradually changing world culture in this direction is the task of the moral economy. Anyone who has the power to change society as radically as necessary to reach the moral economy immediately would have too much power.

Separation of the Economic from other Subcultures

The economic subculture in the moral economy is color blind and gender blind. All persons the world over have the same economic rights and privileges, including to travel, seek employment, buy property, and trade anywhere. Tariffs and other trade restrictions do not exist, except to provide safety and protect the environment. However, this universality will come about only in steps: a borderless world is probably the last step in the moral economy, since others must open the way for it. Only when all world citizens all pay their own way— for health care, social security, education, and the like—will the more developed areas be less of a magnet for the rest of the world. Impossible? Since the 1930s the world has not only formed regional arrangements of free trade, which may easily expand to become worldwide, but many trade restrictions and tariffs have been removed universally. On April 18, 1997, Mongolia abolished all tariffs and trade taxes.[2]

Contract law, business law, instruments of credit, banking, and other institutions of an economic nature may differ from place to place or even in the same place in the moral economy, but all are available to anyone. Money may be issued privately, and different moneys compete with each other—just as different credit cards and mutual funds already do—because control over the money supply should not be entrusted to a single, world central bank. Any person has the right to use any currency. Inflation is controlled not by one man or woman but by individuals shifting to noninflationary currencies because they prefer them. While noneconomic subcultures—such as religion, language and ways of speaking, art and music, clothing, home customs, sports, ideas, and much else—are formally distinct from economics, all interface with and are shaped by the common economic culture. I agree with Fukuyama that "economic life is deeply embedded in social life, and it cannot be understood apart from the customs, morals, and habits of the society in which it occurs."[3] While Buddhists and Christians, and people who eat with chopsticks and those who prefer forks, have distinct cultures, in the moral economy they all interface with the same economic culture.

In our present society, champions—such as presidents, legislatures, and negotiating teams—enhance advantages for both themselves and their constituents. In doing so, they restrict production and trade so that world product does not grow to its potential. Observing this, a visitor from Mars might suggest that individuals and enterprises make their own arrangements for trade with each other directly, without the "benefit" of champions. Why not capture that substantial increment, he, she, or it advises, and work out some way of dividing the positive sums? This visitor cannot understand why champions from Washington, DC, negotiate rules for people as far away as California whom they have never seen but not for those in Mexico, or why the government in Beijing should have sovereignty over business in Hong Kong but not in Singapore.

History and culture, not economics, explain how people are "allocated" to champions and why champions favor their own people. However, the technology of the twenty-first century, where transactors may bypass their champions, is likely to countermand the effects of history and culture. Some writers, such as Peter Huber, argue this case. If you don't like the regulations of one country, just choose another. Ultimately, national borders will vanish.

> In the past you had to vote with your feet. Now you can vote with your modem, too. The Web supplies an instant global storefront. . . . Virtual establishments on the Web already offer incorporation in Belize, bank accounts in Switzerland, currency trading in Germany, brokerage accounts in New Zealand.[4]

The twentieth century has seen great progress in breaking the institutional barriers, starting with the reciprocal trade agreements of the 1930s, continuing through the General Agreement on Tariffs and Trade, and ending with the World Trade Organization. Deregulation, privatization, and shifts in decision making from government pinnacles to grass roots are sweeping the world. Obstacles consist of suspicion of not getting fair or maximum value for one's own nation,

political difficulties when some constituents gain more than others, ethnic prejudices, corruption, mistrust, and above all, the clout of champions wanting to
sustain their personal power.

Two ways to overcome these obstacles are available in the twenty-first
century. The new way is communications technology, and the old is negotiations—giving up one's advantages in exchange for the same from others. Together they may lead to the moral economy.

Economics as a Leading Force

The moral economy recognizes what I believe to be historical truth, that economics is a leading force—though not the only force—in determining culture
and politics. Trade engenders trust; it makes friends more than enemies. A
peaceful world is more likely with widespread economic interaction. The history of Europe since World War II is an example. In the moral economy, people
the world over are encouraged to engage in economic interactions with others
in all parts of the world. Tariffs and trade barriers are eliminated.

Trade sanctions are not used. The United States has applied sanctions
against Burma (Myanmar), China, Cuba, Iran, Iraq, Libya, Nicaragua, South
Africa, and other countries that its government has wished to convert to "our"
way of thinking. Historically, however, liberal ideas have been adopted where
trade has prospered, not where it has been prohibited. Besides, sanctions hurt
the very people intended to be helped: the poor and the politically oppressed.
Usually the powerful people have ways to evade the impact of sanctions on
their own livelihoods. After sanctions on Iraq, the Associated Press reported:

> Iraq's health care system has all but collapsed, the World Health
> Organization said, leaving an acute shortage of the most basic medicines
> and supplies. Electricity blackouts have ruined supplies of polio vaccine,
> which must be refrigerated, and diseases that had been virtually eradi-
> cated are reemerging in Iraq, the agency said. U.N. agencies estimate that
> about 180,000 Iraqi children suffer from malnutrition.[5]

International businesses may be the most effective way to spread Western
values and trading principles. Multinational corporations (MNCs) have had
mixed reviews in less developed countries. On the one hand, they have been
charged with stealing land from peasants, quashing unions, cheating on taxes,
bribing governments, falsifying reports on exports and imports, taking profits
out of the country, racism, and more. Where these charges are true, they generally reflect MNCs living according to the rules of their host countries, and the
same sins are committed by local businesses. In chapter 8, however, it was
noted that U.S. corporations are now forbidden by law to bribe host governments, and a recent treaty would forbid this for all countries of the Organiza-

tion for Economic Cooperation and Development (OECD). On the other hand, MNCs pay their workers well; they negotiate with unions and do not quash them as a rule, and for the most part they pay their taxes. A study by the International Labor Organization showed that MNCs in the Third World pay wages, on average, twice as high as local businesses and offer significantly greater fringe benefits, such as housing, schools, hospitals and health services.[6] In the moral economy, MNCs are no longer distinguished from national companies. Their boards, executives, stockholders, and workers will be from all over the world and their offices in many countries, instantaneously connected by computers. Liberal trade practices become widely diffused when enterprises not only are free to cross borders but span them.

If not by sanctions, how would those rulers who violate international community norms or torture and repress their own people be removed from power? Many ways are possible, and the following is only one suggestion: as the moral economy is slowly being formed, one or more international courts with judges from many nationalities might declare such persons to be *anathema* to different degrees, according to their alleged crimes. Anathema to the first degree would have applied to Adolf Hitler. Anyone who brought to a designated court, for trial, a person labeled anathema to the first degree would receive an enormous reward (although less than the cost of a war or even of sanctions) and would, if necessary, be given a new citizenship and new identity. Slightly lower degrees of anathema might apply to rulers who torture their subjects and much lower degrees to those who violate copyright laws. Once called to such a court but failing to appear, a person with any degree of anathema would be denied the respect of foreigners, the ability to travel outside his or her country, and the right to hold assets in other countries—any already held would be frozen—or would be placed under other restrictions consonant with the alleged crimes. Even within their countries such persons would live in fear of being kidnapped. Upon appearance at the court they might be acquitted—or they might not. How many such courts, where, and what about appeals? All that is for citizens of the moral economy to decide. In July 1998, delegates from 120 countries agreed to establish a standing international court to try "cases of genocide, war crimes, and other crimes against humanity."[7] The United States did not join the agreement. Because questions of jurisdiction and accountability remain unresolved, the terms are still a long way from the courts proposed for the moral economy.

The underlying principle is that the punishment is applied to the person who commits the crime and not to the people who suffer under his or her rule. In this way, also, international trade and communications continue unhindered, and the liberal market may be further spread. International law on anathema would have to be carefully specified to prevent abuse, especially for political reasons. It would be applied only when universally agreed by judges of different nationalities and ideologies.

Social Costs and Benefits Equal
Private Costs and Benefits, Respectively

A social cost is any use of resources—natural, physical, or other—regardless of who pays for it or even whether it is paid for financially, while a social benefit is any increment in resources, regardless of to whom it accrues. Private cost represents payments or sacrifices per individual, while private benefits are the income or increase in assets of the individual. In the world as a whole, aggregate social costs and benefits must equal aggregate private costs and benefits respectively, but some individuals may cause costs, or sacrifices, for others, and some may benefit from the actions of others. North has suggested that the tendency for private to equal social costs and benefits person by person is a principal reason for the amazing economic growth in Europe,[8] and I agree. Where on the other hand transactions constitute private benefits to some parties, at no cost to them, or private costs to others, without benefit to them, economic development and economic justice are less likely to occur, and common resources, such as the environment, are apt to deteriorate. Thus the path to the moral economy will be a tortuous one in which the association of private benefits with private costs is gradually negotiated or else achieved through bypassing champions. In simple language, "you pay for what you get" and "if you damage the environment or use resources, you pay full price for them."

The End of Paternalism

Money, which is fungible, is the common way through which all goods and services are routinely transferred. If the citizens of the moral economy wish to care for the poor—and I fervently hope they will—the poor are paid money, so that they—like the rest of us—experience choosing their goods and services and taking the consequences. The one exception is that donors, usually governments, may stipulate the types of goods—such as food, health insurance, and pension plans—on which certain funds may be spent. In this case, instead of money, vouchers are issued.

This degree of paternalism may be unavoidable, since donors do not want their largesse to be wasted. However, recipients may spend the vouchers here or there as they wish, just so long as they are spent on goods of the type indicated (food, health insurance, and so on). The supplier redeems the vouchers for cash through the government or a private welfare agency. Counterfeit vouchers remain a risk, as does counterfeit money today—they may be controlled by electronic vouchers. So also is power expansion a risk. To the extent that regulations survive at all—who gets which vouchers and under what conditions—regulators will try to extend their power as much as they can, by rule number 1 of chapter 2. They must be controlled by countervailing forces, such as citizens' committees of oversight.

The degree of paternalism which the United States had reached by 1997 is exemplified by President Clinton's proposed tuition tax breaks upon his second inaugural: "a $10,000 tax deduction per family for college tuition fees, and a $1,500-per-child tax credit for the first two years of college. To be eligible for the tuition tax credit, a student must earn at least a 'B' average in college and stay away from drugs."[9] Both of these are good objectives, but one wonders whether a government that bribes its citizens to behave is an ideal form and whether the Internal Revenue Service should give students drug tests and process their grades to see if they qualify for the tax breaks.

A polar case of paternalism resulted in financial tragedy in a less developed country, Albania, early in 1997. Citizens who had lost their sense of personal responsibility during fifty years of communist isolation suddenly found themselves taken in by giant Ponzi schemes, in which investors are promised amazingly high returns—say 100 percent a month. The first are paid off with the money from later investors, so the scheme mushrooms, until suddenly the perpetrators leave the country with their loot. "Hundreds of thousands of Albanians, who on average earn $60 to $80 a month, sold homes and livestock to invest in the pyramid schemes."[10] In more developed countries, while the perpetrator would be punished if caught, the response to the victim might have been "it is your fault for being so stupid and so greedy." In Albania, however, violent rioting ensued against the government, which had been the protector of the people for so long that it became "responsible" for any adversity. "If I'd had some warning from the government at the beginning," one victim said, "I might have thought differently. But the government never said anything."[11] (Some charged that the government itself was perpetrating the schemes).[12] Similar Ponzi schemes had already bilked thousands of investors in Russia, Romania, Bulgaria, and Serbia, where governments had earlier monopolized investment, yielding little experience to the people for discriminate choices when the floodgates of opportunity suddenly opened.[13]

Redistributions of Income

Income distribution over time has tended to become more nearly equal in classic liberal societies but not in power-concentrated societies (see chapter 3). In the past two decades, however, many persons believe that distribution has tended to become more highly skewed in more developed countries. This tendency may be a statistical aberration, as was explained in chapter 3. Those who proclaim it, including well-known media and well reputed economists, may be selectively perceptive in their statistics, and the audience that believes it may be as accepting of widely-disseminated conventional wisdom as were those who believed the sun revolved around the earth in Galileo's time. But it might alternatively be true. To the extent that it is, the maldistribution may be related to the breakup of the family, the shift from one-income to two-income families, rich men and rich women tending to marry each other and the same for the poor, the surge in technology, and the globalization of the economy. None of these events demeans classic liberal economics. All of them are likely to run their course, after which the historic patterns of income distribution will probably be resumed.

If they are not, citizens in the moral economy might decide that income distribution is too highly concentrated, and some redistribution is required. This would occur in the event of social disturbances by the poor, or if the richer groups, finding their markets too limited, decide that greater purchasing power for the poor is desirable for all. Once these motivating forces have been active for a century or more, a relatively egalitarian distribution of income may become accepted morality. In a society in which paternalism is already disapproved, and in which the fungibility of money has become recognized as permitting redistribution of wealth without loss of dignity, the sharing of income would be implemented routinely by cash payments, probably through the negative-and-positive income tax suggested in chapter 8. Persons above a certain level of income would pay tax; persons below a certain level would receive it. Each tax, positive and negative, might be graduated.

Every individual is required to carry health insurance, retirement pension, and unemployment benefits in the moral economy. However, these are bought on the liberal market; those that cannot otherwise afford them receive cash or vouchers to help finance their payments. Vouchers rather than cash may be required so there will be no free riders. ("Free riders" are persons who would fail to buy insurance because a compassionate society would care for them anyway if they became critically ill.) Unemployment, health, and other insurance are divorced from payrolls and purchased in separate markets.

Instead of supplying welfare itself, the government finances private welfare agencies, whose success is judged by their performance in getting clients off welfare and in keeping them off. Welfare clients have their choice among agencies that fulfill minimum conditions. Acceptance of training or seeking jobs may be a condition stipulated by the agencies, not by the government. Thus individuals are encouraged by the liberal market voluntarily to remove themselves from welfare. The government pays the agencies to provide for long-term welfare recipients who—for physical, medical, or psychological reasons—are unable to hold jobs, ever—for example, the retarded—and who do not have enough resources of their own. Thus the objections to the U.S. Welfare Law of 1996—which would cut off many deserving persons after a five-year period—are answered.

Government

As at present with national, state or provincial, and local governments, in the moral economy each person participates in several overlapping governments. The size of a government, territory it covers, and number of personnel needed to manage it, are all determined by its functions. Some functions require greater territorial scope than others, so governments may be local or far reaching; an individual may participate in few or many. As in today's democracies, some positions are held by election and some by appointment.

The moral economy is divided into different subgroups from nations, however. Producing and trading groups, environmentalists, labor unions, and others transcend what are now national boundaries. Today's national boundaries and sizes make little sense economically and will become obsolete with globalization of the economy. The European Union represents a tendency in this direction. In particular, sovereignty over land will expire, thus resolving the war-inducing problems of who "owns" Bosnia, Cambodia, Chechnya, Cyprus, Northern Ireland, Kashmir, the Middle East, Tibet, or the disputed strip between Ecuador and Peru. Individuals may buy land anywhere, and if cultures or people of common ethnic origin wish to live together, they need only buy the land.

In addition to providing vouchers for essential public services to those who cannot otherwise afford them, the government supplies other goods and services, such as maintaining public order. Government courts may enforce contracts, but a preferred way is by private adjudication, with the adjudicators being agreed on in advance by the contractors. Any government business that might alternatively function in the private sector is privatized, and the government offers no subsidies of the sort now considered "corporate welfare" and none to agriculture. Rather, these activities respond to the liberal market and the price mechanism.

The government may be one of many suppliers of information, such as economic data and reports on the quality of foods, drugs, and other consumption products where health or other hazards may be involved. It does not prohibit these substances except in extreme danger, or for danger to third persons, or for the protection of children—born or unborn—or others not competent to make their own decisions. Instead it relies on education and the home to induce citizens voluntarily to respond to this information.

Reorganization of government services according to these principles removes much government power that otherwise would lead to economic distortion and corruption. Corruption and power are closely linked. With limited scope of what a legislator or president can do, the incentive for bribery or campaign contributions is diminished. A president or prime minister becomes like the chairperson of a university department who takes his or her turn out of a sense of duty but who has little real power.

It is widely agreed that campaign contributions in the U.S. presidential election of 1996 exceeded reasonable and even moral bounds. Candidates evaded restrictions by using "soft money," or money contributed to their cause indirectly through political parties or other "educational" organizations, which the Supreme Court foolishly ruled did not violate the laws limiting contributions to candidates. The result has been a widespread demand for tightening the laws to include soft money; opponents argue that such laws would limit freedom of speech. The moral economy, however, offers an alternative response. Campaign contributions are offered because politicians have the power to alter the economic or other prospects of special groups. Limit or remove that power, and the motive for excessive contributions is also removed.

Nongovernmental Agencies

In the moral economy, much of what is now government land in many countries—including national forests and parks in the United States—is deeded to nongovernmental agencies such as the Sierra Club, Audubon Society, or Nature Conservancy. Their charters stipulate that preserving the environment is their principal duty, although they may allow the land to be used for recreation, or lumbered or grazed by private interests for market-rate fees, within the limits of good management. Their separation from central government removes them from political capriciousness. What if their boards of directors, although elected popularly, abuse their powers and thwart these goals? Success depends on wide oversight by a willing citizenry and proper values passed on from generation to generation.

Any agency of government—federal, state, or local—that does not achieve economies of management by being associated with other agencies is split off and made into a nongovernmental entity, such as a private, nonprofit corporation. In this principle, government is similar to private business, where mergers are justified only if the combined entity possesses economies of management not available to the separate units. Government agencies differ from each other according to their purpose, product, technology, and operations. Combining their management into a single government does not always make sense, any more than combining, say, a pharmacy with a shoe repair shop.

Environmental Regulations

Environmental regulations are also removed from politics and placed in the hands of nongovernmental agencies. They are worked out through negotiations by scientists, environmentalists, and business and other groups that use or abuse the environment. However, the rights to pollute are owned by agencies charged by their charters with preserving the environment and may be sold in limited quantities by those agencies only. In final analysis, preserving the environment is a matter of personal morality, based on rules that are mutually agreed upon, and not on government direction imposed on people who wish they could violate it. Continued environmental protection, century after century, depends on how children are brought up, not on regulations imposed by one generation upon the next. The dead cannot rule the living.

Education

Education at all levels is conducted by private enterprise and competes on the basis of product quality. Students or their parents choose the schools or universities. These may be accredited by nongovernmental agencies such as the regional accrediting associations for higher education in the United States, which would confer with each other and with the faculty to establish standards. Alternatively, they may ignore accreditation and establish their own standards, which are judged by the liberal market. Students or parents decide whether to choose an accredited school or not, and employers judge graduates either on the accreditation or on the reputation of a nonaccredited school. For example, Yale might decide to split off from the accrediting agency and set its own standards.

No student is denied any education for which he or she qualifies. One or more educational funds, privately established, make loans at market interest rates, which students pay back according to two or more options, such as a regular payback period, as in ordinary mortgages, or repayment according to income earned over a set period or over one's lifetime. Thus no one is deterred from taking a low-income job as a public or religious service just to pay back a college loan. By paying the debt for their own education, graduates finance the education of the next generation, which is therefore not held in thrall to local or central government finance. Schools and universities would receive "difficult" students by being paid more to do so.

Entrepreneurs, Business Managers, and Universities Have Full Power of Decision over Their Activities and Personnel

No one has a "right" to a job in the moral economy, and managers may discriminate in employment for whatever reason they wish. The liberal market is a better means to affirmative action in employment of women and minorities and in access to education than is government regulation. If a firm does not hire a qualified person because of race, creed, color, gender, sexual orientation, or other characteristic not related to employment, that firm is at a disadvantage in a market where other firms hire by merit. A firm that sells in a multicultural world does well to have a multicultural management and employees who understand that world. A university that does not accept students or hire faculty because of ethnic origin, gender, or similar factor will lose out to others that prefer a multicultural environment as a locus for education. Behaving in this manner becomes a moral imperative, not a legal one. Racial and other discrimination will end only when the social mass *wants* it to end. The lesson must be taught in churches, families, schools and businesses, by their behavior more than by their rules. Government regulation forcing citizens to do what they wish they did not have to does not usually change their hearts and minds. On the other hand, any provider of goods and services to the general market is required by law to sell to all who enter the store dressed and behaving appropriately and not to discriminate according to gender, ethnic origin, or similar quality, so that discrimination in serving customers—such as earlier in the U.S. South—will not reappear. As citizens become less ethnic-conscious after a few generations, this requirement will become obsolete.

Sexual harassment may well be a crime in the moral economy, like assault, burglary, or other physical violence. But it is a crime of the perpetrator, not the employer. Penalizing employers with heavy fines for not providing "appropriate working conditions," as is the custom today in the United States, is like fining an employer if an employee pulls an armed robbery. That would increase costs and prices and decrease employment without necessarily punishing the culprit.

Reorientation of Resources for Litigation and Behavior Control

Billions of dollars are currently spent in controlling behavior all over the world. In the moral economy, drugs are legalized and every dollar now spent to prevent Bolivian farmers from growing coca or to seize imported heroin is instead spent on education about the consequences of drugs; every dollar spent on affirmative-action litigation is instead spent on training to improve the skills of persons now deemed unemployable and in diversity training to persuade bigots to change their values. Persons who abuse their bodies are expected to suffer the consequences. A compassionate society helps them when they have destroyed themselves but does not prevent them from doing so in any way other than by persuasion and example.

Whenever a government legislates behavioral standards out of conformity with existing morality, it creates criminals and needs an expensive police, court, and prison system to control them. This is so whether the speed limit is lower than what motorists will adhere to, or liquor or drugs are banned in a society that craves them. Far better to concentrate on changing the morality of people from below than to legislate the ban from above.

Price Control and the Minimum Wage

All price controls, including minimum wages, are abolished in the moral economy. We have no way to compel people to produce goods whose prices do not cover their costs; often such goods disappear from store shelves. When the price of matches was controlled in Kenya during my residence there in 1972-74, the next day none could be found. They were being smuggled into Uganda, I was told. Likewise, we cannot force an employer to hire a person whose work is not worth his or her wage. Since minimum wages apply to only a tiny percentage of the workforce in the United States, increasing them does not benefit the vast majority. Instead, it prevents the most vulnerable groups—teenagers, African Americans, and single mothers—from experiencing their first employment, in which they would otherwise gain the experience to move up to higher grades. To the small extent that a higher minimum wage does increase money wages (if it does at all), it also increases prices, so that within a few years the real wage is the same as before, and the minimum wage "must" be raised again. (Real wage or real price is measured in commodities that can be purchased with the money wage or price.) The moral economy recognizes—what economists already know—that the real price of a commodity, including the wage of labor, is determined by underlying forces, such as productivity, costs, technology, and demand for that product, and any attempt to change the nominal (money) price other than by modifying the underlying forces distorts output by reducing the quantity or quality of a product or the amount of employment, or in other ways detrimental to the economy.

Using data that other economists find controversial or wrong, two Princeton professors—David Card and Alan Krueger—showed that an increase in minimum wages in New Jersey fast-food outlets was associated with an increase in employment, compared to neighboring Pennsylvania where the minimum wage had not changed.[14] Others have challenged the Card-Krueger data as being insufficient and based on improper sampling.[15] While this chapter is not the venue in which to debate the technical aspects, nevertheless one or a few individual case studies, even if properly done, are hardly sufficient to belie the reasonable generality that an increase in price (wage) does not cause persons to buy more of a product (workers).

Antitrust and the Cyber-Shopper

As this book goes to press, the Justice Department and Microsoft are fussing—surely at a cost of millions of hours—over whether Microsoft should have the right to cajole manufacturers into bundling their software with each new computer, as opposed to allowing consumer choice. Specifically, should the Microsoft browser be coupled with Windows, or might the purchaser choose Netscape instead? Is this an expensive tempest in a teapot? (I think so).

Interstate commerce and antitrust laws in the United States were first passed in 1887 and 1890 to regulate or break up "natural monopolies," such as railroads and utilities, and to combat the Rockefellers, who combined railroads with oil. In the twentieth century, the laws were relaxed to allow operations for which efficiency required large scale, or where new technology turned former monopolies into competitors. In the 1990s, however, the U.S. Justice Department has become concerned about firms such as Microsoft, which have grown "naturally," or not through sole ownership of some resource, but which occupy such a large portion of the market that they are virtual monopolies. The choice is grim, between regulation of Microsoft and its ilk by bureaucrats who may know little about the technology, or allowing them to expand to the limit of their markets, "integrating" their products or signing exclusionary contracts that prevent others from coming in piecemeal.

The excitement about Microsoft may reflect impatience. Since capital may be raised on a worldwide market and is therefore not scarce, and since others exist with knowledge equal to Microsoft's technicians, the most likely solution would be to bide one's time until some massive innovator, such as Java, brings together its own group of "geeks" and creates another whole operating system with the size and capabilities of Windows. The consumer who wishes choice in Internet access will choose the total system that offers it. In the meantime, the consumer is not dissatisfied, and—unlike in the monopolies of the nineteenth century— prices are kept low to expand the market. Balance of power among two or more vast companies may lie in the moral economy.

In such a world, Ms. Computer-Wise clicks on Megawhirl as one of many worldwide shopping services. She is asked what product she wants. Reply: computer. A series of questions follows, about brand name, specifications, price range, and other features, including operating system and browser. She might answer any of these herself, or she might reply "You choose"; if she clicks that, she may then ask "Why?" for an explanation of the choice. If she is not completely satisfied with Windows06, she may click Doors08, which is the complete equal of Windows08, or superior to it. She may also click "Advice" on any choice, whereupon Megawhirl explains the advantages and disadvantages of each alternative. If she knows little about her product, she clicks "Beginner" for elementary explanations. Once she has made her choices, Megawhirl scans the world market, to determine where her computer may be bought most cheaply and how long delivery will take, direct from the manufacturer in Zambia or elsewhere. A final question will be "Breakdown on price? (Y/N)." If she types "Y," she will discover how much she is paying for transportation, sales tax, import duties, and the rest. (Once these questions are answered for many purchasers, an understanding of the cost of import duties will dawn on the public, and support will grow for free trade.) Before she signs off, Ms. Computer-Wise asks what alternative products would offer the same features at lower price. She then agrees to a charge on her credit card for Megawhirl's service and turns to select a vacuum cleaner. She might repeat her search with Maxibuy, to compare with Megawhirl's results, or she might not. If she does, next time she will call on whichever served her better. Microsoft is no longer able to cajole computer manufacturers into installing its operating system or browser, not because the government protects the consumer but because the competition outwits Microsoft.

What about Mr. Computer-Illiterate, who has never used a telephone? Intermediate stores will open, where computer-wise people will appear in remote villages to perform these tasks for him. If electricity is lacking, they will use their own generators, solar power, or batteries. One problem remains: sociability. We may not like a world in which every person sits by a computer all day long, communicating with colleagues, fellow workers, pastors and priests, students and teachers only in cyberspace. (Want a Catholic service? Click on Roman or Orthodox. Want a Quaker meeting? Turn off the computer.) We may miss the water cooler, coffee breaks, the huge vault of the church, and saying hello to neighbors on the mall. But we can still have these if we want them. In the moral economy, we will have the choice.

War

The United States now possesses the strongest military capability in the world, "based on the application of information technology to weapons. It involves gathering huge amounts of data; processing them so that relevant information is displayed on a screen; and then destroying targets, at much greater accuracy than was previously possible."[16] This capability is reflected in the eastward march of the North Atlantic Treaty Organization (NATO), which at the time of writing is considering the admission of eastern European countries, an eventuality that Russia finds disquieting. This movement follows rule number 1 of chapter 2: *power expands until other power stops it.* Now that Russia is weak, the West moves into the former Soviet orbit.

Yet the United States and its allies face a threefold hazard. First is the prevalence of guerrilla warfare and terrorist attacks. The second—and most consequential—is that despite fifteen hundred years of technological progress, the political ramifications of *Pax Americana* are not much different from those of *Pax Romana.* The Roman Empire also followed rule number 1, expanding to the point of its weakness, whereupon it collapsed from within as much as from without. The third is the likelihood that other nations will gain the same technology as the United States. If that occurs, say within the next two centuries, the optimal scenario would be a new military balance of power.

However, a worldwide military balance in the twenty-second century may be no more successful than the balance of power of the nineteenth in Europe. Except for the Crimean War of 1853-56 and the Franco-Prussian war of 1870-71, this balance kept relative peace in Europe for only a century, 1815-1914. Likewise, a twenty-first century of peace through balance of power may not be a sufficient bulwark for a world that has speeded up in many senses. It may hold no better than the balance of the nineteenth.

To increase the probability of peace, balance of power is also needed in economic capability, political prowess, education, law, money, and other institutions of economic and political development. While nothing can assure that the world will not dissolve in nuclear holocaust, nevertheless the moral economy is designed to create a multidimensional balance of power for peace.

Cross-Cultural Property Transactions

In the moral economy, anyone in the world will have the right to buy property anywhere else in the world. But what about the meantime? How does a classic liberal society, based on private property rights, confront other societies whose land rights are different, for example communal? Native Americans, Australian Aborigines, and New Zealand Maori are examples. In all these societies, the first encounter was "resolved" by capture of the lands through force. In the United States, peace treaties allowed Native Americans to retain their national rights only on reservations—a land grab of major proportions. Since then, Native Americans have claimed more rights over their lands in courts, but with little success except the right to permit gambling casinos. In Canada, in December 1997, the Supreme Court awarded rights over mining concessions to native tribes, which may therefore be able to claim royalties, but details are yet to be worked out.[17] In Australia, European settlers at first declared the land to have been unoccupied—*terra nullis*—as if the Aborigines were not real people. By the Mabo decision of the High Court in 1992, enshrined in the Native Title Act, these lands were found to have been illegally confiscated and subject to return. The Wik decision of 1997 extended the coverage to pastoral lands.[18] Farmers, sheepherders, and mining companies that now occupy the land would presumably pay rent to Aborigine groups. The issue—who pays, to whom, and how much?—is still in limbo, as it is in Canada, and probably has diminished investment. In New Zealand, the Waitangi Treaty of 1840 allowed European settlers to buy land from the Maori, but claims remained that land was illegally seized or confiscated by the Crown or bought for a pittance under false pretences. Late in 1996 the New Zealand government apologized to the Maori and restored to the Ngai Tahu people a land and cash package worth $117 million.[19] The question is moral more than economic: following their own rules in their own classic liberal societies, settlers should either buy land at agreed prices without coercion, or refrain from settling. William Penn did so with the Native Americans in Pennsylvania, but his action has not been much emulated.

Early in the twentieth century, the government of South Africa effectively confiscated the lands of many blacks and turned them over to whites. The transfers were legal purchases. Certain areas were designated as white, and blacks owning land there were required to sell at fire-sale prices. Now, generations later, the black-led government must decide whether white farmers who inherited these lands, improved them, increased their productivity, and built homes and raised families there, must return their fields, and if so, what compensation they should receive. There is no just answer. In November 1997, the president of Zimbabwe has declared that white farms will be confiscated with no compensation, since any moral obligation belongs to the British, who took the land from the natives over a century ago.[20]

To solve these and similar disputes, the world appears to be converging on two international rules of morality in property rights. Call them the sovereignty rule and the limitations rule, respectively. Though full agreement eludes us, let us consider them as interim morality, valid while the moral economy lies yet in the future:

Under the sovereignty rule, each country or community has the moral right to specify its own property laws; a foreigner wishing to buy property within any country must conform to the laws of that country. The morality of any country invading another and taking the property of its citizens was ended after colonialism. Under the limitations rule, a "statute of limitations" applies to the taking of property from another society, in quotation marks because no one knows how long it runs. This rule says that the United States need not return land to the Mexicans or the Native Americans. However, current morality might require a country to compensate for past injustices, as in the case of Australia, Canada, New Zealand, and the United States vis-à-vis their indigenous peoples.

These rules, if recognized by Arabs and Israelis, might be the basis for settling their dispute. Although their Arab ancestors took the land from the Romans (Byzantines) in the seventh century, the Palestinians should own it now under the limitations rule. Since the sixteenth century, however, Palestinians have not had the opportunity to write their own land laws, because they have been continuously occupied by Ottomans or British. The early Zionists who acquired land in Palestine under Ottoman or British-mandate law did not recognize the sovereignty rule, which would have required that they purchase only under the nonexistent Palestinian law. By that rule, they should not have purchased at all.

By the limitations rule, the land Israelis have already taken is theirs, for surely the "statute of limitations" has run out in fifty years, but by the sovereignty rule they should take no more. As this book goes to press, the Israelis, not yet recognizing that rule, continue to press into territory in which Palestinians have lived for centuries. Those Palestinians who commit violence upon Israelis do not recognize the limitations rule. The United States is pushing both parties to accept both rules. Only when these two rules become so accepted internationally that abiding by them becomes requisite for respect in the world community will Arabs and Israelis resolve their dispute. They are not the final rules for the moral economy, but they are probably the best we have, for now.

Palestinians do not want to sell land to Israelis because doing so (many believe) would totally change the surrounding culture. Their familiar sights, language, laws, and other institutions would disappear. If by the sovereignty rule, an Israeli should not buy land from a willing Palestinian seller, by the same rule should a black in the United States be precluded from buying property in a predominantly white neighborhood, turning it into predominantly black? While others equally moral may differ, my morality says blacks should be allowed into white neighborhoods in the United States but Israelis not into the West Bank (eastern Palestine). Inconsistent? In one way, yes, but in another, no: these positions consistently reflect sympathy for the underdog and a search for balance of power, that is, strengthen the weak relative to the strong. Furthermore, the sovereignty rule is temporary in the long course of history, and the time to relax it may have come in the United States but not yet in Palestine.

Converting an interventionist society, such as the former Soviet Union, into a classic liberal one will be the most difficult task of all. Classic liberalism and private property encompass a whole culture, an idea of what is right and what is wrong, how and by whom decisions are made, how property is managed, and a liberal set of institutions of credit, supplies, markets, and knowledge. This culture is not easily copied or even grasped in nonliberal societies. Russia, Ukraine, and other countries of the former Soviet Union have lived for centuries with collective farms (with only brief exceptions such as 1907-30) where command—earlier by landed aristocracy, then by *mir* (community) rulers, and later by Soviet authorities—has always been the norm. Collective farms have failed as engines of economic development, and—prodded by the West—governments are trying to engineer privatization from on top. But top-down mandate does not normally work. Credit, equipment, and seeds and fertilizer are not always available, since institutions to supply them must be totally changed. "Bosses" of collective farms, still operating by command, try to preserve their power; farmers who try to move to private farms often find themselves bullied, and the law will not protect them.[21] The best strategy of the former Soviet countries would be to pass laws allowing privatization, to enforce those laws to the extent possible, which may not be great, but to leave implementation to the people concerned, who will work out the manner of privatization—and the time period (slow)—by their own agreements. In the meantime, collective farms would remain, side by side with the new private ones.

While people in less developed areas—Bosnia, Middle East, Ecuador, Peru, and others—are still fighting over territory, it is only in the more developed world that twinges of conscience cause compensation to be given for land taken, even if not in full measure. Economic development helps lead us toward the moral economy.

Compromise

The moral economy is founded on negotiation and compromise. Before it is formed, issues in each generation appear intractable, but with a later generation they are resolved. The wars of religion, the nationality of Alsace-Lorraine, and rivalry over colonizing Africa are among these. Negotiation humanizes, while power—vicarious or other—demonizes.

One of today's issues is abortion. One side wishes to make it totally illegal, the other totally legal. There are many possible compromises. One would be to make it legal during the first so many months. Education on birth control, psychological counseling, and other antipregnancy methods might be popularized more than they are now. Once a child is conceived, social organizations might work harder to find ways for the parent to keep it or to make adoption possible. Yet in the United States many political groups are still confrontational, demanding nothing short of total victory. Candidates and voters are torn between two extremes, and politicians dare not speak for compromise. But the late Russell Kirk and his wife, Annette—he was the author of *The Conservative Mind*—put their money where their mouths were. Strongly opposed to abortion, they provided a home for expectant mothers and facilitated the way to adoption.

Other potential compromises may be found for virtually any conflict, such as territorial in Northern Ireland, the Middle East, Bosnia, and elsewhere. Instead, government backing of small groups of belligerent citizens has fanned these conflicts. If governments would back off and conflict resolution were entrusted to nongovernmental citizens' groups, perhaps compromises would come more easily. Whether central European countries (Ukraine, Hungary, Moldova, Romania, Bulgaria) would align themselves with West or East would become as obsolete a question as whether Britain is European or not (some say that question is not obsolete). Australia need not decide between its history (Western) and its geography (Asian). Religious and tribal wars would pass into history in the Middle East and Africa just as they did in western Europe except Northern Ireland. Since today's conflicts are different from the past, no one yet knows the exact route by which these changes will occur. But hope is grounded in the idea that many solutions are sensible and free people—with power relatively well balanced—ultimately find sensible solutions. While the idea is clear, the path must be sought by trial and error.

For obvious reasons, negotiation and compromise as personal qualities evolve more readily in situations of balance of power than under concentrated power. Instead, concentrated power led to two major world crises in the 1990s, that of Mexico and that of east Asia. Both reflected the characteristics of lesser development.

Mexico in the 1990s: The Case of a Less Developed Country

Crisis in Mexico during the first half of the 1990s illustrates the abuse of power. Inflation resumed after it had presumably been conquered; the peso was devalued by more than 50 percent; unemployment spread; and more migrants fled to the United States. Why? Evidence is abundant that the crisis was man-made; that the elite families brought it on specifically if not purposefully; and that they gained from it.[22] That their gains were far more than offset by the losses of everyone else mattered little to them. It is most unlikely that the same scenario could have happened in any country of the more developed zone, where countervailing power is more prepared to defend itself.

After a currency crisis in 1982, the Mexican government nationalized all banks, expelling foreign influence in them. Hundreds of small businesses, which had been owned by banks, became owned by the government. Banks were required to convert their dollar deposits into pesos at a less-than-market exchange rate; exchange controls were decreed; and imports were made subject to license.

From 1988 to 1993 these banks increased their loans to the private sector by 1,327 percent.[23] Had these loans financed productive investment, gross domestic product (GDP) at 1980 prices would surely have increased by far more than the 16 percent that it did. Apologists for the government argue that the officers of the newly nationalized banks, being inexperienced in banking, did not know how to analyze loans well, and many bad loans slipped in. Another— to me more likely—explanation is that loans were made largely to the elite families who "run" Mexico and to other favorites, and their purpose was risky investment or extravagant consumption. With scant increase in GDP, however, these borrowers could only support their follies with increased imports. The increase in demand for foreign goods would normally have driven down the value of the peso, so that the cost of imports would have increased, thus offsetting the benefits for the few. To avoid this, the banks supported the peso by buying it in the foreign exchange market, so that its depreciation was contained to about one-third, or from 3.07 pesos to the dollar in 1988 to 4.23 in 1993. In so doing, however, the Bank of Mexico came close to using up its foreign exchange reserves. To prevent that, it held the domestic interest rate high, reaching 69 percent in 1988, to encourage the influx of "hot money" (short-term funds that travel from country to country seeking high rates; in Mexico *capital golondrino*). By so doing, they were able to build up foreign reserves from $5,279 million dollars in 1988 to $28,919 million in 1993. The foreign investors who loaned this money were duped by the ahistorical supposition that sovereign powers do not default on their obligations, such as to convert the currency at a specific rate.

Even the reprivatization of the banks in the early 1990s is suspect. Critics argue that "Mexican officials erred in two ways: First, they allowed buyers to pay exorbitant prices, instead of ensuring that the new financial groups would be adequately capitalized and knew how to run a bank. . . . Second, they didn't set up an adequate regulatory framework until several years after the banks were in private hands."[24] If these criticisms are correct—and I presume they are—they might be explained either by carelessness on the part of both bankers and government or by favoritism. Believing that those with the finance to buy banks must be able to analyze their worth, my supposition is that if they paid too much they expected some kind of favored political treatment in return. If the government did not set up adequate regulation for two years, I would suppose that this too was no mistake.

In 1993, the foreign investors woke up to the imminence of a financial crisis, since the Bank of Mexico did not have enough foreign exchange reserves to repay them. The result was panic: hot money was withdrawn; the market interest rate fell to 16 percent in 1993; reserves fell to $8,189 million in 1993 and appeared to be headed for zero; the peso dropped precipitously to 7.77 per dollar at the end of 1993, causing losses to foreign investors who had to pay more pesos for every dollar they withdrew. Early in 1995, the government of the United States loaned or guaranteed loans of $50 billion, but even this amount was far from enough to prevent an economic skid. Opponents argued that on the pretext of shoring up the Mexican economy President Clinton had bailed out U.S. investors who should have borne the losses on risks they took voluntarily.

Unemployment spread in Mexico for several reasons. First, industries depending on imports were undercut by the devaluation of the peso—the cost of imports suddenly more than doubled. While exports surged—their prices became low for foreigners—the increase in employment in export industries could not quickly absorb the losses in import industries. The multiplier effect caused a decrease in demand, as those who had lost their jobs scaled back their consumption. Second, in order to recoup their capital speedily, many banks loaned funds furiously. As the quality of their portfolios deteriorated, they still paid high dividends to appease their investors, using new capital as in a Ponzi scheme. Doing so is consistent with past behavior, in which Mexican bankers have always expected the government, or government banks such as the Nacional

Financiera, to bail them out. This time, however, the losses were too great. Banks failed; the government took over the failing ones; and businesses were foreclosed. Third, in order to attract foreign capital again, the Bank of Mexico raised the interest rate once more, this time to about 60 percent by 1994. Credit for ordinary enterprise, let alone new entrepreneurial activity, became scarce. Bankers suddenly became fearful to make any loans at all, and more businesses—unable to borrow—failed.

The economic crisis spread to the political scene, as blame was passed out on all sides. The new president, Ernesto Zedillo, did not belong to the traditional elite; he correctly blamed the crisis on the previous presidency of Carlos Salinas de Gortari. Salinas's brother, Raúl, was arrested, suspected of the murder of a high official in the Zedillo administration. Raúl's wife was found to have $84 million in deposits in Swiss banks, and there were reports of much more elsewhere.

Defenders of the $50 billion in loans and guarantees point out that the Mexican economy did rebound in 1996, and the loan was paid off. Looking back on the crisis from 1997, *The Economist* suggests three ways to prevent a recurrence: more information, so that foreign investors can foresee the problems; international cooperation for a bailout; and a readiness to act by the International Monetary Fund. Joseph Stiglitz, vice-president of the World Bank, said that "Mexico's crisis in 1994-95 taught us the importance of disclosure and transparency, so that investors can make informed sensible decisions."[25] Does he suppose the Mexicans did not know that or that they did not have their own reasons for being less than fully transparent? All these suggestions are fine palliatives that should be tried, but unless the characteristics of lesser development are addressed, there is every reason to believe that the same scenario, or something like it, may some day recur. (After I had written the preceding sentence, and while this book was in press, it did recur, this time in East Asia.)

The East Asian Crisis of 1997-98

In 1994, I wrote the following about East Asia. Since little attention was paid to these ideas at the time, I repeat:

> The twentieth century may turn out to have been for the four dragons [Hong Kong, Singapore, South Korea, and Taiwan] what the thirteenth was for Novgorod and the fifteenth was for the Italian city states.
>
> Contemporary occupants of power in the four dragons may perceive that their interest lies in the free market and export promotion, provided they command it. But the balanced forces to maintain this are not present.[26]

This section is written as the events occur, and it is slipped in while the manuscript is already in press. Yesterday (December 3, 1997) the International Monetary Fund (IMF), World Bank, Asian Development Bank, and at least seven governments of rich nations agreed to lend South Korea $55 billion[27]—the largest bailout loan the IMF has ever arranged—to cover losses that threatened to scuttle the economy and probably spread to other nations. By today (February 4, 1998) the IMF-led rescue package for all of East Asia has reached $118 billion.[28]

The Asian crisis had begun in Thailand, which—along with other southeast Asian countries—had been employing free-market policies. However, these countries had tied their currencies to the dollar, while also promoting economic expansion at home. Borrowing extravagantly for sound and unsound ventures from overindulgent banks operating under government guarantee, businesspeople converted their borrowed currency into dollars, swallowing up the countries' foreign exchange reserves. In South Korea, banks fueled by the central bank had been lending to business "families" known as *chaebol,* which had expanded into activities beyond their capacity to sustain, while the financial markets were too permissive to restrain them through downsizing or bankruptcy. Essentially, the Asian crisis was a repetition of the one in Mexico a few years earlier. This time, however, the reverberations hit the currencies and stock markets of all of East Asia, including Japan, and even of Brazil, Argentina, Europe, and the United States.

The point I tried to make in 1994 still has not been heard by economists. They are right that the *proximate* causes of the crisis are the bad economic policies of governments, especially Indonesia, Japan, South Korea, and Thailand. Banks expected their governments to rescue them if necessary, as they always had. Krugman finds that the cause of the crisis lay primarily in government guarantees. Businesses borrowed up to the "Pangloss" value of investments: values that would be realized under the best of circumstances, with no discount for risk.[29] But so far economists have supposed that governments follow these policies from exuberance, stubbornness, or ignorance. The *underlying* explanation is different: the rulers had *power* to follow these policies without the counterweights found in Western societies. The most benign interpretation is that they used their power in a well-intentioned effort to direct the flow of resources into development projects that would benefit all, but that they made human errors. The least benign (and more probable) is that they grossly and flagrantly cheated their people for their own benefit, in two ways. First, diverting public resources to private chaebol built up their political support. Second, the rulers and favored companies might buy imports cheaply with an overvalued currency, thus satisfying their material greed.

The political backlash from the IMF bailout shows that these rulers have not been chastised enough to recognize their immorality and their mortality. "Politicians from both the governing and opposition parties attacked the South Korean government Thursday for yielding to the key demands of the International Monetary Fund . . ."[30] In a major cultural gaffe, Michel Camdessus, Director General of the IMF, allowed himself to be photographed. arms akimbo, towering above President Suharto of Indonesia, who was crouched down to sign the IMF document.[31] The photo was published throughout East Asia, a symbol of IMF humiliation of national sovereigns.

President Suharto had parceled out the most weighty enterprises of his country to members of his family, who ran them inefficiently and milked them of what was left. With the IMF bailout, he has promised not to do that any more.[32] In the long run, however, the problem is not that he *did* it but that he had the *power* to do it, and so will his successor after the IMF restrictions expire. *Only the Indonesian people can erode that power, and they will not do it if they believe the IMF and not their rulers is the cause of their problems.* Having vision limited to their own discipline, economists stop at the proximate cause, failing to dig down to the underlying one, an excess of power. Short-sighted investors have also not realized this truth.

Feldstein puts the blame on Japan for having kept interest rates low instead of reducing taxes, thus allowing the yen to be overvalued.[33] The low interest rates had encouraged other Asian countries to borrow from Japan, enabling them also to maintain overvalued currencies. When debt burdens became too great and governments could not maintain the currency pegs, a rash of devaluations ensued. As in Mexico, foreign investors perceived the crisis belatedly, and the investment outflow hemorrhaged. Some economists thought the IMF restrictions would be so severe as to dissuade governments from repeating their errors, since they had discovered the bitter pill of their rescues. Possibly, but nothing could restore the legal diversions they had enjoyed up to that point.

What is the alternative? To let these governments muck in their own juices would cause widespread economic hardship to innocent people. However, the IMF bailout preserves the power of the "stationary bandits" (Olson's term) or their successors to do it again. History has varying experiences. In the fourteenth and fifteenth centuries, the Estates of Germany bailed out their princes from analogous iniquities, as did the nobility of England and France for their wasteful kings. In the South Sea Bubble of 1720 and the Ponzi schemes in Albania and eastern Europe today, on the other hand, no one bailed out the losers.

To summarize: Rulers with power took the foreign exchange that investors had provided and diverted billions into extravagances or risky investments that could not pay their way with self-generated income. The apparent Asian miracle drew in more investors, just like any Ponzi scheme. When the inevitable bankruptcy loomed, the Asian governments turned to the IMF and foreign governments to bail them out, with the realistic threat that with no bailout, the world might be plunged into serious depression. Finding themselves in a corner, the IMF and foreign governments put up the cash to rescue the malefactors, insisting on blunt instruments to prevent recurrence. But ordinary people and businesses are the ones who suffer through those blunt instruments—higher taxes, credit restrictions, and other austerity measures.

Did the IMF do right? That depends on whether one thinks in the short run or the long. In the short run, the IMF may command good behavior, minimizing the further financial suffering of millions of people, though far from preventing it. In the long run, once the current fuss has died down (say, in ten years or so), the IMF may have preserved the power of the next generation of rulers to do it again, placing yet another obstacle in the way of the moral economy. Stiglitz recommends "establishment of an effective regulatory system, improving corporate governance and enhancing transparency more broadly."[34] Once again he is thinking in the culture of the more developed world, where if fiscal and monetary managers behave morally (in this respect, anyway) it is only because their power to behave immorally has been weakened over centuries, a theme in my previous work.[35] As in Mexico, so in East Asia Stiglitz would entrust the solution to the very people who caused the problem, apparently believing that with a bit of explanation they will behave like "us."

How to diminish central power? Abolishing the link between currencies and governments, as proposed in chapter 7, would be a major way. Firms like Techno would issue money based on the market capability of borrowers. Unlike the case of a central bank, Techno's own hide would depend on the soundness of its judgments.

Another way would be to downsize governments, making them functional instead of territorial. Nongovernmental agencies, as suggested in chapters 4 and 5, would take over much of their power and would spread it about. A third way is already in progress—privatization of government monopolies—but its cronyistic[36] counterpart—private monopolies—has not yet been tackled. These are the real changes the IMF should demand, but it will not do so because the governments of rich countries are not yet ready to relinquish their power in these ways either.

As the reader has surely surmised, this section was rewritten many times as the crisis unfolded, and as this book lumbered its way through the editorial process that anxious authors always find too long. On February 3, 1998, Schultz, Simon, and Wriston published the prescription that comes closest to the one suggested above, but not quite so radical. "The promise of an IMF bailout," they wrote, "insulates financiers and politicians from the consequences of bad economic and financial practices. . . . The IMF is ineffective, unnecessary, and obsolete. Once the Asian crisis is over, we should abolish [it]."[37]

From Here to There

In chapter 1, twelve current, momentous changes in economic society were cited as harbingers of the moral economy: globalization of the economy; greater access to technology and markets; bypassing of government restrictions by using other jurisdictions through the Internet; fall in trade barriers; deregulation and declines in government intervention; loss of financial credibility of governments; intolerance of corruption and campaign contributions; privatization of production facilities throughout the world; land reform; decentralization of welfare; the collapse of socialism and decline of the welfare state; and the move toward magnet schools, charter schools, and home education. Each of these has a trajectory of its own, yet the trajectories intertwine. Where I count twelve, others may count more or fewer, since some are parts of others. As a step is taken in one trajectory, the next step becomes more likely in some other trajectory, since the idea of classic liberalism is promoted overall.

In part 1, seven major problems were cited—poverty, population growth, environment, ethnic and gender bias, welfare, social security, and health care. For each of these, a classic liberal solution was supplied. All such solutions are possible within a democratic society; they require the determination of the electorate in opposition to the desire of politicians to retain their power. A continuation of the power-diffusion process—in motion in northwestern Europe and Japan since the late Middle Ages—is also required. As classic liberalism becomes more appreciated, each of these solutions—which now seem distant—becomes more likely.

Thus not one single trajectory but many intertwining ones promote the moral economy. Although this chapter has provided a survey, nothing in this book has set forth the details of the moral economy, which is a way to transact economic affairs, not the affairs themselves. Its characteristics are balance of power, social discipline, incentives rather than regulation, compromise and negotiation rather than litigiousness, presumption of "goodness" and positive-sum moves, separation of the economic from other subcultures with equal economic rights for all, the end of nationalism, the end of paternalism, new governments functionally oriented, nongovernmental agencies, private equaling social costs and benefits respectively, private money, liberal markets, private property, regular redistributions of income but not of property, limited government services, economic decision power reserved for entrepreneurs and businesspeople rather than government, religion separated from politics, and education decided upon by parents and students. All of these are ideology or values that will gradually be internalized as the many intertwining trajectories are pursued. None is a specific organization or even an institution. Thus the moral economy is a way for people to live. Impossible? The road from the present to the moral economy implies social changes of no greater order—indeed, much less—than the changes the world has experienced in the two hundred years just past.

The moral economy may be reached in many ways; no one can tell now which will be taken. Optimism arises out of the many positive-sum moves awaiting us if the power-diffusion process continues: intelligent citizens in a power-diffuse society can find these moves. Therefore, this book does not propose the detailed steps of each trajectory.

Built-in reversals are a prime reason why steps are slow and uncertain. Consider the following model. An inability to satisfy human needs, in defiance of the liberal market, causes waste of resources and government bankruptcy. Reform, shifting from wrong methods to right ones, deprives constituents of services they have come to accept as "rights" in the old socialist or welfare state. Inefficient state enterprises are closed, and workers are unemployed in the interim period before new, efficient enterprises are formed. By strikes, protests, and sometimes violence, they restore the earlier arrangements in part, but not completely. Many of the distortions reappear, but not all. Thus the move toward the moral economy is five steps forward, four back, repeat the process, and continue—three centuries? a millennium?—until the distortions approach a limit of zero. A cycle is set up, running several turns until the moral-economy philosophy comes to occupy the social mass.

According to evolutionary scientist Richard Dawkins, in *Climbing Mount Improbable*,[38] the degree of complexity achieved by modern physical life is so great as to be highly improbable when seen from an early evolutionary stage. He adopts the analogy of a mountain: sheer cliffs would seemingly be climbed. Yet evolution is always in small steps: modern creatures do not spring forth in a generation. If Mount Improbable is examined closely, one sees many gentle slopes along which a route was selected, each step of which was taken for a smaller purpose that had little or nothing to do with the final destination. Furthermore, it would have been impossible to say—millions of years ago—what the bodies of all creatures would be like today. Other creatures of equal complexity might have evolved instead.

It is because the same will be so over the next millennium that we cannot define the moral economy as a *there*. Power diffusion, freedom of enterprise, and democracy were not sought in the past for themselves but were by-products of millions of smaller outcomes. All we can cite now are the smaller outcomes that we foresee in the next century, such as reforms in education and health care, and the general principles that point us toward a successful evolution. Indeed, that is all we have done in this book. Proposals such as nongovernmental agencies and education funds are illustrations, not predictions.

Yet several characteristics of the moral economy are already visible. Fiscal stringency and the failure of socialist planning are forcing governments the world over to downsize, outsource, and privatize. Health care and social security are on the list in many countries. In the United States, the Clean Air Act of 1990 employs market principles in the sale of pollution permits. Accountability and trust have greatly increased in classic liberal societies, compared to two centuries ago. Firms increasingly discover that equality of opportunity for men and women and for ethnic minorities is good business. World population growth is slowing down. The Welfare Act of 1996 has led firms to make proposals to state governments on private management for welfare,[39] though adequate funds for the moral-economy programs are not yet voted. Alternatives to public education are widely explored. In Europe, "businessmen . . . are adapting to globalization as fast as or faster than the politicians, and are doing just what the single market encourages: treating Europe as one giant area, rationalizing production across frontiers."[40] From 1973 to 1995, the European Commission disallowed 168 cases of state aid, forcing the recipients to repay, and it has rejected mergers proposed by national governments.[41] Only a little imagination is required to see these events as precursors to the full moral economy.

Attempts to specify the exact route would, however, violate the principles of the moral economy, whose way is selected by negotiation and not by the dictums of an intellectual or political elite, or any author. But I can make three observations.

First, the principal obstacle is power groups, mainly the distributional coalitions (Olson's term) for which subsidies, such as corporate welfare and agricultural benefits, are voted or that have the power to demand "rights." Add government as a special power group. Every right is another person's obligation, but the assignment of obligations is often not specified. Besides government itself, power groups include business corporations, sugar producers, ranchers, and loggers. But they also include those righteous people, growing out of religious or charitable societies, who think they know the way, and whose vicarious power stands behind political power. The present-day ethos of seeking victory for one's own idea or group and defeat for the other, whether abortion, antiabortion, the religious right, the religious left, health care providers, protectionists, free traders, or what, must give way to one of respect for the integrity of the social mass, which requires attention to the ideas of adversaries. Our present concept of democracy, of victory or defeat, must lead instead into a democracy of negotiation.

Yet do not despair. That society has been in the making for centuries—democracy is far more "negotiating" than any other system. It is only necessary to continue on that path, not to find it anew. In less developed countries, electoral outcomes are increasingly honored—not always upset by military coups—so that the electorate may choose gradually to wean itself away from overarching power. The election in 1997 of an Iranian moderate, Mohammed Khatami, is a case in point.[42]

Otherwise, power groups might be subdued in various ways. One is to defeat a nation militarily, as Germany in World War II, so that previous power groups lose their legitimacy. Olson tells about this. However, defeat implies a victor, whose distributional coalitions remain or are strengthened. Another is debt repudiation, or the logical end of welfare states in which citizens demand more than they are willing to pay for in taxes. Although debt repudiation has happened in England, Spain, Germany, and many other countries, it does not seem likely for Western democracies in the immediate future. Rough political times are ahead, with strikes and electoral upsets, but ultimately—as citizens become more impatient with their loss of autonomy—Western democracies and Japan will, I believe, settle into governments that favor democracy, classic liberalism, and balanced budgets. Most of all, the people must learn to pay for what they demand. This lesson is slow in coming, but just as it happened for the kings of Europe and the shogun and emperor of Japan, it is likely to happen for the rest of us.

Second, once the path is started, methods of one entity are absorbed by another, then another, then another. In the last two decades, the idea of seeking the optimal size and shape of firms spread rapidly from one to another. Downsizing, outsourcing, new enterprises, and changing conditions of employment came in clusters. Perhaps these ideas will also spread to government. Once that happens along with a responsibility to balance budgets, then downsizing, outsourcing, and privatizing may spread from one government agency to another. These moves will not lead to unemployment, any more than they did in the private sector. Rather, the original government functions, now bundled under the supervision of a much-too-stretched president or prime minister, would be divided among agencies more capable of handling them efficiently. Citizens might choose their policies individually—a citizen's line veto.

Third, a power group may be bought off. For example, the privatization of inefficient government enterprises is often opposed by laborers who might lose their jobs. Henderson has suggested that this opposition should be neutralized with shares of stock, a strategy followed by Margaret Thatcher that was "responsible for the successful waves of privatization . . . during her 12 years as prime minister." [43] Environmentalists often "hug trees" to prevent loggers from cutting them down. If instead they would pay the loggers for their de facto (if not de jure) right to cut and focus on new jobs for them, they might be more successful. Cattle ranchers in the West believe they have the "right" to low-cost use of government land. They do not have that right, but if we behaved as if they did, we might buy it from them, thus splitting with them the environmental gains in the cheapest and most effective solution possible. In the American farm act of 1996, farmers were compensated, with lump-sum payments for a period of years, for losing their "rights" to subsidies. The British bought off their farmers in Rhodesia as they turned the land over to Africans who named it Zimbabwe. Ample precedent exists for buying off power groups.

The moral economy lies on the horizon, and the path to it will be slow and piecemeal. Gradually, citizens may become aware that governments are unable to protect the environment because they cater to special interests. One nongovernmental agency might be set up cautiously as the vested interests of a power group are "bought." Another would follow when the virtue of the first is grasped, and so on. In addition, citizens may gradually resent the loss of their autonomy, as did residents of company towns, and they might try to regain it through smaller government. If the moral economy comes about at all, it will be democratically.

A principal obstacle to improving the balance of power under democracy is the widespread misunderstanding of economics. Olson argues that if citizens knew the harm that distributional coalitions were doing to them, they would not permit it. He is right for some places and wrong for others, since vested interests are sometimes more powerful than an enlightened citizenry. The same may be so for minimum wages, tariffs, affirmative action, and the many government regulations that go far beyond the need for environmental protection, equity, and security. Formal education appears not always to provide the necessary knowledge—see chapter 9. Since education tends to confirm the belief set of those who provide it, it sometimes teaches "untruth" instead of "truth." But experience in living and operating in the economy does provide this information, ever so gradually. Citizens understand far more about how the economy functions today than they did one thousand years ago, and in the next thousand years they will understand much, much more.

The slowest path will be that of eastern Europe and the less developed areas. Turn-of-the-century diplomacy is enthusiastic about the new liberalism and privatization, but it is not sufficiently wary of the characteristics of lesser development, as set forth in chapter 3. Present reforms, imposed by the more developed countries upon the less developed countries as the price of financial assistance, all have been tried before and have failed because they also did not address those characteristics.[44] Let us recall the remark of my interpreter/professor in Zaporizzia, Ukraine: "All our lives the government has taken care of us, and now that it has failed us, we have no idea of how to take care of ourselves." Fifty years, at least, are necessary for the world to become aware of all present deficiencies, and by then a new generation may have forgotten some of them, just as the present generation has forgotten some of those of the past. Lessons come piecemeal and cyclically. Our grandchildren will learn them that way, until they just might approach a horizon called the moral economy.

If they do, another horizon—totally beyond our vision now—will loom in the distance.

Notes

Introduction

1. Expressed in Charles Murray's *What It Means to be a Libertarian* (1996).
2. Pinkerton, James P., *New York Times Book Review,* 1/19/97.

Chapter 1

1. *The Economist,* 4/19/97.
2. *Washington Post Weekly,* 7/14/97.
3. Farmers were given "transition payments" of $30 billion, diminishing each year from 1997 to 2002, when they will be ended. They do not depend on crops or acreage planted, or on prices in the market. See *The Economist,* 7/12/97.
4. Powelson and Stock 1990.
5. Yergin and Stanislaw 1997.
6. *New York Times,* 7/23/97.
7. Kramer, Peter, *New York Times,* 5/6/97.
8. Rothschild 1990.
9. Smith, *The Theory of Moral Sentiments,* 1776 (reprint, Oxford 1979):166.
10. *New York Times,* 6/26/96.
11. *The Economist,* 12/21/96.
12. Soros 1997:55.
13. Dodgson, Charles Lutwidge (Lewis Carroll), *Through the Looking Glass,* Chapter 6.

Chapter 2

1. Yergin and Stanislaw, 1997: subtitle.
2. How market prices are actually determined, based on the underlying forces, is taught in courses in microeconomics.
3. Lewis 1995:171.
4. Unless otherwise specified, "Western" means United States, Canada, western Europe, Australia, and New Zealand.
5. Fitzpatrick 1994:134-36.
6. Fukuyama 1989.
7. Freeman, 1996.
8. Drucker, Peter, letter to the editor, *The Economist,* 1/6/96.

9. Powelson 1994.

10. *Washington Post National Weekly,* 1/6/97.

11. *New York Times,* 7/21/97.

12. Ridley 1997:33.

13. Hosking 1997:14.

14. *Wall Street Journal,* 3/19/97.

15. *New York Times,* 7/15/97.

16. *New York Times,* 8/11/97.

17. *New York Times,* 12/8/97.

18. Quill 1996:7.

19. Samuelson 1980:38.

20. Economists distinguish among monopoly profit, profit due to risk, and "interest," which is the market return on capital and not interest in the popular sense. These distinctions are not warranted in this nontechnical book.

Chapter 3

1. Gray 1975.

2. Harms 1981.

3. De Soto 1989; Dietz and Moore 1979.

4. *New York Times,* 10/11/97.

5. *New York Times,* 10/6/81.

6. Starr 1977:54.

7. Wells 1984:203.

8. Herlihy 1977:8; Cipolla 1980:10.

9. Kunt 1983:53.

10. Cipolla 1980:106.

11. Mathias 1979:186-89; also Mathias 1983:27.

12. Hibbert 1987:289.

13. Jain 1975.

14. *New York Times,* 2/5/98.

15. *New York Times,* 7/20/97.

16. Tuchman 1984:135.

17. *The Economist,* 2/22/97.

18. Olson 1996:6.

19. Olson 1996:16.

20. Olson 1996:21.

21. Olson 1993.

22. North (1995): "The ruler faces a trade-off between the increased income he can obtain and the increased threat to his security that the relaxed restrictions result in because his constituents have both more freedom of action and resources to overthrow him." My only amendment would be to include the enjoyment of power along with income.

23. *The Economist,* 11/5/94.

24. *New York Times,* 3/14/97.

25. Hacker 1997.

26. "Nature does not jump," from Marshall 1890 (5th ed. 1938), front material.

27. This example is borrowed from Furchtgot, *Wall Street Journal,* 6/30/95.

28. Hacker 1997.

29. Madrick 8/14/97.

30. Calculated from *Statistical Abstract of the United States,* 1996, tables 665 (for employment cost index) and 745 (for consumer price index).

31. Boskin, Michael, "Prisoners of Faulty Statistics," *Wall Street Journal,* 12/5/96.

32. Moulton 1996.

33. Madrick 3/6/97.

34. Gordon and Griliches 1997.

35. Gordon and Griliches 1997.

36. *Wall Street Journal,* 6/14/95.

37. Judson and Orphanides, 1996.

38. *New York Times Magazine,* 8/18/96.

Chapter 4

1. *New York Times,* 5/14/95; *Wall Street Journal,* 5/22/95.

2. *Washington Post Weekly,* 6/15/92.

3. *New York Times,* 6/21/93.

4. *New York Times,* 9/23/91.

5. *New York Times,* 8/29/88, 10/11/88, 5/22/92.

6. *The Economist,* 6/12/93.

7. *New York Times,* 8/13/89.

8. *New York Times,* 4/4/97.

9. *The Economist,* 10/4/97.

10. *New York Times,* 12/10/95.

11. Smil 1993, also *New York Times,* 7/25/94.

12. *New York Times,* 12/9/90.

13. *New York Times,* 5/29/92.

14. *New York Times,* 4/16/95.

15. *New York Times,* 8/10/95.

16. *New York Times,* 11/26/93.

17. Holloway, David, in a review of Feshback and Friendly 1992, *New York Times Book Review,* 6/10/93. See also *New York Times,* 12/27/88; *Washington Post Weekly,* 7/26/92.

18. Solomon, Lawrence, "The Best Earth Day Present: Freedom," *New York Times,* 4/20/90.

19. *New York Times,* 11/28/97.
20. More details on this are found in *The Economist,* 12/13/97.
21. *Washington Post Weekly,* 5/25/92.
22. *New York Times,* 2/15/89.
23. *New York Times,* 6/11/92.
24. *Wall Street Journal,* 10/3/97.
25. *New York Times,* 5/19/97.
26. Bovard 1994:35.
27. Bovard 1994:34.
28. *The Economist,* 1/18/97.
29. Munro, Mark, *New York Times,* 3/29/97.
30. *New York Times,* 4/11/95.
31. *New York Times,* 8/6/96.
32. Melloan, George, *Wall Street Journal,* 4/3/95.
33. *New York Times,* 9/23/97.
34. *Wall Street Journal,* 12/26/95.
35. *New York Times,* 6/18/96.
36. *Washington Post Weekly,* 6/30/97.
37. *Wall Street Journal,* 10/29/97.
38. *New York Times,* 9/24/95.
39. *Wall Street Journal,* 12/4/97.
40. *New York Times,* 4/23/93.
41. *Philadelphia Inquirer,* 4/23/93, in article reproduced from *Washington Post.*
42. *New York Times,* 8/27/94.
43. Melloan, George, *Wall Street Journal,* 4/3/95.
44. Wager 1995-96:1-2.
45. *The Economist,* 10/25/97.
46. *New York Times,* 6/28/97.
47. *The Economist,* 6/14/97.
48. Clark 1968 for the earlier data; United Nations Fund for Population Activities for projection; see *New York Times,* 5/15/90.
49. *New York Times,* 7/24/93.
50. *New York Times,* 10/27/97.
51. Sen 1994:66.
52. *New York Times,* 11/17/96.
53. *The Economist,* 11/16/96.
54. Simon 1996. See also his article in *Wall Street Journal,* 11/18/96.
55. Avery, Dennis T., "Mother Earth Can Feed Billions More," *Wall Street Journal,* 9/19/91.
56. Sen 1994:63, who draws his figures from the National Academy of Science.
57. Calculated from Clark 1968:108.

58. United Nations, *World Population Prospects: The 1996 Revision,* reviewed by Wattenberg, Ben J., *New York Times Magazine,* 11/23/97.

59. *New York Times,* 8/17/97; *Wall Street Journal,* 10/20/97.

60. *The Economist,* 7/30/94; *New York Times,* 9/4/94.

61. *New York Times,* 1/2/94.

62. Sen 1994:70.

63. William Nordhaus in his review of Joel E. Cohen, *How Many People Can the Earth Support?* New York, Norton, 1995, in *New York Times Book Review,* 1/14/96.

64. United Nations, *Demographic Yearbook,* 1993:129.

65. United Nations, *Food and Agricultural Organization Yearbook,* 1994:65.

66. Eberstadt, Nicholas, *Wall Street Journal,* 10/16/97.

67. Williamson and Higgins, 1997.

68. Mason, Lee, and Miller, 1997.

69. *The Economist,* 9/13/97.

70. *New York Times,* 10/2/9

71. Wandycz 1992:22.

72. Kissinger, Henry, "Bosnia: Only Just Beginning . . ." *Washington Post,* 9/11/95. Reference is to ethnic groups in the former Yugoslavia.

73. Wandycz 1992:23.

74. Colbourne 1956:111.

75. Landes 1965:358.

76. Takekoshi 1930:2:273, 281.

77. Parry 1976:181.

78. Richmond 1977:88.

79. Harms 1981.

80. Fukuyama 1995:26.

81. Cannon and Griffiths 1988:58.

82. Holborn 1959:5.

83. Finley 1987:63-66.

84. Braunstein 1988:614.

85. Lynch 1981:1:226.

86. Alpers 1982.

87. Marques 1976;85.

88. Murray 1993:40.

89. *Encyclopedia Britannica* 1968:8:42; Bowman 1986:131.

90. Rouche 1987:465.

91. Tuchman 1984:214.

92. Gilles 1986:124.

93. de la Roncière 227, writing about Tuscany.

94. Ozment 1980:428.

95. Dewey 1977:53.
96. Furet 1989:446.
97. Reid 1988:147.
98. *New York Times,* 7/29/92.
99. *New York Times,* 8/16/94.
100. *New York Times,* 4/23/92.
101. *The Economist,* 3/11/95:29.
102. *The Economist,* 6/17/95:69.
103. Hochschild 1995.
104. Davidson and Grofman 1994.
105. *Wall Street Journal,* 3/20/95.
106. *Wall Street Journal,* 12/27/95.
107. Bovard 1994:171.
108. *Wall Street Journal,* 6/29/95.
109. *Wall Street Journal,* 12/19/93.
110. *New York Times,* 7/23/95.
111. *The Economist,* 4/15/95.
112. *Wall Street Journal,* 3/1/95.
113. *Washington Post Weekly,* 5/19/97.
114. *New York Times,* 1/28/95.
115. *New York Times,* 6/29/95.
116. *Washington Post Weekly,* 11/7/94.
117. *New York Times,* 8/30/95.
118. *Wall Street Journal,* 12/2/96.
119. *Wall Street Journal,* 6/9/97.
120. *New York Times,* 5/23/97; *The Economist,* 7/19/97.
121. Inglehart 1997.

Chapter 5

1. *The Economist,* 9/20/97.
2.   International Monetary Fund, *Government Financial Statistics*, 1995.
3. *New York Times,* 2/2/95.
4. *International Herald-Tribune*, 10/26/96.
5. *New York Times,* 12/12/86, 12/14/86.
6. *New York Times,* 11/19/95.
7. *The Economist,* 7/28/90.
8. *New York Times,* 2/28/98.
9. *The Economist,* 7/9/94.
10. International Monetary Fund, *Government Financial Statistics*, 1995.
11. Kaus, Mickey, "The Welfare Mess—How It Got That Way," *New York Times,* 9/12/94.

12. *Wall Street Journal,* 9/28/95.

13. *Wall Street Journal,* 8/23/96.

14. de Parle, Jason, *New York Times Magazine,* 12/18/94.

15. Holt, Tom, *Wall Street Journal,* 12/1/94.

16. *Wall Street Journal,* 1/20/95.

17. *Wall Street Journal,* 1/21/97.

18. *The Economist,* 3/8/97.

19. *New York Times,* 8/1/96.

20. *The Economist,* 1/25/97.

21. *New York Times,* 9/15/96.

22. *Washington Post Weekly,* 5/19/97.

23. Social security taxes in the United States are paid into a social security trust fund, which invests its entire assets in U.S. government obligations.

24. *New York Times,* 3/3/98.

25. *Wall StreetJournal,* 1/7/97.

26. Schieber, Sylvester, "Your Retirement, Your Social Security," *Wall Street Journal,* 1/8/97.

27. *The Economist,* 8/3/96.

28. *The Economist,* 4/10/93; see also *The Economist,* 8/13/94, 12/9/95; *New York Times,* 8/28/92; *Wall Street Journal,* 3/30/94, 12/12/94.

29. *Wall Street Journal,* 1/8/97.

30. Piñera 1995.

31. For further on Chilean social security, see *Wall Street Journal,* 8/18/95; Graham 1994, Chapter 2.

32. *The Economist,* 9/13/97.

33. *The Economist,* 3/8/97.

34. *The Economist,* 3/15/97.

35. *New York Times,* 11/13/95.

36. *New York Times,* 12/9/95.

37. *The Economist,* 6/20/92:84.

38. Lakonishok, Schleifer, and Vishny 1992.

39. *New York Times,* 12/20/92, 7/11/93; *Washington Post Weekly,* 1/4/93, 1/11/93, 11/29/93; *Wall Street Journal,* 2/4/93, 9/2/93.

40. Reich, Robert, in a letter to the editor, *Wall Street Journal,* 10/26/94.

41. *Washington Post Weekly,* 1/11/93.

42. *New York Times,* 11/20/92.

43. *New York Times,* 11/2/93.

44. US Department of Commerce, *Statistical Abstract of the United States, 1995,* page 109.

45. *Wall Street Journal,* 11/12/91.

46. Calculated from *Statistical Abstract,* 1995, pages 109 and 451.

47. *Wall Street Journal,* 12/16/91.

48. *Wall Street Journal,* 1/25/96.

49. *New York Times,* 3/17/98.

50. *New York Times,* 8/17/97.

51. *New York Times,* 3/26/97.

52. *Wall Street Journal,* 3/31/97.

53. *Encyclopedia Britannica,* Macropedia, 1974:2: 1083, and 1974: 8:113.

54. Newspaper articles by those favoring the Canadian health plan include Goad, *Wall Street Journal,* 12/3/91; and Cohen, *Wall Street Journal,* 2/6/92. Articles bringing out the criticisms mentioned previously include Walker, *Wall Street Journal,* 10/18/91, Munro, *Reader's Digest,* September 1992; Farnsworth, *New York Times,* 10/4/92; Swardson, *Washington Post Weekly,* 7/5/93; Arnett, *Wall Street Journal,* 8/6/93; Goodman, *Wall Street Journal,* 9/16/93; Crittenden, *Wall Street Journal,* 3/31/94; Farnsworth, *New York Times,* 9/17/95; Swardson, *Washington Post Weekly,* 10/16/95; and De Palma, *New York Times,* 12/15/96.

55. *New York Times,* 6/16/94.

56. *Wall Street Journal,* 7/05/84.

57. *The Economist,* 9/23/95.

58. *New York Times,* 1/30/97. For more evidence, see *The Economist,* 3/15/97.

59. *The Economist,* 11/18/95.

60. *The Economist,* 3/7/98.

61. *New York Times,* 11/08/94.

62. *Washington Post Weekly,* 4/11/94.

63. Graham 1994:226-7.

64. *New York Times,* 11/23/94.

65. *Wall Street Journal,* 10/12/93.

66. *New York Times,* 12/28/92.

67. Herzlinger 1996.

68. *Washington Post Weekly,* 1/15/96.

69 *The Economist,* 3/7/398.

70. *The Economist,* 12/23/95, page 74.

71. *Encyclopedia Britannica,* Macropedia, 1974:13:802.

72. *The Economist,* 12/23/95, page 74.

Chapter 6

1. Williamson 1985; this book is excellently summarized by Alchian and Woodward 1988.

2. Webber and Wildavsky 1986:210.

3. Fairbank, Reischauer, and Craig 1978:181.

4. Webber and Wildavsky 1986:127.

5. Webber and Wildavsky 1986:213.

6. Berman 1983:443.
7. Hogue 1966:63.
8. Prestwich 1979:83.
9. Miller 1987:27.
10. Cannon and Griffiths 1988:408.
11. Bossenga 1989:586.
12. Powelson 1994:78.
13. Carsten 1959.
14. Webber and Wildavsky 1986:208.
15. Hill 1961:49-50.
16. Miller 1987:171. See also Sicard 1986:195.
17. Behrens 1977:578.
18. Gauchet 1989.
19. Powelson 1994.
20. Powelson 1994:14.
21. Takekoshi 1930:1:273.
22. Bloch 1971:250.
23. Braunstein 1988:550.
24. Asakawa 1929:186.
25. Takekoshi 1930:3:90.
26. Crawcour 1961:342.
27. Takekoshi 1930:2:450.
28. Wigmore 1969:16.
29. *New York Times,* 12/06/92.
30. *New York Times,* 11/24/92.
31. Drucker, Peter, *Wall Street Journal,* 12/1/92.
32. Abelson, Reed, *New York Times,* 6/23/96.
33. "Chile: Forest Fire," *The Economist,* 2/3/96.
34. Mikesell 1995:1.
35. Coulborn 1956:185.
36. Berman 1983:393.
37. Epstein 1991:66.
38. Black 1984:37.
39. Webber and Wildavsky 1986:130.
40. Glamann 1977:267.
41. Haskell 1985:2:551-3.
42. Bloch 1961:1:124. See also Rueschemeyer 1986:57.
43. Powelson 1994:98 ff.
44. *New York Times,* 4/23/96.
45. Hughes 1993.
46. Fukuyama 1995. A summary of the argument is found on pp. 335-38.

47. Bruton 1967.
48. Jones 1971:343.
49. Lynch 1984:2:145.
50. Neale 1969:8.
51. Fryde and Fryde 1971:448.
52. de Roover 1971:73.
53. Powelson 1994:27.
54. *The Economist*, 5/11/96.
55. Ridley 1997:23.
56. Berman 1983:344.
57. Berman 1963:345.
58. Bordewich 1986.
59. *New York Times*, 7/7/96.
60. *The Economist*, 7/13/96.

Chapter 7

1. Gregg 1976:294.
2. Landes 1969.
3. Manin 1989:835.
4. My translation
5. Buchanan 1975:25-34.
6. Demsetz 1967. For the relationship between the Coase theorem and a theory of property, and a further development of property price theory (beyond the scope of this book), see Demsetz 1964.
7. Leacock 1954.
8. Nigam 1975; Powelson 1988:190.
9. Powelson 1988:155.
10. Black 1984:35.
11. Bowman 1986:98.
12. Except for those who held *precaria,* lands obtained by prayer to the master, which could be confiscated at the will of the master.
13. Takekoshi 1930: 1:27.
14. Lefebvre 1947:223.
15. Powelson 1988, 1994.
16. Black 1984:36.
17. Blum 1978:262.
18. Hogue 1984:7-8.
19. Hogue 1984:14.
20. Powelson 1988:31.
21. Hall 1970:180.

22. Cohen et al. 1980:9.
23. Mary Anastasia O'Grady, "Squatter Rights vs. Private Property Rights," *Wall Street Journal,* 2/16/96.
24. *The Economist,* 5/3/97.
25. See letters to the editor by executives of power companies, *Wall Street Journal,* 12/26/97.
26. *The Economist,* 2/29/92.
27. *The Economist,* 7/2/94.
28. *The Economist,* 9/13/97.
29. *New York Times,* 5/33/97.
30. *Washington Post Weekly,* 10/28/96.
31. *Wall Street Journal,* 4/15/94.
32. Powelson 1960.
33. See Bartley, Robert, and Malpass, David, two separate articles in *Wall Street Journal,* 12/20/96.
34. Bowman 1986:92.
35. Bastid 1985:51.
36. Eberhard 1977:15.
37. Yang 1952:21.
38. Yang 1952:21.
39. Takekoshi 1930:1:94.
40. Lewis 1988:37, 1995:157-178.
41. Lawrence 1978:25.
42. Luzatto 1961:37.
43. Cannon 1988:68.
44. Cannon 1988:72; Cantor 1993:191.
45. Holt, Lambton, and Bernard 1970:525.
46. Lewis 1988:37.
47. Fairbank, Reischauer, and Craig 1978:138.
48. *Wall Street Journal,* 1/21/98.
49. Friedman, Milton, *Wall Street Journal,* 9/24/96.
50. In Belgium, payments for small purchases may be made by a introducing a customer's plastic card, called Proton, into a store's machine. It is honored by many banks, and inter-bank balances are cleared daily. This is a step toward techno, but it is not there yet, since only one currency (the Belgian franc) is involved. See *The Economist,* 4/26/97.
51. *The Economist,* 3/22/97.
52. *The Economist,* 7/26/97.
53. US Department of Commerce, Bureau of the Census, *Historical Statistics of the United States, Colonial Times to 1970,* Series E 135-166, page 211.
54. Ibid., Series E 40-51, page 200.
55. Angell, Wayne, "Understanding 1929," *Wall Street Journal,* 3/7/97.

Chapter 8

1. Powelson 1994:chapter 6.
2. *Wall Street Journal,* 8/10/94.
3. *Wall Street Journal,* 10/5/94.
4. *The Economist,* 5/25/96.
5. *The Economist,* 7/27/96.
6. Glendon 1994; Howard 1994.
7. Glendon 1994:18.
8. Williams 1995.
9. *New York Times,* 3/10/97.
10. Pryce-Jones, 1997:27.
11. *New York Times,* 7/22/90.
12. *New York Times,* 1/16/91; *The Economist,* 1/19/91.
13. *New York Times,* 6/18/92, 8/21/92, 8/25/92.
14. *New York Times,* 11/12/93.
15. *The Economist,* 1/29/94.
16. Weber 1947:352.
17. Browning 1971:50.
18. Webber and Wildavsky 1986:148.
19. Hibbert 1987:140.
20. Black 1984:106.
21. Cipolla 1980:45.
22. Berman 1983:445.
23. Tuchman 1984:292.
24. Gregg 1981:34.
25. *Encyclopedia Britannica,* 1968:21:284.
26. Gregg 1961:83.
27. Cannon and Griffiths 1988:459.
28. Duby 1988:71.
29. Tuchman 1978:73.
30. Webber and Wildavsky 1986:220.
31. Miller 1987:89.
32. Sicard 1986:186 (my translation).
33. Sicard 1986:188.
34. Bossenga 1989:587.
35. Asakawa 1903:279.
36. Grossberg 1981:20.
37. Jacobs 1958:39.
38. Takekoshi 1930:1:204.
39. Wigmore 1969:98.

40. Bix 1986:27.
41. Bix 1986:110.
42. Takekoshi 1930:3:227.
43. Fairbank, Reischauer, and Craig 1978:514.
44. *Encyclopedia Britannica,* Macropedia, 1974:14:476.
45. Gueniffey 1989:227.
46. Maurois 1948:481.
47. Hall 1970:320.
48. *New York Times,* 7/30/87.
49. *The Economist,* 1/5/91.
50. *New York Times,* 8/28/92.
51. *Washington Post Weekly,* 9/14/92.
52. *New York Times,* 10/11/92.
53. *New York Times,* 9/10/95, *Washington Post Weekly,* 9/18/95.
54. Creel 1980:40.
55. Bastid 1985:51; Yan Meng 1988:1:10; Eberhard 1977:82.
56. Eberhard 1977:283.
57. For example, Eberhard 1977: 93, 226, 262; Fairbank, Reischauer, and Craig 1978:78; Miyazaki 1980:71; *Encyclopedia Britannica* 1974:4:338; Santangelo 1985:270, 281, 283, 287; Yang 1952::99
58. *New York Times,* 2/17/84, 7/1/92.
59. *New York Times,* 7/10/88.
60. *New York Times,* 7/2/89.
61. MacFarquhar 1983:174.
62. *New York Times,* 5/8/88; *Newsweek,* 6/6/88.
63. *New York Times,* 6/2/95.
64. *Wall Street Journal,* 5/6/96.
65. For Africa, several countries, *New York Times,* 5/25/95; for Argentina, *The Economist,* 6/25/94, *New York Times,* 7/17/94; *Wall Street Journal,* 12/11/95; for Asia as a whole, *The Economist,* 5/27/95; for Brazil, *The Economist,* 11/54/94; for Cambodia, *The Economist,* 12/2/95, *New York Times,* 2/6/95; for China, *New York Times,* 6/2/95, 8/10/95, *The Economist,* 2/3/96; for Colombia, *New York Times,* 2/15/96; for Dominican Republic, *New York Times,* 7/23/87; *Wall Street Journal,* 12/9/88; for Egypt, *New York Times,* 11/2/81; 7/12/92; for El Salvador, *New York Times,* 1/31/84, *Wall Street Journal,* 3/17/89; for Ghana, *New York Times,* 6/15/79, *Wall Street Journal,* 4/17/87, *The Economist* 8/22/92; for Guatemala, *Wall Street Journal,* 1/5/96, *New York Times,* 2/7/96; for Haiti, *Wall Street Journal,* 6/9/86, 12/2/86, 10/15/93; for India, *New York Times,* 2/14/82, 10/26/83, 2/21/85, 2/14/85, 4/18/87,6/27/91, 11/10/92; 1/22/96; *The Economist,* 1/20/96; for Indonesia, *New York Times,* 6/3/79, *The Economist,* 8/4/90, 6/25/94; for Iran, *New York Times,* 1/10/79, 11/25/79; Saikal

1980:60; for Kenya, *New York Times*, 10/21/91, 11/12/91, 11/17/91, 11/20/91, 12/12/95, 7/8/96; for Korea, *New York Times*, 11/27/88, 10/11/92, 5/8/93, 12/6/95; for Latin America as a whole, *The Economist*, 4/6/96; *New York Times*, 7/8/96, *Wall Street Journal*, 7/1/96; for Liberia, *New York Times*, 3/26/90; for Mexico, *New York Times*, 12/16/79, 9/6/81, 1/31/84, 4/17/87, 1/12/89, 1/30/92, 7/19/96, 8/19/94, 7/22/96, 8/8/95, 9/3/95, 10/19/95, 11/25/95, 2/15/96, 7/5/96, 7/13/96, *New York Times Magazine*, 4/9/95, *The Economist*, 2/3/96, *Wall Street Journal*, 1/12/84, 1/18/84, 1/12/89, 7/29/94, 10/5/94, 12/9/94, 3/11/95, 11/27/95, 1/12/96, *Washington Post Weekly*, 11/28/94, 3/13/95; for Nicaragua, *New York Times*, 2/11/90, 3/9/90, *Wall Street Journal*, 4/23/90; for Nigeria, *New York Times*, 1/30/84, 11/20/93, 12/18/94, *The Economist*, 10/22/94, 6/8/96; for Pakistan, *The Economist*, 9/9/95, *Wall Street Journal*, 6/10/96; for Panama, *New York Times*, 5/9/94, *Wall Street Journal*, 7/10/87; for Paraguay, *The Economist*, 6/11/94, *New York Times*, 1/7/95; for Peru, Randall 1977:4:55, de Soto 1989; for Philippines, *New York Times*, 11/8/85, 7/3/89; for Saudi Arabia, *New York Times*, 1/1/81; for Singapore, *New York Times*, 6/5/96, 6/6/96; for Venezuela, *Wall Street Journal*, 8/16/91, 2/4/94, *The Economist*, 6/10/95, 6/1/96; for Vietnam, *New York Times*, 5/8/94; for Zaire, *New York Times*, 10/6/83, 6/10/95, *The Economist*, 11/2/91, 12/17/94; for Zambia, Graham 1994:163, 171, 174; for Zimbabwe, *New York Times*, 12/10/89, *The Economist*, 3/2/96.

66. *New York Times*, 7/19/96.

67. *The Economist*, 4/19/97.

68. *New York Times*, 2/16/97.

69. *The Economist*, 7/27/96.

70. *The Economist*, 7/27/96.

71. *The Economist*, 7/27/96.

72. Friedman, Milton, *Wall Street Journal*, 9/24/96.

73. *The Economist*, 7/27/96.

74. Bovard, James, *Wall Street Journal*, 5/16/97.

75. *Wall Street Journal*, 5/19/97.

76. *The Economist*, 5/3/97.

77. Smith 1776 (reprint, Oxford, 1979):817-828.

78. *The Economist*, 6/1/96.

79. Bastid 1985:51; Yang 1952:3, 52.

80. Loewe 1985:263.

81. Loewe 1985:264.

82. Eberhard 1977:215.

83. *New York Times*, 5/19/93.

84. Grant 1978:359.

85. Luzzatto 1961:17.

86. Morgan 1986:164-65.

87. Lambton 1953:83.
88. Morgan 1986:102.
89. Bobrick 1987:45.
90. Blum 1961:233.
91. Lawrence 1978:153.
92. Kunt 1983:80.
93. Parry 1976:182.
94. Ludden 1985:142.
95. Takekoshi 1930:1:43.
96. Takekoshi 1930:1:125, 225, 265, Fairbank Reischauer and Craig 1978:417; Bix 1956:70.
97. Hirschmeier 1964:105.
98. Henry Simons's students, Herbert Stein and James Buchanan, remember his advice fondly in *Wall Street Journal*, 1/30/96.

Chapter 9

1. *The Economist*, 12/21/96.
2. Eberhard 1977:64, 77, 103.
3. Grant 1978:382.
4. Cantor 1993:81.
5. Cantor 1993:152-3.
6. Cannon and Griffiths 1988:32.
7. Findley 1980:28.
8. Kahan 1989:191.
9. Holborn 1964:276.
10. Kahan 1989:172.
11. *New York Times*, 7/22/90.
12. *New York Times*, 3/21/95.
13. *New York Times*, 5/18/96.
14. Ozment 1980:262.
15. Black 1984:115-6.
16. Holborn 1964:126-7.
17. Baker 1989:211.
18. Hall 1970:219.
19. *Washington Post Weekly*, 8/18/86; *Wall Street Journal*, 10/30/87.
20. *New York Times*, 8/30/92.
21. *New York Times Magazine*, 2/17/97.
22. *New York Times*, 4/30/91, 1/28/94.
23. Lefkowitz 1996.
24. D'Souza, Dinesh, *Wall Street Journal*, 9/24/91.
25. Bloom 1987.

26. *Wall Street Journal*, 7/29/92.

27. *Wall Street Journal*, 10/5/94.

28. *Wall Street Journal*, 6/29/95.

29. Windschuttle, Keith, 1996. Quotation is from a review in *Wall Street Journal*, 8/8/96.

30. *New York Times*, 5/18/86.

31. *Wall Street Journal*, 11/13/90, 3/19/96; *New York Times*, 8/6/95.

32. *New York Times*, 6/20/92. Kristol, Irving, supports this position in *Wall Street Journal*, 7/31/91.

33. *The Economist*, 6/28/97.

34. *New York Times*, 9/10/96.

35. *New York Times*, 7/14/97.

36. *New York Times*, 2/20/95.

37. *New York Times*, 9/13/96.

38. *Wall Street Journal*, 10/1/96.

39. *New York Times*, 8/13/96.

40. *New York Times*, 9/18/97; *Wall Street Journal*, 9/18/97.

41. *Wall Street Journal*, 9/16/94.

42. *New York Times*, 1/31/96.

43. *New York Times*, 3/1/95.

44. *The Economist*, 12/2/95.

45. *New York Times*, 6/26/96.

46. *Wall Street Journal*, 1/9/95; *New York Times* editorial, 2/12/96.

47. *New York Times*, 8/26/96.

48. This idea was suggested to me by Stephen Williams.

49. Drucker, Peter, *Wall Street Journal*, 5/9/91.

50. *New York Times*, 7/18/97.

51. *International Herald-Tribune*, 11/28/97.

52. *New York Times*, 3/12/97.

53. Many Catholics were entrepreneurial.

54. Lewis 1995:133.

55. Grant 1978:410.

56. Browning 1971:55.

57. Bowman 1986:48.

58. Lewis 195:138.

59. Fairbank , Reischauer, and Craig 1978:109.

60. Berman 1978:573.

61. Mayr-Harting 1990:92.

62. Poly and Bournazel 1991:142.

63. Gilles 1986:148.

64. Berman 1983:320; Powelson 1994:64.

65. Barraclough, ed., 1979:122.
66. Gueniffey 1989:310.
67. Holborn 1964:387.
68. Holborn 1964:491.
69. Cantor 1993:252.
70. Berman 1983:30.
71. Courvoisier 1986:112.
72. Marques 1976:131.
73. *New York Times*, 12/20/91.
74. Berryman 1987.
75. Fukuyama 1995:154.
76. Fukuyama 1995:155.

Chapter 10

1. *The Economist*, 7/5/97.
2. Ridley 1997:182.
3. Gregg 1967, chapters 21-25. Quotation is from page 500.
4. Yankelovich 1996:6.
5. *New York Times*, 3/13/95, 4/5/95.
6. *New York Times*, 5/14/85.
7. *New York Times*, 3/3/97.
8. *New York Times*, 5/14/85.
9. Kahn 1986:16.
10. Netanyahu 1995, reviewed in The *New York Review*, 2/1/96.
11. Seward 1987:117.
12. Hughes 1986.
13. Banks, Day, and Muller 1996:144.
14. *New York Times*, 3/3/84, 10/5/86, 7/12/87, 5/11/89, 1/16/90, and other dates.
15. *New York Times*, 1/31/86.
16. *New York Times*, 1/6/96, 1/9/96, *Wall Street Journal*, 1/11/96, 2/1/96.
17. Rouche 1987:456.
18. Bloch 1961:298.
19. Hibbert 1987:73-4.
20. Hibbert 1987:92.
21. Fabre 1989:560.
22. Vaillant 1962:90-1.
23. *New York Times*, 11/3/96.
24. *New York Times*, 12/2/84.
25. Wilson 1993.
26. Dawkins 1976.

27. Ridley 1996:249.
28. Lea 1866 (reprint, University of Pennsylvania Press, 1973):viii.
29. Shapiro 1983:205-6.
30. Haskell, April 1985:339.
31. Hibbert 1987:454.
32. Sicard 1986:211.
33. Fabre 1989:560.
34. Henderson 1980:278.
35. Henderson 1980:282-83.
36. Henderson 1980:292.
37. Ridley 1997.
38. Haskell, June 1985:547.
39. Powelson 1994.
40. Asakawa 1916:314.
41. Berman 1983:556.
42. Berman 1983:107.
43. Henderson 1975:14.
44. Henderson 1975:47.
45. *Wall Street Journal,* 12/13/96.
46. *New York Times,* 1/30/89, 1/22/91. 3/28/91.
47. *New York Times Magazine,* 9/24/95.
48. Rebel 1983:245-6.
49. *New York Times,* 6/10/86, 1/28/87.
50. Fairbank, Reischauer, and Craig 1978:915.
51. *New York Times,* 1/17/80, 9/17/81, 2/27/84.
52. My source is officials of the Bolivian government. I was present in La Paz as advisor to the government when the incident occurred.
53. *New York Times,* 3/31/94.
54. McEwan and Maiman 1984, cited in Wilson 1993:70.
55. Kahn 1986:13.
56. From an epistle by pope Leo the Great forbidding usury by clerics. See *The Economist,* 12/25/93:103.
57. *Harvard College Class of 1941, Fifty-Fifth Anniversary Report,* Cambridge, MA, Office of the University Publisher, 1996, p. 38.
58. Powelson 1994:3.
59. Olson 1971, 1982.
60. Olson 1989:299.

Chapter 11

1. *New York Times,* 6/12/94.
2. *New York Times,* 6/27/96.
3. Powelson 1994:218-19.

Chapter 12

1. Friedman, Thomas, *New York Times,* 2/2/97.
2. *The Economist,* 4/26/97.
3. Fukuyama 1995:13.
4. Huber 1996:142.
5. Associated Press report, in *New York Times,* 2/28/97.
6. International Labor Organization, 1973.
7. *New York Times,* 12/14/97.
8. North 1981:5.
9. *The Economist,* 1/18/97.
10. *New York Times,* 1/27/97.
11. *Washington Post Weekly,* 2/10/97.
12. This was told to me by an economic consultant who had just returned from Albania.
13. *New York Times,* 1/29/97.
14. Card and Krueger 1995.
15. *The Economist,* 4/8/95.
16. *The Economist,* 3/8/97.
17. *New York Times,* 12/12/97.
18. *The Economist,* 4/19/97.
19. Associated Press, in *Boulder (CO) Daily Camera,* 10/5/96.
20. *International Herald Tribune,* 11/29/97.
21. For Romania, *New York Times,* 2/12/92; for Russia, *The Economist,* 12/8/90; for Ukraine, *New York Times,* 7/15/96, Pedersen 1992.
22. Guillermoprieto 1996:31-36.
23. All data in this section are calculated from International Monetary Fund, *International Financial Statistics,* except for exports for 1995, which are taken from *Business Week,* 11/6/95.
24. *Wall Street Journal,* 1/25/96.
25. *New York Times,* 10/31/97.
26. Powelson 1994:310-2.
27. later increased to $57 billion.
28. *Wall Street Journal,* editorial, 2/4/98.
29. *The Economist,* 1/10/98.
30. *International Herald-Tribune,* 12/5/97.
31. That photo was published in the Business Section of *New York Times,* 2/1/98
32. *New York Times,* 1/16/98.
33. *Wall Street Journal,* 11/25/97.
34. *Wall Street Journal,* 2/4/98.
35. Powelson 1994.

36. Beginning with *Centuries of Economic Endeavor,* it is now my practice to coin one new word with each book.

37. Schultz, George P.; Simon, William H.; and Wriston, Walter B., *Wall Street Journal,* 2/3/98.

38. Dawkins 1996.

39. *New York Times,* 9/15/96.

40. *The Economist,* 3/15/97.

41. *The Economist,* 3/15/97.

42. *New York Times,* 4/25/97.

43. Henderson, David R., in *Wall Street Journal,* 7/13/96.

44. These failed experiments are explained in *Centuries.*

Bibliography

Alchian, Arman A. and Woodward, Susan. "The Firm Is Dead: Long Live the Firm: A Review of Oliver E. Williamson's *The Economic Institutions of Capitalism.*" *Journal of Economic Literature* 26, no. 1 (March 1988).

Alpers, Edward A. "Eastern Africa," chap. 7, in Gray 1982.

Ariès, Philippe. "Introduction," in Chartier 1989.

Ariès, Philippe, and Duby, Georges, general editors. *A History of Private Life,* 4 vols. 1987-91. Cambridge, MA: Belknap at Harvard.

Asakawa, Kanichi. "The Early Sho and the Early Manor: A Comparative Study." *Journal of Economic and Business History* 50, no. 2 (January 1929).

Asakawa, Kanichi. "The Life of a Monastic Sho in Medieval Japan." *Annual Report of the American Historical Society for 1916,* pp. 311-42, Washington, DC, 1916.

Asakawa, Kanichi. "The Origin of Feudal Land Tenure in Japan." *American Historical Review* 20, no. 1 (October 1914).

Asakawa, Kanichi. *The Early Institutional Life of Japan.* Tokyo: Shueisa, 1903.

Baker, Keith. "Condorcet," in Furet and Ozouf 1989.

Banks, Arthur S.; Day, Alan J.; and Muller, Thomas C. *Political Handbook of the World: 1995-1996.* Binghamton, NY: CSA Publications, State University of New York, 1996.

Barber, Malcolm. *The Two Cities: Medieval Europe, 1050-1320.* London: Routledge, 1992.

Barraclough, Geoffrey. *The Crucible of Europe: The Ninth and Tenth Centuries in European History.* Berkeley: University of California Press, 1976.

Barraclough, Geoffrey, editor. *The Times Atlas of World History,* rev. ed. London: Times Books, 1979.

Barro, Robert J. *Determinants of Economic Growth: A Cross-Country Empirical Study.* Cambridge, MA: M.I.T. Press, 1997.

Bastid, Marianne. "The Structure of the Financial Institutions of the State in the Late Qing" in Schram 1985.

Behrens, Betty. "Government and Society," in Rich and Wilson 1977.

Berman, Harold J. *Law and Revolution: The Formation of Western Legal Tradition.* Cambridge, MA: Harvard University Press, 1983.

Berman, Harold J. "The Background of the Western Legal Tradition in the Folklaw of the Peoples of Europe." *University of Chicago Law Review,* 45, no. 3 (spring 1978).

Berman, Harold J. *Justice in the U.S.S.R: An Interpretation of Soviet Law.* Cambridge, MA: Harvard University Press, 1963.

Berryman, Phillip. *Liberation Theology*. New York: Pantheon Books, 1987.

Bix, Herbert P. *Peasant Protest in Japan, 1590-1884*. New Haven and London: Yale University Press, 1986.

Black, Antony. *Guilds and Civil Society in European Political Thought from the Twelfth Century to the Present*. Ithaca, NY: Cornell University Press, 1984.

Bloch, Marc. "The Rise of Dependent Cultivation and Seignorial Institutions,." in Postan 1971.

Bloch, Marc. *Feudal Society*. Chicago: University of Chicago Press, 1961.

Bloom, Allan. *The Closing of the American Mind*. New York: Simon and Schuster, 1987.

Blum, Jerome. *Lord and Peasant in Russia from the Ninth to the Nineteenth Century*. Princeton, NJ: Princeton University Press, 1978.

Bobrick, Benson. *Fearful Majesty: The Life and Reign of Ivan the Terrible*. New York: Putnam, 1987.

Bordewich, Fergus M. "Yugoslavia since Tito." *New York Times Magazine,* April 13, 1986:54 ff.

Bossenga, Gail. "Taxes," in Furet and Ozouf 1989.

Bovard, James. *Lost Rights: The Destruction of American Liberty*. New York: St. Martin's Press, 1994.

Bowman, Alan K. *Egypt after the Pharaohs, 322 BC-AD 642*. Berkeley: University of California Press, 1986.

Braudel, Fernand. *The Wheels of Commerce: Civilization and Capitalism, Fifteenth-Eighteenth Century,* vol. 2, English translation. New York: Harper and Row, 1982.

Braunstein, Philippe. "Toward Intimacy: the Fourteenth and Fifteenth Centuries," in Duby 1988.

Brissaud, Jean. *A History of French Private Law*. Boston: Little, Brown & Co., 1912.

Browning, Robert. *Justinian and Theodora*. London: Thames and Hudson, 1971.

Bruguières, Marie-Bernadette; Gilles, Henri; and Sicard, Germain. *Introduction aux Institutions Françaises*. France: Privat, 1986.

Brundage, Burr C. "Feudalism in Ancient Mesopotamia and Iran," in Coulborn 1956.

Bruton, Henry J. "Productivity Growth in Latin America." *American Economic Review* 57, no. 3 (December 1967).

Buchanan, James M. *The Limits of Liberty: Between Anarchy and Leviathan*. Chicago: University of Chicago Press, 1975.

Butler, William E., editor. *Russian Law: Historical and Political Perspectives*. Leyden, A. W. Sijthoff, 1977.

Cambridge Economic History of Europe, 7 vols. New York: Cambridge University Press, 1966-78.

Cannon, John; and Griffiths, Ralph. *The Oxford Illustrated History of the British Monarchy.* New York: Oxford University Press, 1988.

Cantor, Norman F. *The Civilization of the Middle Ages.* New York: Harper Collins, 1993.

Card, David; and Krueger, Alan. *Myth and Measurement: The New Economics of the Minimum Wage.* Princeton, NJ: Princeton University Press, 1995.

Carsten, F. L. *Princes and Parliaments in Germany: From the Fifteenth to the Eighteenth Century.* Oxford: Clarendon Press, 1959.

Chartier, Roger, editor. *A History of Private Life,* vol. 3, *Passions of the Renaissance.* Cambridge, MA: Belknap at Harvard, 1989.

Chaunu, Pierre, editor. *The Reformation.* New York: St. Martin's Press, 1986.

Cipolla, Carlo M. *Before the Industrial Revolution: European Society and Economy, 1000-1700.* 2d ed. London: Methuen, 1980.

Clark, Colin. *Population Growth and Land Use.* New York: Macmillan, St. Martin's Press, 1968.

Cohen, Jerome A.; Edwards, R. Randle; and Chang Chen, Fu-mei, editors, *Essays on China's Legal Tradition.* Princeton, NJ: Princeton University Press, 1980.

Cohen, Joel E. *How Many People Can the Earth Support?* New York: Norton, 1995.

Coulborn, Rushton, editor. *Feudalism in History.* Princeton, NJ: Princeton University Press, 1956.

Courvoisier, Jaques. "Zwingli," in Chaunu 1986.

Crawcour, Sydney. "The Development of a Credit System in Seventeenth-Century Japan." *Journal of Economic History* 21 (1961).

Creel, Herlee. "Legal Institutions and Procedures during the Chou Dynasty," in Cohen, Edwards, and Chang Chen 1980.

Davidson, Chandler; and Grofman, Bernard. *Quiet Revolution in the South: The Impact of the Voting Rights Act.* Princeton, NJ: Princeton University Press, 1994.

Davis, Richard, editor. *The Origins of Modern Freedom in the West.* Stanford University Press. 1995.

Dawkins, Richard. *Climbing Mount Improbable.* New York: Norton, 1996.

Dawkins, Richard. *The Selfish Gene.* New York: Oxford, 1976.

de la Roncière, Charles. "Tuscan Notables on the Eve of the Renaissance," in Duby 1988.

Demsetz, Harold. "Toward a Theory of Property Rights." *American Economic Review* 57, no. 2 (May 1967).

Demsetz, Harold. "The Exchange and Enforcement of Property Rights." *Journal of Law and Economics,* October 1964.

de Roover, R. "The Organization of Trade," in Postan, Rich, and Miller 1971.

de Soto, Hernando. *The Other Path: The Invisible Revolution in the Third World.* New York: Harper and Row, 1989.

Dewey, Horace W. "Morality and the Law in Muscovite Russia," in Butler 1977.

Diamond, Jared. *Guns, Germs, and Steel: The Fates of Human Societies.* New York: Norton, 1997.

Dietz, Henry A.; and Moore, Richard J. *Political Participation in a Non-Electoral Setting: The Urban Poor in Lima, Peru.* Papers in International Studies, Latin America Series No. 6, Ohio University Center for International Studies, Latin America Program. Athens, Ohio University, 1979.

Duby, Georges, editor. *A History of Private Life.* Vol. 2, *Revelations of the Medieval World.* Cambridge MA: Belknap at Harvard, 1988.

Eberhard, Wolfram. *A History of China.* Richmond: University of California Press, 1977.

Epstein, Steven. *Wage Labor and Guilds in Medieval Europe.* Chapel Hill: University of North Carolina Press, 1991.

Ehrlich, Paul. *The Population Bomb.* New York: Ballantine, 1968.

Ehrlich, Paul, and Ehrlich, Anne H. *The Population Explosion.* New York: Simon and Schuster, 1990.

Fabre, Daniel. "Families: Privacy versus Custom," in Chartier 1989.

Fairbank, John K.; Reischauer, Edwin O.; and Craig, Albert M. *East Asia: Transition and Transformation.* Boston: Houghton Mifflin, 1978.

Feshbach, Murray; and Friendly, Alfred, Jr. *Ecocide in the USSR: Health and Nature under Siege.* New York: Basic Books, 1992.

Findley, Carter V. *Bureaucratic Reform in the Ottoman Empire: The Sublime Porte, 1789-1922.* Princeton, NJ: Princeton University Press, 1980.

Finley, M. I.; Smith, Denis Mack; and Duggan, Christopher. *A History of Sicily.* New York: Elisabeth Sifton Books, 1987.

Fitzpatrick, Sheila. *Stalin's Peasants: Resistance and Survival in the Russian Village after Collectivization.* New York: Oxford University Press, 1994.

Freeman, Diane. "Salaries for U.S. Managers Far ahead of Other Countries," *Boulder County Business Report,* Boulder, CO, 1960.

Fryde, E. B.; and Fryde, M. M. "Public Credit, with Special Reference to North-Western Europe," in Postan, Rich, and Miller 1971.

Frykenberg, Robert E., editor. *Land Control and Social Structure in Indian History.* Madison: University of Wisconsin Press, 1969.

Fukuyama, Francis. *Trust: The Social Virtues and the Creation of Prosperity.* New York: Free Press, 1995.

Fukuyama, Francis. "The End of History?" in *The National Interest,* September 1989.

Furet, François. "Civil Code," in Furet and Ozouf 1989.

Furet, François; and Ozouf, Mona, editors. *A Critical Dictionary of the French Revolution.* Cambridge, MA: Belknap at Harvard, 1989.

Galbraith, John Kenneth. *American Capitalism: The Concept of Countervailing Power.* Boston, MA: Houghton Mifflin, 1952.

Gauchet, Marcel. "Rights of Man," in Furet and Ozouf 1989.

Gilles, Henri. "La France Mediévale," in Bruguières 1986.

Glamann, Kristof. "The Changing Patterns of Trade," in Rich and Wilson 1977.

Glendon, Mary Ann. *A Nation under Lawyers: How the Crisis in the Legal Profession Is Transforming American Society.* New York: Farrar, Straus, and Giroux, 1994.

Gordon, Robert J.; and Griliches, Zvi. "The Cost of Living: An Exchange." *New York Review of Books,* June 26, 1997.

Graham, Carol. *Safety Nets, Politics, and the Poor.* Washington, DC: Brookings Institution, 1994.

Granott, A. *The Land System in Palestine: History and Structure.* London: Eyre and Spottswood, 1952.

Grant, Michael. *A Social History of Greece and Rome.* New York: Scribner's, 1992.

Grant, Michael. *History of Rome.* New York: Scribner's, 1978.

Gray, Richard, editor. *Cambridge History of Africa,* vol. 4: *c.1600-1790.* New York: Cambridge University Press, 1975.

Gregg, Pauline. *Black Death to Industrial Revolution: A Social and Economic History of England.* New York: Barnes and Noble, 1976.

Gregg, Pauline. *Modern Britain: A Social and Economic History since 1760.* New York: Pegasus, 1967.

Gregg, Pauline. *Freeborn John: A Biography of John Lilburne.* Westport, CT: Greenwood Press, 1961.

Grossberg, Kenneth A. *The Laws of the Muromachi Bakufu.* Tokyo: Sofia University, 1981.

Gueniffey, Patrice. "Lafayette" and "Robespierre," in Furet and Ozouf 1989.

Guillermoprieto, Alma. "Mexico: Murder without Justice." *New York Review of Books,* October 3, 1996.

Habbakuk, H. J.; and Postan, M., editors. *The Cambridge Economic History of Europe,* Vol. 6: *The Industrial Revolutions and After.* New York: Cambridge University Press, 1965.

Hacker, Andrew. *Money: Who Has How Much and Why.* New York: Scribner's, 1997.

Hardin, Garrett. *Living within Limits*. New York: Oxford University Press, 1993.

Hardin, Garrett; and Baden, John, editors. *Managing the Commons*. San Francisco: W.H. Freeman, 1977.Hall, John Whitney. *Japan: From Prehistory to Modern Times*. New York: Dell Publishing, 1970.

Harms, Robert W. *River of Wealth, River of Sorrow: The Central Zaire Basin in the Era of the Slave and Ivory Trade, 1580-1891*. New Haven, CT: Yale University Press, 1981.

Haskell, Thomas J. "Capitalism and the Origins of the Humanitarian Sensibility." Parts 1 and 2. *American Historical Review* 90:2 (April 1985); 90:3 (June 1985).

Henderson, Dan Fenno. "Chinese Influences on Eighteenth-Century Tokugawa Codes," in Cohen, Edwards, and Chang Chan 1980.

Henderson, Dan Fenno. *Village "Contracts" in Tokugawa Japan: Fifty Specimens with English Translations and Comments*. Seattle: University of Washington Press, 1975.

Herlihy, David. *Tuscans and Their Families: A Study of the Florentine Catasto of 1427*. New Haven, CT: Yale University Press, 1985.

Herlihy, David. "Family and Property in Renaissance Florence," in Miskimin, Herlihy, and Udovitch 1977.

Herrenstein, Richard J. and Murray, Charles. *The Bell Curve: Intelligence and Class Structure in American Life*. New York: Free Press, 1994.

Herzlinger, Regina E. *Market-Driven Health Care*. Reading MA: Addison-Wesley, 1996.

Hibbert, Christopher. *The English: A Social History, 1066-1945*. New York: W. W. Norton, 1987.

Hill, Henry Bertram, translator. *The Political Testament of Cardinal Richelieu*. Madison: University of Wisconsin Press, 1961.

Hilton, Rodney H. "Agrarian Class Structure and Economic Development in Pre-Industrial Europe." *Past and Present*, August 1978.

Hilton, Rodney H. *Bond Men Made Free*. London: Temple Smith, 1973.

Hirschmeier, Johannes. *The Origins of Entrepreneurship in Meiji Japan*. Cambridge MA: Harvard University Press, 1964.

Hobbes, Thomas. *Leviathan, of the Matter, Form, and Power of a Commonwealth, Ecclesiastical and Civil*, 1651.

Hochschild, Jennifer L. *Facing up to the American Dream: Race, Class, and the Soul of a Nation*. Princeton, NJ: Princeton University Press, 1995.

Hogue, Arthur R. *Origins of the Common Law*. Bloomington: University of Indiana Press, 1966. Indianapolis: Liberty Press, 1984.

Holborn, Hajo. *A History of Modern Germany, 1648-1840*. Princeton, NJ: Princeton University Press, 1964.

Holborn, Hajo. *A History of Modern Germany: The Reformation.* Princeton, NJ: Princeton University Press, 1959.

Holt, J. C.; Lambton, Ann K. S.; and Bernard, Lewis, editors. *The Cambridge History of Islam.* vols. 1 and 2. New York: Cambridge University Press, 1970.

Hosking, Geoffrey. *Russia: People and Empire.* Cambridge, MA: Harvard University Press, 1997.

Howard, Philip K. *The Death of Common Sense: How Law is Suffocating America.* New York: Random House, 1994.

Huber, Peter. "Cyber." *Forbes,* December 2, 1996.

Hughes, Robert. *Culture of Complaint: The Fraying of America.* New York: Oxford, 1993.

Hughes, Robert. *The Fateful Shore.* New York: Random House, 1986.

Hulsewe, Anthony. "The Influence of the Legalist Government of Qin on the Economy as Reflected in the Texts Discovered in Yunmeng County," in Schram 1985.

Inglehart, Ronald. *Modernization and Postmodernization: Cultural, Economic, and Political Change in Forty-Three Countries.* Princeton, NJ: Princeton University Press, 1997.

International Labor Organization. *Wages and Working Conditions in Multinational Corporations.* Geneva, 1976.

Jacobs, Norman. *The Origins of Modern Capitalism and Eastern Asia.* Hong Kong: Cathay Press, 1958.

Jain, Shail. *Size Distribution of Income: A Compilation of Data.* Washington, DC: World Bank, 1975.

Jones, Philip. "Italy." in Postan 1971.

Judson, Ruth; and Orphanides, Athanasius. "Inflation, Volatility, and Growth." Washington, DC: Board of Governors of the Federal Reserve System, May 1996.

Kahan, Arcadius. *Russian Economic History: The Nineteenth Century.* Edited by Roger Weiss. Chicago: University of Chicago Press, 1989.

Kahn, Arthur D. *The Education of Julius Caesar: A Biography, A Reconstruction.* New York: Schocken Books, 1986.

Kamarck, Andrew M. *Economics and the Real World.* Philadelphia: University of Pennsylvania Press, 1983.

Kamarck, Andrew M. *The Tropics and Economic Development.* Baltimore, MD: The Johns Hopkins University Press, 1976.

Kirk, Russell. *The Conservative Mind, from Burke to Eliot.* 6th rev. ed. Chicago: Regnery Gateway, 1978.

Kunt, I. Metin. *The Sultan's Servants: The Transformation of Ottoman Provincial Government, 1550-1650.* New York: Columbia University Press, 1983.

Lakonishok, Josef; Schleifer, Andrei; and Vishny, Robert. "The Structure and Performance of the Money Management Industry." *Brookings Institution Papers on Economic Activity*. Washington, DC: Brookings Institution, 1992.

Lambton, Ann K. S. *Landlord and Peasant in Persia*. New York: Oxford University Press, 1953.

Landes, David S. *The Wealth and Poverty of Nations*. New York: W. W. Norton, 1998.

Landes, David S. *The Unbound Prometheus*. New York: Cambridge University Press, 1969.

Landes, David S. "Technological Change and Development in Western Europe, 1750-1914," in Habbakuk and Postan 1965.

Lawrence, John A. *A History of Russia*. New York: New American Library, 1978.

Lea, Henry Charles. *Torture: With Documents on the Theory and Practice of Judicial Torture*, 1866. Reprint, Philadelphia: University of Pennsylvania Press, 1973.

Leacock, Eleanor. "The Montagnais 'Hunting Territory' and the Fur Trade." *American Anthropologist* 56, no. 5, part 2, memoir no. 78, 1954.

Lefebvre, Georges. *The Coming of the French Revolution*. Translated by R. R. Palmer. Princeton, NJ: Princeton University Press, 1947.

Lefkowitz, Mary. *Not Out of Africa: How Afrocentrism Became an Excuse to Teach Myth as History*. New York: Basic Books, 1996.

Lewis, Bernard. *The Middle East: A Brief History of the Last 2,000 Years*. New York: Scribner, 1995.

Lewis, Bernard. *The Political Language of Islam*. Chicago: University of Chicago Press, 1988.

Locke, John. *Two Treatises of Government*. 1690. A Critical Edition with an Introduction and Apparatus Criticus, by Peger Laslett. New York: Cambridge University Press, 1960.

Loehr, William; and Powelson, John P. *The Economics of Development and Distribution*. New York: Harcourt Brace Jovanovich, 1981.

Loewe, Michael. "Attempts at Economic Co-ordination during the Western Han Dynasty," in Schram 1985.

Ludden, David. *Peasant History in South India*. Princeton, NJ: Princeton University Press, 1985.

Luzzatto, Gino. *An Economic History of Italy from the Fall of the Roman Empire to the Beginning of the Sixteenth Century*. London: Routledge and Kegan Paul, 1961.

Lynch, John. *Spain under the Habsburgs*, vol. 1, *Empire and Absolutism, 1516-1598*; volume 2, *Spain and America, 1598-1700*. New York: New York University Press, 1984.

MacFarquhar, Roderick. *The Origins of the Cultural Revolution: The Great Leap Forward, 1958-60*. New York: Columbia University Press, 1983.

Madrick, Jeff. "In the Shadows of Prosperity." *New York Review of Books*, August 14, 1997.

Madrick, Jeff. "The Cost of Living: A New Myth." *New York Review of Books*, March 6, 1997.

Manin, Bernard. "Rousseau,." in Furet and Ozouf 1989.

Mankiw, N. Gregory. *Principles of Economics*. Fort Worth, TX: Harcourt Brace, Dryden Press, 1997.

Marques, A. H. de Oliveira. *A History of Portugal*, vol. 2: *From Empire to Corporate State*. New York: Columbia University Press, 1976.

Mason, Andrew; Lee, Ronald; and Miller, Timothy. "Saving, Wealth, and the Demographic Transition in East Asia." East-West Center Working Papers, population series, no. 87-88, August 1997.

Marshall, Alfred. *Principles of Economics*. London: Macmillan, 1890; 5th ed. 1938.

Mathias, Peter. *The First Industrial Nation: An Economic History of Britain. 1700-1914*, 2d ed. London: Methuen, 1983.

Mathias, Peter. *The Transformation of England: Essays in the Economic and Social History of England in the Eighteenth Century*. New York: Columbia University Press, 1979.

Maurois, André. *History of France*. New York: Minerva Press, 1948.

Mayr-Harting, Henry. "The West: The Age of Conversion (700-1050)," in McManners 1990.

McEwan, Craig A.; and Maiman, Richard J. "Mediation in Small Claims Court: Achieving Compliance through Consent." *Law and Society Review* 18 1984:11-49.

McManners, John, editor. *The Oxford Illustrated History of Christianity*. New York: Oxford University Press, 1990.

Mikesell, Raymond F. "Green Accounting as a Tool in Environmental Economics." Paper presented at University of Oregon Department of Economics seminar, May 18, 1995.

Miller, John. *Bourbon and Stuart: Kings and Kingship in France and England in the Seventeenth Century*, New York: Franklin Watts, 1987.

Miskimin, Harry A.; Herlihy, David; and Udovitch, Abraham L. *The Medieval City*. New Haven, CT: Yale University Press, 1977.

Miyazaki, Ichisada. "The Administration of Justice during the Sung Dynasty," in Cohen, Edwards, and Chang Chen 1980.

Morgan, David. *The Mongols*. Oxford and New York: Basil Blackwell, 1986.

Moulton, Brent R. "Bias in the Consumer Price Index: Where Is the Evidence?" in *Journal of Economic Perspectives*, fall 1996.

Munro, Ian R. "How Not to Improve Health Care," *Reader's Digest*, September 1992.

Murray, Charles. *What It Means to Be a Libertarian*. New York: Broadway Books, 1996.

Murray, Oswyn. *Early Greece,* 2d ed. Cambridge MA: Harvard University Press, 1993.

Neale, Walter G. "Land Is to Rule," in Frykenberg 1969.

Netanyahu, B. *The Origins of the Inquisition in Fifteenth Century Spain*. New York: Random House, 1995.

Nigam, Shyamsunder. *Economic Organization in Ancient India*. Delhi: Munshiram Manoharlal, 1975.

North, Douglass C. "The Paradox of the West," in Davis 1995.

North, Douglass C. *Institutions, Institutional Change, and Economic Performance*. New York: Cambridge University Press, 1990.

North, Douglass C. *Structure and Change in Economic History*. New York: Norton, 1981.

Olson, Mancur. "Big Bills Left on the Sidewalk: Why Some Nations are Rich, and Others Poor." *Journal of Economic Perspectives* 10, no. 2 (spring 1996).

Olson, Mancur. "Democracy, Dictatorship, and Development." *American Political Science Review* 87, no. 3 (September 1993).

Olson, Mancur. "Is Britain the Wave of the Future?" *L.S.E. Quarterly, winter 1989*.

Olson, Mancur. *The Rise and Decline of Nations*. New Haven, CT: Yale University Press, 1982.

Olson, Mancur. *The Logic of Collective Action*. Cambridge, MA: Harvard University Press, 1971.

Ozment, Steven. *The Age of Reform, 1250-1550: An Intellectual and Religious History of Late Medieval and Reformation Europe*. New Haven, CT: Yale University Press, 1980.

Parry, V. J. *A History of the Ottoman Empire to 1730*. New York: Cambridge University Press, 1976.

Pedersen, Jamie. *No Shortcuts: The Limits of the Law in Remaking Ukrainian Agriculture*. Manuscript, University of Colorado Law School, 1992.

Piñera, José. "The Success of Chile's Privatized Social Security." *Cato Policy Report* July/August 1995.

Poly, Jean-Pierre; and Bournazel, Eric. *The Feudal Transformation, 900-1200*. New York: Holmes & Meyer, 1991.

Postan, M. M. *The Medieval Economy and Society: An Economic History of Britain*. Berkeley: University of California Press, 1972.

Postan, M. M., editor. *The Cambridge Economic History of Europe:* Vol. 1, *The Agrarian Life of the Middle Ages*. New York: Cambridge University Press, 1971.

Postan, M. M.; Rich, E. E; and Miller, Edward, editors. *The Cambridge Economic History of Europe*, vol. 3: *Economic Organization and Policies in the Middle Ages*. New York: Cambridge University Press, 1971.

Powelson, John P. *Centuries of Economic Endeavor: Parallel Paths in Japan and Europe and Their Contrast with the Third World*. Ann Arbor: University of Michigan Press, 1994.

Powelson, John P. *The Story of Land: A World History of Land Tenure and Agrarian Reform*. Cambridge MA: Lincoln Institute of Land Policy, 1988.

Powelson, John P. *National Income and Flow-of-Funds Analysis*. New York: McGraw-Hill, 1960.

Powelson, John P. and Stock, Richard. *The Peasant Betrayed*. 2d ed. Washington, DC: Cato Institute, 1990.

Prestwich, Michael. "Italian Merchants in the late Thirteenth and Early Fourteenth Century England," in University of California at Los Angeles 1979.

Prost, Antoine; and Vincent, Gérard, editors. *A History of Private Life*. vol 5, *Riddles of Identity in Modern Times*. Cambridge, MA: Belknap at Harvard, 1991.

Pryce-Jones, David. "Corruption Rules the World," *The American Spectator*, December 1997.

Quill, Timothy E. *A Midwife through the Dying Process: Stories of Healing and Hard Choices at the End of Life*. Baltimore: The Johns Hopkins University Press, 1996.

Randall, Laura. *A Comparative Economic History of Latin America*, 4 vols. New York: University Microfilms, 1977.

Rebel, Hermann. *Peasant Classes: The Bureaucratization of Property and Family Relations under Early Habsburg Absolutism, 1511-1636*. Princeton, NJ: Princeton University Press, 1983.

Reid, Anthony. *Southeast Asia in the Age of Commerce, 1450-1860*, volume 1: *The Lands below the Winds*, New Haven, Yale University Press, 1988.

Rich, E. E.; and Wilson, C. H. editors. *The Cambridge Economic History of Europe*, vol. 5: *The Economic Organization of Early Modern Europe*. New York: Cambridge University Press, 1977.

Richmond, J. C. B. *Egypt, 1798-1952: Her Advance towards a Modern Identity.* New York: Columbia University Press, 1977.

Ridley, Matt. *The Origins of Virtue: Human Instincts and the Evolution of Cooperation.* New York: Viking, 1996.

Rothschild, Michael L. *Bionomics: The Inevitability of Capitalism.* New York: Henry Holt, 1990.

Rouche, Michael. "The Early Middle Ages in the West," in Veyne 1987.

Rueschemeyer, Dietrich. *Power and the Division of Labour.* Palo Alto, CA: Stanford University Press, 1986.

Sachs, Jeffrey, and Warner, Andrew. "Economic Reform and the Process of Global Integration." *Brookings Institution Papers on Economic Activity,* Washington, DC: Brookings Institution, 1995.

Saikal, Amin. *The Rise and Fall of the Shah.* Princeton, NJ: Princeton University Press, 1980.

Samuelson, Paul A. *Economics.* 11th ed. New York: McGraw-Hill, 1980. Subsequent editions have been written by Samuelson and William Nordhaus.

Santangelo, Paolo. "The Imperial Factories of Suzhou: Limits and Characteristics of State Intervention during the Ming and Qing Dynasties," in Schram 1985.

Schram, Stuart R., editor. *The Scope of State Power in China.* London: St. Martin's Press, 1985.

Schultz, Charles P.; Simon, William E; and Wriston, Walter B. "Who Needs the IMF?" *Wall Street Journal,* 2/3/1998.

Schumpeter, Joseph A. *The Theory of Economic Development: An Inquiry Into Profits, Credit, Interest, and the Business Cycle.* Cambridge, MA: Harvard University Press, 1936.

Sen, Amartya. "Population: Delusion and Reality." *New York Review of Books,* September 22, 1994.

Seward, Desmond. *Henry V: The Scourge of God.* New York: Viking, 1987.

Shapiro, Barbara J. *Probability and Certainty in Seventeenth-Century England: A Study of Relationships between Natural Science, History, Law, and Literature.* Princeton, NJ: Princeton University Press, 1983.

Sicard, Germain. "La France Moderne," in Bruguière, Gilles, and Sicard, 1986.

Simon, Julian. *The Ultimate Resource 2.* Princeton, NJ: Princeton University Press, 1996.

Smil, Vaclav. *China's Environmental Crisis: An Inquiry into the Limits of National Development.* Armonk, NY: M. E. Sharpe, 1993.

Smith, Adam. *An Inquiry into the Nature and Causes of the Wealth of Nations.* 1776. Reprint, Oxford: Clarendon Press, 1979.

Smith, Adam. *The Theory of Moral Sentiments.* 1759. Reprint, New York: Oxford University Press, 1979. Indianapolis, Liberty Press, 1982.

Soros, George. "The Capitalist Threat." *Atlantic Monthly,* February 1997.

Soros, George. *Underwriting Democracy.* New York: Free Press, 1995.

Starr, Chester G. *The Economic and Social Growth of Early Greece, 800-500 BC.* New York: Oxford University Press, 1977.

Takekoshi, Yosoburo. *The Economic Aspects of the History of the Civilization of Japan.* 3 vols. New York: Macmillan. 1930.

Thurow, Lester C. *The Future of Capitalism: How Today's Economic Forces Shape Tomorrow's World.* New York: William Morrow and Company, 1996.

Tuchman, Barbara. *A Distant Mirror: The Calamitous Fourteenth Century.* New York: Alfred A. Knopf, 1984.

Udovitch, Abraham L. *Bankers without Banks: Commerce, Banking, and Society in the Islamic World of the Middle Ages.* Los Angeles: University of California Press, 1979.

University of California at Los Angeles. *The Dawn of Modern Banking.* New Haven, CT: Yale University Press, 1979.

Vaillant, George C. *Aztecs of Mexico: Origin, Rise, and Fall of the Aztec Nation.* Garden City, NY: Doubleday, 1962.

Vaughn, Karen Iversen. *John Locke, Economist and Social Scientist.* Chicago: University of Chicago Press 1980.

Veyne, Paul W., editor. *A History of Private Life* vol. 1: *From Pagan Rome to Byzantium.* Cambridge, MA: Belknap at Harvard, 1987.

Wager, Janet S. "Double Exposure." *Nucleus, The Magazine of the Union of Concerned Scientists* 17, no. 4 (winter 1995-96).

Wandycz, Piotr. *The Price of Freedom: A History of East Central Europe from the Middle Ages to the Present.* London: Routledge, 1992.

Webber, Carolyn, and Wildavsky, Aaron. *A History of Taxation and Expenditure in the Western World.* New York: Simon and Schuster, 1986.

Weber, Max. *The Theory of Social and Economic Organization,* translated by A. M. Henderson and Talcott Parsons. New York: Oxford University Press, 1947.

Wells, Colin. *The Roman Empire.* Palo Alto, CA: Stanford University Press, 1984.

Wigmore, John H. *Law and Justice in Tokugawa Japan.* Part I, *Introduction.* Tokyo: Japan Cultural Society, 1969.

Williams, Stephen. "Accountability, Popular Will, Interest Groups, and Invisible Hands." Address at the University of Pennsylvania Law School, March 25, 1995.

Williamson, Jeffrey; and Higgins, Matthew. "Age Structure Dynamics in Asia and Dependence on Foreign Capital." *Population and Development Review*, June 1997.

Williamson, Oliver E. *The Economic Institutions of Capitalism: Firms, Marketing, Relational Contracting*. New York: Macmillan, Free Press, 1985.

Wilson, James Q. *The Moral Sense*. New York: Free Press, 1993.

Windschuttle, Keith. *The Killing of History: How a Discipline Is Being Murdered by Literary Critics and Social Theories*. Paddington NSW, Australia: Macleay Press, 1996

World Bank. *World Tables, 1997*. Washington, DC: World Bank, 1997.

Yang, Lien-shing. *Money and Credit in China: A Short History*. Cambridge, MA: Harvard University Press, 1952.

Yankelovich, Daniel. "How Changes in the Economy Are Reshaping American Values." *Human Economy: Economics as if People Mattered* 15, no. 2 (spring 1996).

Yan Meng. "A Review of Law in Traditional China: I and II." Papers prepared at University of Colorado, Boulder, 1988.

Yergin, Daniel, and Stanislaw, Joseph. *The Commanding Heights: The Battle Between Government and the Market Place That Is Remaking the Modern World*. New York: Simon and Shuster, 1997.

Young, Alwyn. "The Tyranny of Numbers: Confronting the Statistical Realities of the East Asian Experience." Working Paper no. 4680, New York: National Bureau of Economic Research, 1994.

Index

C